Raising Musical Kids

Raising Musical Kids

A guide for parents

DR. ROBERT A. CUTIETTA
Illustrated by Harvey Mercadoocasio

OXFORD
UNIVERSITY PRESS

OXFORD
UNIVERSITY PRESS

Oxford   New York
Auckland   Bangkok   Buenos Aires   Cape Town   Chennai
Dar es Salaam   Delhi   Hong Kong   Istanbul   Karachi   Kolkata
Kuala Lumpur   Madrid   Melbourne   Mexico City   Mumbai
Nairobi   São Paulo   Shanghai   Taipei   Tokyo   Toronto

First published by Oxford University Press, Inc.
First issued as an Oxford University Press paperback, 2003
198 Madison Avenue, New York, New York 10016

www.oup.com

Oxford is a registered trademark of Oxford University Press

Library of Congress Cataloging-in-Publication Data
Cutietta, Robert A.
Raising musical kids: a guide for parents /Robert A. Cutietta;
illustrated by Harvey Mercadoocasio.
p. : ill./ cm.
Includes bibliographical references.
ISBN 0-19-512922-9 (CLOTH) ISBN 0-19-512923-7 (PBK.)
1. Music—Instruction and study—Parent participation.
2. Mercadoocasio, Harvey. II. Title.

MTI C94 2001
649'.51—dc21
00-069300

Book design by Adam B. Bohannon

9 8 7 6 5 4 3 2

Printed in the United States of America

*Dedicated to my family, without whose help this book
would have been finished three years earlier
. . . but would not have been nearly as good.*

And to my dad, who somehow never needed this book.

Contents

Introduction

What On Earth Prompted Me to Write This Book?

It was a normal morning. Our son had already caught the morning bus to high school and our two daughters were waiting for their bus at the end of the driveway. My wife had already left for work, and I was getting a few last things together to take to the office. I would leave as soon as I heard the school bus stop in front of the house and arrive perfectly on time at work. The routine was well practiced.

But this morning the sound of the bus didn't come. Instead, the front door flew open. DAD, WE MISSED THE BUS!!! ALL THE OTHER KIDS ARE GONE ALREADY!!! Suddenly everything was in high gear as we all rushed to get in the car and head to school.

At the school I was just one more parent with a cup of coffee and children pouring out of the minivan. Unfortunately we arrived after the final bell had rung and I had to go into the main office to sign the girls in. They went to their classes while I walked past classrooms filled with students and teachers who were just beginning their day together.

Later that day I was in another middle school across town observing a student teacher who was, somewhat awkwardly, teaching an eighth-grade music class. You see, in addition to being a parent, I am a professor who specializes in training music teachers and therefore spend many of my days in schools. But that day, as I watched this young man, something occurred to me that never had before. It struck me how different the school looked to me as an educator than it had to me as a parent just a few hours earlier.

This thought stuck with me. The more I pondered it, the more intriguing it became. It became even more intriguing as I mentally expanded the view from two perspectives (university music teacher and parent) to four different perspectives. I could do this because in the music world I actually wear four different "hats."

The first hat I wear is that of professional musician. I have been a working musician for the past twenty-eight years and have played many styles of music from classical to jazz to gospel. I have performed in venues as diverse as the Oregon Bach Festival, the Montana Rodeo, the concert stage, and the corner bar. I have worked as a studio musician playing commercials, a lute player in a Renaissance music ensemble, a bass player in a jazz band, an orchestra conductor, a choral director, and just about everything in between.

The second hat is that of a music teacher. For several years I taught middle and high school choir and general music in the public schools of the suburbs of Cleveland, Ohio. While I was doing that, I taught in the evenings in an inner-city community music school. More recently, I have been a music professor at the university level. I have taught countless private piano and guitar lessons, music theory to third graders, and note reading to college students. I have conducted college bands and eighth-grade guitar ensembles. I have taught preschoolers and mentally handicapped adults.

The third hat I wear is that of a researcher. I have devoted the past twenty-one years to conducting research into the way young people learn about music. I have compared various teaching techniques, studied how middle school children form concepts, and examined factors that encourage youngsters to continue studying music. From this perspective we often ask "what if"; we strive to find what teaching techniques *would* work under certain circumstances and examine how the proposed practice is different from how it is actually done.

Fourth, I am a parent. We have three teenage children and have helped guide them through the often confusing path of music instruction. This, to me, is probably the most important credential I have because it brings practicality, common sense, and a real sense of humility to all the book knowledge and experience I have.

The process of children learning music "looks" different depending on which of these hats I am wearing. Interestingly, the most difficult view to focus was when I was wearing the parent hat. If I have trouble, how must other parents view the complex issue of teaching children about music?

I found the best view was when I was wearing all four hats at the same time. I started seeing how the complexities of helping children learn about music are actually woven together. This is the perspective that became truly helpful. I figured that if I could somehow write a book from this vantage point, it might actually help parents guide their children toward becoming musical.

To create this view of music learning from these separate, and sometimes contradictory, perspectives, I had to continually balance the ideal and the practical, the intellectual and the emotional, and the professional and personal. The goal was to explain the process of developing musicality in children in a way that would make sense first to me as an "insider" and then to you as a parent. Depending on the topic, this balance had to shift throughout the book, but I worked to have some degree of all four perspectives in every discussion.

My original thought was to write a series of articles for parenting magazines exploring music education. But the more I watched, observed, and pondered, and outlined, the more I found. It was like the proverbial onion; the more layers I exposed the more layers there were waiting underneath. It soon became clear that an article here and there would not provide enough scope for the information I had learned.

This book is the result. It outlines ways parents can provide a musical environment that will nurture musicality in children. It is primarily intended for use with children from the day they are born until they graduate from high school.

I will begin with what to do for your child from birth through the preschool years, then move into the different levels of education from elementary school through the early adolescent and high school years. I conclude with ideas of possible careers in music. Topics will include creating a musical environment in the home, choosing the proper instrument for your child, expectations of your school music program, finding a teacher, ages your children should begin their musical journey, and keeping them on track once they begin their travels. I have tried to provide a complete road map for developing your child's inherent musical abilities.

There are no fictitious characters in this book; all are real. I have taught hundreds and hundreds of students over the course of my career as a music teacher. You will meet many of these students, although I have changed their names. But being a teacher was only half the learning experience for me. To really understand this topic, I also had to be a parent (one of two) who was responsible for the musical development of my kids outside of the forty-seven-minute class period they received in school. You will hear about my three kids, not because they are musically special in any way, but because I know their development the best. I will introduce them now. Nathan is my fifteen-year-old son. He plays drums in the school marching and jazz bands and also has his own rock band. Madeline is my thirteen-year-old daughter. She is in the senior company of the Tucson Regional Ballet and plays the harp. Melanie is my eleven-year-old daughter. She plays the piano and sings in the Tucson Girl's Chorus. In addition, you will meet several of their friends and many of my former and current students.

As often happens, the fact that Madeline and Melanie missed the bus to school that day turned out to be a very good thing. It was the seed for this book. I hope this book will be the seed for the musical growth of your children.

Raising Musical Kids

Chapter 1

The Ground Rules

Let's stop and review before we go any further. The title of this book is *Raising Musical Kids*. This title is not to be taken lightly. It is intended to imply something that I have come to believe in very strongly over the last twenty-five years of teaching music, research-ing musical learning, and raising three children. What I believe is simply this: *musical children are not born—they are raised.*

While there are certainly child geniuses such as Mozart and Yo Yo Ma, these are not the children this book is about. Instead, it is about your children and mine. Children who, given the right environment, nurturing, and instruction, will grow up to be musical. What is most important to realize is that you, the parent, may be the single most influential person in your child's development as a musician. This book is intended to be your guidebook to lead your child along this path. Along the way we will look at ways to make your home more musical, how to pick the right instrument for your child, how to get her to practice, what age to begin music instruction, and a host of other issues.

What is meant by "being musical"?

No one seems to agree on what it means to be musical. Therefore, I will only assert what I believe it to mean. In this book, when I say that someone is musical I mean that he has met at least one of two criteria.

First, the person possesses the desire to make music for personal enjoyment and expressive release in some form. Notice that it is not enough to simply play an instrument. Many people can play an instrument, such as a trumpet, but seem to get nothing out of it besides pushing the buttons or the opportunity to wear a fancy uniform. To be musical, a person has to be able to "feel" the expressive part of music. A musical person feels something when performing music that is impossible to put into words. This feeling of the music is the foundation of what it means to be musical. I would hate to have to measure this feeling, but it is there, it is real, and it is very important.

The second measure of being musical is whether the person can resonate with the expressive qualities and then judge music based on them. Uh-oh, there is that word—judge. Yes, a musical person can and will judge a piece of music based on the quality of the music. If you believe that all music is created equal and no one should tell someone else what is good and bad music, then we are at an impasse. This book is based on the belief that music compositions are not all equal and some are better, often much better, than others.

But that does not mean good music is confined to one style such as classical or art music. There is quality country, rock, jazz, pop, and any other style that you can name. So I am not talking here about liking a certain style of music. All I am advocating is that people who are musical can hear and appreciate the quality aspects in whatever style of music they are listening to.

So, this is what I mean by being musical. It is fairly straightforward and simple. I believe that in most cases the first criterion, that of being able to make music, is a prerequisite for the second, although I have met many people who possess the second and have never played an instrument. Therefore, I will proceed on the assumption that most people must be involved in music making to get to the second stage, while realizing that this is not always the case. I have no problem with that inconsistency. I *do* have a bigger problem with the reverse, and more common, inconsistency: the person who can play an instrument, but has not developed any degree of musicality.

Why be musical?

My last book was one that reviewed all the research showing that studying music helps a child to do better in academic classes such as math, foreign language, and reading. There is also research indicating that music study will increase self-concept, social skills, and cooperation.[1] But I have rejected the temptation to use these arguments in this book to support why children should be nurtured to be musical. Instead, this book will be based on the premise that creating music is one of the important factors that makes us civilized; it is one of the key factors that makes us human. No culture, regardless of how distantly past or how geographically remote, has ever been found that did not have music.[2] It is so interwoven into the human experience that it almost needs no justification. Studying music will give one's life a deeper meaning.

Most parents want their children to lead happy and successful lives. Unfortunately, too many parents have bought into the argument that good academic grades in school are the main road to this success. I have met many parents who allow their children to drop out of band, choir, or orchestra so they can fit in an advanced math class. Although this may be justified for some students, it is probably a mistake for many others.

I can hear many of you disagreeing with me, so I will offer some support for my assertion. Parents want their children to be happy and fulfilled as adults. This is their ultimate goal and they are really less concerned about whether they have that life as an airline pilot, dancer, store manager, or homemaker. This is good. What is misunderstood by many parents (and other adults) is the road to this successful life. With the best of intentions, many parents guide their children down less than effective avenues. Consider this: The American College Testing Service (the company that created and administers the ACT) completed a self-study that compared four possible predictors of future success.[3] Success was defined as both self-satisfaction and participation in a variety of activities two years after college graduation. The factors explored were (1) major achievement in extracurricular activities such as music, (2) high grades in high school, (3) high grades in college, and (4) high scores on the ACT.

Three of the four factors were found to have no value as a way of predicting success later in life. Grades and ACT scores did not relate to a person's eventual success. The only factor that did was major achievement in extracurricular activities. This could be used as a predictor of success in later life.

Similarly, Jennings and Nathan[4] compared the SAT for its ability to predict success in a person's chosen career after graduation. They found that "the SAT offered virtually no clue to capacity for significant intellectual or creative contributions in mature life" (p. 589). There was no correlation between high SAT scores and success in life. Further, they found that the best predictor of success in later life was a childhood full of hobbies, diverse interests, and participation in extracurricular activities such as music.

Don't get me wrong—grades are important. They get your child into college, garner scholarships, and do say *something* about your child. But an "A" received at the expense of a well-rounded life is evidence of misplaced priorities. A good example of these misplaced priorities are schools that will not allow students to participate in music because of low grades in academics. These schools are missing the point and certainly do not have the well-being of the child in mind. Parents who support policies such as this have never had a child who enjoys going to school mainly for the opportunity to play in the school orchestra, regardless of how hard the rest of the subjects are. They also do not realize that being in those so-called extracurricular activities may be more beneficial to success later on than the subjects in their general curriculum.

It should be clear that this book is not intended to create an army of professional musicians. Heaven knows the field is crowded enough. Instead, this book is based on the premise that everyone needs to be musical to experience a more meaningful life. Being musical is something everyone should be. Without a developed musicality, an individual goes through life missing the beauty of the sound landscape surrounding her. She may see it, but does not resonate with the intricacies of the music that reflects so much about our culture, past, present, and future.

Without being musical, a person also misses the opportunity to know a part of himself. Studying music is one of the few things children learn from what Charles Fowler calls inside out rather than outside in.[5] Children are taught that "2 + 2 = 4," "C-A-T spells cat," and the capital of the United States is in Washington, D.C. This type of learning takes facts on the "outside" and inserts them into the

> It sounds naively idealistic, but I firmly believe that if everyone were musical, this would be a much better world.

"inside" of the child. In music, two children, even very young children, performing the same simple piano piece will make it sound different in ways that reflect who they are. These children are developing their musicality on the inside and reflecting it out to the world. Unlike learning the correct spelling of "school," the correct answer in music is constantly changing as it interacts with, and is recreated by, the child. It is through this process that children will learn something very meaningful about themselves as well.

Becoming musical develops a child in ways that are at the core of being a vibrant human being. It sounds naively idealistic, but I firmly believe that if everyone were musical, this would be a much better world.

Can all kids be musical?

As I said at the start of this chapter, I believe all children can be musical if raised in the proper environment. Therefore, it seems logical that I would believe there is no such thing as talent. That is not the case. Talent, or aptitude for music, does exist and it is something your child is born with to some degree.

Although all people can achieve a degree of musicality, for some it will be easier than others. Given the same set of environmental circumstances, two individuals experience it quite differently. That is because people have aptitudes for certain subjects. Some people's brains are simply wired in such a way that musical information is easy to sort out. Similarly, others will feel more at ease with math, language, athletics, or science. For the areas in which a person is not naturally inclined, they have to be learned. So the techniques in this book will be received differently by different children. For the child with a high musical aptitude these activities will sink in like water on sand. For a child with a lesser musical aptitude, the learning will be slower. Therefore, the child with the high aptitude will always be ahead when provided with the same environment.

This book is intended to help parents nurture and develop the level of musical aptitude with which their children are born. Like many other skills, such as language, developing musicality is most easily accomplished when children are young and naturally exploring and making sense of the world around them.[6] It becomes harder to go back and develop musicality as an adult. Therefore, the focus here is on what can be done with children from birth through approximately age eighteen.

An interesting question is whether a child with high musical aptitude who gets no nurturing will be better than a child with average musical aptitude who receives extensive musical training. I would put my money on the average child who had been exposed to a high degree of musical activities as a child. That bet is what this book is all about.

Chapter 2

What Does Music Study
Do for Your Child?

A few months ago I was reading our local newspaper. In it was a reprint from the *Los Angeles Times* with the headline "Music boosts brain power, researchers say." Almost unbelievably, an article on the same page from the Associated Press had the headline "Music study helps students recall words." These articles follow on the heels of the discovery of the so-called Mozart Effect that supposedly found that listening to five minutes of Mozart will make you smarter. I am just waiting for the next round of studies that will show that listening to two minutes of Beethoven each day will burn off ten pounds of fat per week. I am ready!

Yes, I am skeptical, not so much about the research, but by how it is reported and embraced in the popular press. To see why, we need to examine some of this research. We will start with the highly publicized study that started the public interest in the Mozart Effect. This article described the results of a pilot study[1] concerning music and one aspect of intelligence—namely, spatial intelligence. This is the brain's ability to deal with objects in a three-dimensional world. When a person is able to predict the trajectory of a football (and therefore time the speed needed to run to be at the proper point to catch it), that person is using spatial intelligence. When a person designs a bridge and can visualize it in three dimensions from the blueprints, he or she is using spatial intelligence. When you build a puzzle, you are solving problems using spatial intelligence. This is a skill that is necessary in some advanced math operations.

Obviously, it is an important mental ability. To measure spatial intelligence, there are tests that examine up to seven different aspects of this skill. These seven aspects combine to create what we call spatial intelligence. In the research so widely publicized, scores on *one* of the seven subtests were slightly higher after music instruction. This difference was so small that it only became apparent after looking at the results (statistically) in many different ways. There were no differences in the other six tests.

Since that first exploratory study, a host of other studies have had mixed results, but overall have confirmed that studying or listening to music will help a child perform better on spatial intelligence tests. Two highly respected researchers in this area, Ellen Winner and Lois Hetland, both from Harvard University, conducted an in-depth review of all available research on this topic and concluded that there is "a medium-sized causal relationship . . . between listening to music and temporary improvement in spatial-temporal reasoning."[2] In most studies, the increase lasted just a few minutes. They go on to conclude that there is "a large causal relationship . . . between learning to make music and spatial-temporal reasoning."

Another line of research has physically examined the brains of musicians and nonmusicians and found some striking differences. The area of the brain that processes sound, the planum temporale, has been found to be larger in the left hemisphere of musicians than in nonmusicians.[3] Likewise, the corpus callosum, the organ that carries communication between the two hemispheres of the brain, has been shown to be 10 to 15 percent larger in musicians who began music study before the age of six than in nonmusicians or even musicians who started music later in childhood.[4]

As a researcher, these findings really excite me. They may help us understand how the brain specifically deals with music and, in turn, bring us closer to understanding how the brain works overall. Therefore, the research community is right to explore this avenue of findings. However, as a teacher and parent, these findings hold little, *if any*, practical application for helping children become musical. Most of the score increases have been small and temporary. The larger area of the brain is seemingly due to using it for musical tasks, but the musicians who have this larger area are apparently no better musicians.

Nevertheless, the news media has fallen in love with the Mozart Effect and created a major issue out of a little information. The governor of Georgia has even gone so far as to propose that all babies born in the state receive a CD of Mozart music to make them smarter. The National Academy of Recording Arts and Sciences made a CD available for every child born in the United States for an entire year. Even the program of the last school concert I went to had a note to parents saying that "research has proven that playing in band will make children smarter." I think we had better examine what is really going on.

So what does the research say?

In my last book, *Spin-offs: The Extra Musical Advantages of a Musical Education*[5] (co-authored with two colleagues), we looked at all the research available since 1960 that examined the benefits of music study on such other areas as math reading skills and creativity. I will save you from having to purchase that book by telling you the ending. The basic conclusion is that the evidence is pretty weak for non-musical academic skills being developed by learning music.

There appears to be some support for the fact that if children learn to read music at the same time they learn to read words, both skills will be enhanced. There is also data to support the notion that the isolated spatial intelligence discussed earlier is enhanced by music study. Interestingly, there is little, if any, objective support for music increasing actual math skills, language skills, or overall academic achievement.

So why do we hear about this improved academic achievement so often? The problem lies in the fact that the studies previously described, which are seemingly finding true differences, are reported in the same articles, often in the same sentence, with the results of another avenue of research. For example, after stating that studying music makes a section of the brain larger, the articles often report as further evidence that children who study music have higher SAT scores. These two "facts" sound logical together, but actually have little to do with one another.

The problem lies in finding what is causing the differences. In the spatial intelligence tests, for example, experiments are devised to find out if the music instruction is causing the increase in spatial intelligence. The research studies on SAT scores are not designed that way.

Almost all the research conducted with standardized test scores looks at correlations or relationships between studying music and something else. For example, folklore has it that people who drive red cars get more speeding tickets. This is called a correlation and may in fact be true. Explaining correlations is usually a guess at best. The red car drivers say the correlation exists because the police are out to get

Just because a child is good in two subjects doesn't mean that one is causing the other.

drivers in red cars. A far more likely explanation would be that people who drive fast are attracted to (and thus own) red cars. A third, but less likely, explanation is that red cars make a person drive faster.

The truth is that we have no way of knowing which of the three possible explanations is the reason for the correlation. Instead, people choose the explanation that they want to believe. This is exactly what happens in music. Students who study music in high school, as a group, have higher SAT scores than those not in band. Consequently, we end up with statements like the one in the band program that tell the audience that music makes you smarter and the proof is that the kids in band have higher grade point averages, or higher SAT scores, than kids not in band. True, there is a strong correlation between playing in band and grades, but there is no proof that music study causes these increases. Instead, it is very likely that the kids who are better academically play in band. This seems a logical conclusion. It takes self-discipline, social skills, concentration, and perseverance to perform in a high school band, orchestra, or choir. Those same traits would probably also result in better grades. I would find it hard to believe that if the band were canceled tomorrow all the SAT scores would fall.

I think the safest conclusion from the research is that any nonmusical benefits from studying music are probably secondary and small. Learning just about anything has some spin-offs. Learning American history could be useful as an aid to making conversation at a cocktail party. Fortunately, I have never heard this as a justification for teaching it in the schools. Most people think there is an inherent value to studying American history.

I think there is a very good reason we are hearing about these latest developments. For a long time, music skill was viewed as something that was the result of talent. People believed either they had it or they didn't. The general public did not realize the amount of work, money, and sweat that went into becoming a great musician. Musicians have always known that music making was a skill requiring a great deal of mental energy. But only now is everyone starting to realize that. A parallel example is evident in the old stereotype that football players were kind of dumb. You do not hear that stereotype much anymore as we became aware of the level of mental strategies and highly coordinated physical skills necessary to be successful in the game.

So too with musicians. Every now and again a genius is born who sits down at the piano and plays beautiful music, yet the reality is that for most musicians it takes a combination of mental, physical, and emotional skills developed through years of hard work. As everyone begins to accept this, and downplays talent as the sole cause, we naturally start looking for ways to enhance these mental skills that are so basic to musical thought. It would be totally amazing (and thus more newsworthy) if researchers were finding that studying music did *not* enlarge the brain or increase the brain's overall mental capacity.

So what's the problem?

The problem with these reports is that they send the wrong message. They say that learning about music, or learning to play music, is not important unless there is some other reason for doing it. Because of this thinking, learning music is held to a higher standard than other disciplines. Music is required to justify itself because of unrelated learning. A math teacher is judged on how well her students learn math, an English teacher is judged on how well his students learn English. But, in music, how well a student learns music is often regarded as secondary if the child does not also show an increase in some other academic area.

Music is one of the great joys of being human. Being involved with music in a meaningful (and knowledgeable) way will add greatly to the quality of your child's life. If it increases brainpower along the way, great, but that alone is not a good enough reason to study it. Instead, we have to remember that there is an inherent value for studying music or any of the arts. The late Charles Fowler summed it up beautifully in his book *Strong Arts, Strong Schools.*

> The arts are part of what makes people well educated. Take them away and people will be less well educated. There is no replacement. You either acquire the capacity to unlock artistic insights and responses, or you are deprived of these insights and the joys they offer. Children made to live without the arts are inevitably poorer for it. This is why every young person, without exception, should be given access to the study of the arts, not to become an artist, but to be better educated.[6]

Claims of justifying music study for increasing math or other skills demean the true value of music and learning about it. It would be akin to saying the reason to get married would be to get a break on your income taxes. Am I being overly dramatic? Imagine the following headline: "Studying math increases musical ability, researchers say." Would parents demand more math study to increase their children's musical ability? Of course not. If the goal is better musical skills, common sense dictates more daily music study, not math study. Yet somehow we are supposed to get excited about music study increasing math skill.

There is another problem with the acceptance of all these reports. The result of the research presented earlier makes it clear that making music is much more powerful than listening to music. Yet the media has made it seem that simply handing a CD of classical music to parents and telling them to play it for their children will make those children smarter. This is simply dishonest. I truly wish it were that easy, but there is no evidence to support that claim.

Another Way to Look at Things

Then do we want our children to study music *only* to learn music? Actually, no. We want our children to develop in a variety of ways—emotionally, spiritually, and mentally.

Mental development is clearly enhanced by studying music, but not necessarily in the simplistic way that results in higher SAT scores or math grades. Current theories of intelligence take into account the

> The truly intelligent child is one who
> has had an opportunity to develop all
> seven areas of intelligence.

multifaceted and overlapping skills the brain is capable of managing
simultaneously. For example, the theories of Howard Gardner are
becoming widely accepted as a view of intelligence that is measured
by more, much more, than the traditional view of math and reading
ability.

In Gardner's theory,[7] intelligence is viewed as having seven different but equal components. These seven components are:

- *Verbal/Linguistic Intelligence*—The ability to use words and language both written and spoken.
- *Logical/Mathematical Intelligence*—The ability to use inductive
and deductive thinking, numbers, and abstract patterns.
- *Visual/Spatial Intelligence*—The ability to visualize an object and
create mental images.
- *Body/Kinesthetic Intelligence*—The ability to coordinate mind and
body in physical movement.
- *Musical/Rhythmic Intelligence*—The ability to recognize and be
sensitive to musical patterns.
- *Interpersonal Intelligence*—The ability to communicate in person-
to-person situations.
- *Intrapersonal Intelligence*—The ability to relate to inner states of
being and spirituality.

What is clear from this model is that thinking in music is a type of
intelligence just like thinking in words. Although a young child will
learn language just by being around other people, we acknowledge
that that is not enough. We encourage the child to learn more than
this basic level. We want her to possess enough knowledge to allow
her to "think" better by possessing more sophisticated verbal tools

with which to work. Likewise, children will develop some musical mental skill by being in a society that has music. But we encourage them to study music to develop their ability beyond this basic functional level.

Unfortunately, most schools only deal with two types of intelligences in a systematic way: verbal/linguistic and mathematical/logical. These two intelligences are usually bundled together and called the academic subjects or the three Rs. This emphasis on developing just a limited part of one's overall intelligence is the reason so many people think it is important to justify music by enhancing those areas.

But that argument misses the point. The truly intelligent child is one who has had an opportunity to develop all seven areas of intelligence. All children have some level of intelligence in each of the seven areas. Children will be clearly stronger in some areas and weaker in others, but the seven areas overlap and interact. The best way to increase overall intelligence is to develop each area to its highest potential. Think of the seven intelligences as poles on a circus tent. The most effective way to raise the entire tent is to raise each pole at the same time to the same level. Although you can raise just one or two, the resulting tent will be uneven and the amount of energy used would be enormous. Most important, if only two poles are used, the overall tent will never be as high, as broad, or as useful, as if all the poles were used.

So too with intelligence. All seven areas need to be developed because they all are connected and overlapping. This is most likely the real reason that research is finding that developing one area helps another area.

Musicians have been found to possess larger planum temporale and thicker corpus callosum in the brain because their musical mental ability has been developed. If they had not had musical exposure and training, this area would have been neglected and thus underdeveloped. It would be as if one of the circus tent poles was shorter than all the rest. This is turn would negatively affect all the other areas of the tent as well.

As our understanding of the brain increases, it is becoming clear that by and large we have underestimated the extent of mental abilities that must be developed in childhood. It is conceivable that at some point in the future schools that restrict their instruction to the so-called academics without giving equal attention to the rest of the child's mental development could conceivably be held accountable for neglecting their mission to educate children.

The clear reason we study music is to develop our musical intelligence as an equal component of our overall intelligence.

But I digress. The clear reason we study music is to develop our musical intelligence as an equal component of our overall intelligence. It is only when all aspects of our mental ability are developed that we are truly intelligent. In that way, studying music does make us smarter. Since the areas overlap, studying music helps us with non-musical skills. But the goal of studying music is not to develop the other mental areas. That is really backward thinking. We want children to study music to develop their musicality and develop all the mental capacities they were born with. When one area of intelligence is developed, all areas are enhanced. When they are all developed equally, the circus tent is high, broad, and well balanced.

When our children study music, they should do so to become musical and develop the musical parts of their brains. These musical children will receive those other benefits as a freebie. Now *that* is a great deal.

Chapter 3

What Age to Begin
Music Lessons

There is no question asked of music teachers more than "When should I begin lessons for my child?" As might be expected, the answer is usually not as simple as most parents would like. Fortunately, there *is* an answer; it just takes some explanation. This chapter will provide that explanation.

First, I want to clarify that this chapter will deal with what parents need to do with their children outside of any music education in the public schools. Often school music does not begin in a systematic way until first grade, which leaves the parents on their own for the first six or seven years of their child's life. Also, even when school music does start, it will be designed to provide a foundation for musical learning, but is not intended to supply all that is needed for complete musical development. Therefore, this chapter will focus on what can be done outside of school music as a complement to what the music teacher is doing for your child.

To truly understand your child's musical development, we need to understand the difference between two very important concepts: musical aptitude and musical achievement. This is where we will begin.

Musical aptitude is the term used for a person's natural potential to become a musician. The popular term for this is simply talent. We say a certain person is talented in music, acting, math, or any of a variety of disciplines. We are referring to that person's natural potential for the specific area. Aptitude is outwardly apparent in many ways. For example, in music, a person with high musical aptitude is able to learn music quickly, can perceive subtle nuances in music easily, or can play

Aptitude determines what a child is capable of achieving. Actual achievement is determined by how a child uses his or her talents.

a song in a musical style with relatively little practice. We see these signs and conclude: "This person is really talented." This is especially true when we observe it in a young person. Children who can learn songs quickly or are constantly singing or tapping out rhythms are quickly labeled talented.

Musical achievement, on the other hand, is what a person can do with music. The most common way to judge a person's musical achievement by how well she can play an instrument. Quite simply, aptitude tells of a child's potential in a given area; achievement is how far she takes her potential.

Aptitude and achievement have an interesting relationship. I have taught many children whom I feel have more aptitude than achievement. In other words, they have talent, but do not spend the time needed to become really good musicians. On the other hand, I have seen many children who have achieved a great deal of skill on an instrument, but can never be really outstanding because they have limited aptitude.

This distinction is not unique to music. A child may have great potential (aptitude) in sports, but lack the self-discipline for daily practice. Another child may have great potential in computer programming, but come from a family lacking the resources to have a computer. In either case, the result is unused potential.

As you can see, having aptitude does not guarantee that a child will become good at something. Without the self-discipline to practice, good teachers and parents to instruct, and proper resources (instruments, supplies, music) to support, the child will not rise to the achievement level of his or her aptitude. Aptitude can also be limited by physical characteristics such as motor skills, dexterity, or a range of other factors. It should be clear that having high aptitude would not always lead to becoming a great musician. However, without aptitude for music, the chances of becoming a good musician are probably slim.

It may be impossible for your children to live up to their potential in music (or any other area). If children have several strong potentials, eventually they are going to have to decide where to focus their attention. However, aptitude should never be wasted simply because the child is watching television, lacking parental guidance, or needing self-discipline.

Obviously, both aptitude and achievement are important. But it is important for you, the parent of a young child, to focus on the development of your child's musical aptitude in the early years. Why? Quite simply because the musical environment surrounding a child when she is young can have a substantial impact on her musical aptitude. Citing a variety of research studies done over five years with more than 10,000 children, music researcher Daryl Walters reports that "musical aptitude for children younger than nine appears to be developmental. Environmental variables exercise a push and pull upon younger children's innate potential at rates that vary among children. Consequently, young children are constantly changing their relative positions in terms of musical aptitude depending on the kind of 'nurture' that is interacting with their 'nature'."[1] Somewhere around the age of nine, a child's aptitude tends to stabilize and remain constant throughout the rest of childhood and adult life. Therefore, you, as a parent, have a great opportunity to enhance your child's aptitude while it is still forming. The more musical experiences you can provide for your child, during these preschool years, the greater the enhancement of his or her aptitude. An enhanced aptitude is a gift you can give your child for life.

You may be wondering what happens to children who do not have musical activities during these developmental years. Fortunately, we live in a society in which most children are exposed to great amounts of music. Movies, television, radio, theater, preschools, churches, and recorded music on CDs surround children throughout their early formative years. Therefore, most young children will have some degree of musical stimulation on a regular basis and will develop a basic aptitude for music. To move beyond this minimal level takes more than these basic, casual experiences.

It appears that everyone is born with some degree of musical aptitude and that it is normally distributed.[2] This means that most children are born with average aptitude and about a quarter are born with above average and a quarter below average. Regardless of the level, all children have some degree of musical aptitude that can be enhanced, "Parents can proceed to offer musical experiences on the assumption that all possess some level of musical aptitude and that all can learn to the level allowed by that aptitude."[3]

It is becoming clear why these early years are so critically important for the mental and musical development of children. When a child is born, his brain has somewhere around 100 billion neurons.[4] These neurons are not yet connected into the networks that define a more mature brain. The young brain is extremely adept at creating connections between these neurons with what are called synapses. Synapses form quickly when the child is young. Synapses are created when the environment surrounding the child stimulates parts of the brain. If these synapses are used over and over during the developmental time, the resulting neural pathways become part of the child's permanent brain circuitry. However, if they are not used repeatedly during these years, they are gradually eliminated starting around age ten.

The nature and extent of these pathways determine how a child thinks and learns. The more complex and rich the connections, the easier it is to learn and think. Basic neural pathways in the musical part of the brain will be developed in most children simply by their exposure to the music around them on television, computers, radio, and in the home. However, to create the musically rich neural connections that benefit a child throughout life takes repeated and somewhat systematic exposure to a wide variety of musical activities during this time when the brain is developing.

To provide the atmosphere that will be most conducive to this musical development, it is necessary to divide musical aptitude into two separate, but equal components. One component is related to a person's rhythmic potential and the other is related to his or her melodic (or tonal) aptitude. Both are important for musicians, but "it is possible to be strong in one dimension while weak in another."[5] Therefore, a child with high rhythmic aptitude and lower tonal aptitude may be more drawn to dance, a rhythmic instrument such as drums or guitar, or even sports (where timing is crucial). Likewise, a student with high tonal aptitude but lower rhythmic aptitude might be more drawn to a melodic instrument such as the violin, flute, or voice.

Regardless of the instrument, some degree of both types of aptitude is required for skillful playing. Also, regardless of the type of aptitude, they both originate with the child at birth (or before) and are developed during the first nine years of life. Therefore, the goal of early music activities is to help children hold onto every ounce of musical aptitude they were born with. Obviously, the first nine years of life are a critical window of opportunity for your child's musical future.

We now have our answer to what age to begin musical study. Age-appropriate music study can start as soon after birth as possible. Most experts would suggest beginning some sort of systematic music experiences no later than eighteen months.

Whoa, hold the horses! Does this mean that we should have a generation of one-year-olds sitting at the piano practicing Bach etudes for a half-hour a day? Quite simply, no. The key words in my recommendation are age appropriate. As you read other chapters in this book, you will see that you can actually do more harm than good by trying to push children into some types of activities before they are ready. The same is true here as well.

As the name implies, age-appropriate music study changes with the child as he or she gets older. There also are no absolutes regarding age cutoffs—these will vary from child to child. Still, the general categories outlined later in the chapter can provide a useful guide for all children.

What does early music study actually do?

Clearly, the goal of early music instruction is to enhance the aptitude of your child by developing your child's innate musical abilities. The most effective ways to develop children's ability are through what noted British music psychologist John Sloboda calls enculturation or training.[6] Enculturation is quite different from training. Enculturation is what happens as your child is exposed to, and interacts with, the music around him. Training, on the other hand, refers to actual instruction to be able to *do* something musical. The most common example is taking lessons to learn to play a musical instrument or learning to dance.

Musical Enculturation

Enculturation refers to what the brain learns about music from simply being exposed to it. Naturally, the music surrounding your child would be different if you were in raising her in China, Brazil, or the

United States—thus, the base word "culture" in enculturation. But even if your child is raised in one country, such as the United States, he will still be influenced by a culture. The music a child hears will be greatly different depending on the musical culture you, the parent, participate in. Your child will hear different music if you are a country music fan as opposed to a classical music fan.

A young child's brain is geared to make sense out of the world around her. One of the primary functions of the young brain is to sort what it sees and experiences into categories. These categories are sometimes referred to as concepts. The brain is also geared to find patterns in everyday life, and it is actually these patterns that help to put everything around us into categories.

The reason the brain creates categories is to deal with the large amount of information coming into our senses. Think about it. Imagine if every time you walked into a room you had to make sense out of the windows, the doors, the light fixtures, the wall covering, the electrical outlets, the furniture, the carpeting, the ceiling, and all the other things in that room. Instead, we have learned that rooms are rooms and that you can expect certain things. We have categories for bedrooms, living rooms, kitchens, and bathrooms. As long as everything is in order, we deal with it as a unit. But imagine walking into a bedroom with a stove and sink. You immediately realize something is not right. It does not fit your definition of a bedroom.

Young children are creating these categories at a very basic level. For example, a toddler first learns that a woman is "mommy" and men are "daddy." For a while, all women are mommies and all men are daddies. This is a basic categorization, and, while incorrect, is totally appropriate for a first concept because it can be easily modified later. Eventually the child learns that only one specific woman is mommy and one man daddy. At this point the concept expands.

The brain does this with everything it encounters.[7] All living things are first sorted as either people or animals. Later, plants are added to the group of living things. Slowly, animals start becoming different things as well: cows, horses, dogs, or lions might be first. In time this category will be refined to include zebras, mules, collies, mountain lions, and quarter horses.

How is this done? It is done through the child talking with parents, adults, and other children. Parents are constantly reinforcing and correcting children when they label something. If a child labels something correctly, the parents make a big fuss. If children get it wrong, they are corrected. This is a very powerful way of learning.

But how many parents help their child learn how to sort music? Not many. A study by Cathy Zwink has shown that children sort their entire musical world into just a few categories.[8] The most common categories are farm music, parents' music, happy music, rock music, or church music. These are odd categories. With the exception of rock music, these cannot be expanded or modified into adult musical categories later (what style is farm music?) and this creates a big problem. If the first categories are inherently wrong, they cannot be expanded or refined later to accommodate new types of music. Therefore, we find that teenagers still use basically these same categories as preschool children to make sense of their musical world.[9] Because these categories cannot be used to sort their increasingly complex musical world, they create new (and also musically useless) categories such as cool or uncool music, music they like or dislike, music they are *supposed to* like or dislike. What makes a piece of music fit into one of these categories is anybody's guess.

One of the goals of early instruction, therefore, should be to help the child create appropriate musical categories that can be modified and refined throughout life. Research has shown that this can be done.[10] For example, a study by Nancy Lineburgh taught first-grade children to classify classical music by the composer who wrote the piece. After a very short amount of consistent exposure, the children were able to classify music they had never heard before if it was written by one of the composers studied. What was interesting in this study was how readily these children's brains grabbed onto the game of classifying composers. For these children, the basics of later appreciation and enjoyment of music were laid down at this time.

In addition to the basic mental goal of sorting music, your child should start to learn to identify patterns in music. In just about all

Young children group everything into categories.

music the pitches go up and down (or stay the same) in patterns. The same is true of rhythms and harmony. There are common patterns repeated throughout the piece of music whether it is a song, symphony, hymn, or jingle. If there were no patterns, the music would sound random and pointless. Likewise, without patterns we could not put music into categories because each style (rock, jazz, classical) has its own set of acceptable patterns. Even if there are patterns in the music, if we have never learned to hear them, the music can still sound pointless anyway. One of the reasons music from other countries sounds so strange to us is that we did not learn the patterns for that music when we were children. Therefore, early music instruction should also work to help your child learn the basic patterns of music.

We can take this a step further. The reason music sounds like music to us is because we recognize patterns in the sound. Your child will start noticing these patterns at a very young age. Several researchers found that babies as young as five or six months old are already sensitive to patterns in music.[11] By studying the heart rate of babies who listen to music, they have concluded that five-month-old babies can, and do, identify rhythm and melody patterns.

Knowing and using these patterns can be viewed as thinking in sound much like most of our thought is in words. Children learn to do this by learning and improvising chants, writing music, and being exposed to a wide variety of music. Children will do this naturally on the playground, the bus, at home,[12] but it is the parent's role to try to expand and focus this learning. You probably think in sound also. Have you ever had a song stuck in your head? That is thinking in sound.

Beyond learning these basic patterns, early instruction should also work to help the young child learn to sense a feeling of tonality (the feeling that something is in a certain key), steady beat, and the idea that small pitch and rhythm patterns combine into larger structures called phrases. These types of patterns are learned later, when your child is around five years old.[13]

Lastly, from the mental standpoint, a growing body of research indicates that so-called perfect pitch is something that can be learned between the ages of four and six.[14] Perfect pitch is the ability to name a pitch by just hearing it. For example, a person who hears an A played on the piano will know it is an A without looking at the keyboard. It is controversial among musicians whether this is a beneficial skill. For example, it creates real problems for the musician who is transposing music (playing it in a different key than what is written on the page) or who is playing or singing in a group that might be using an alternate tuning. Still, despite the controversy, I think most musicians would find this a handy tool to have.

The research tends to show that there is a window of opportunity for developing this skill in youngsters. Between the age of four and six children seem to be able to learn to identify pitches if they are trained to do so. In other words, if the parents regularly were to play a game in which they played pitches on a piano and then had the child try to identify them, it seems that the child will develop perfect pitch.

Notice that I carefully said the research "tends" to show the ability to learn perfect pitch. It is by no means certain that this is true. Part of the problem is the difficulty inherent in doing this type of research (to completely prove it, you would probably have to separate twins at birth and give one of each pair the training). The second problem is that the worth of perfect pitch is very controversial. Great harm can be done if the pitches are learned on an instrument not accurately tuned. For example, it would be a true hindrance if a child learns the pitch names on a piano that is out of tune.

If you are a parent with some degree of musical skill, you should make the decision about whether you want your child to have perfect pitch. If you do, I suggest you do a pitch-naming activity on a regular basis between the ages of four and seven. Please be sure the pitches you are naming are accurate. If you have no musical background, I would suggest skipping this idea.

Musical Training

Whereas musical enculturation is intended to develop your child's mental skills to process music, musical training is intended to develop specific skills such as playing an instrument, singing, or composing. "Very broadly, we may say that, in our Western culture, musical enculturation is the dominant process up to the age of 10; thereafter musical training plays an increasingly important part."[15]

Further, enculturation happens (to some extent) to just about all children and is somewhat common to every child in a given culture. Training, in contrast, is only undertaken by certain children and is focused on specific skills not common to all. For example, one child may choose to pursue no musical training, a second will learn to play the trumpet, and a third could choose to sing. All three would learn very different skills.

How does aptitude fit into all of this? Plainly, the higher the musical aptitude or degree of musical development prior to training, the easier the training will be. Even if training is not pursued, the pattern recognition and music-processing skills developed during this time will help with a lifetime of musical enjoyment for your child.

Music in the Prenatal Stage

Your child's musical learning begins before he or she is born. Fetuses in the eighth or ninth month of gestation have been shown to recognize music as different from sounds such as voices or noise.[16] Further, they appear to be able to recognize a specific piece of music. In one study, fetuses were exposed to the same piece of music on a daily basis. For some of the fetuses the music was stopped between weeks 32 and 38. When the music playing was resumed, the fetus heartbeats reacted as if they had never heard the music before, whereas the fetuses that had continued to hear the music reacted to hearing the music as something familiar.[17] This learning remains after birth. When a piece of music was played throughout a woman's pregnancy, the newborn baby seemed to recognize it when played with other pieces of music.[18]

Although none of these studies has direct suggestions about whether it is, in fact, beneficial for a pregnant mother to listen to music, it seems clear that the unborn child is already attempting to make sense out of the sounds it is hearing in the womb. To have the unborn baby begin to recognize music as one of these sounds would seem to be something of benefit.

Age-appropriate Music Study during the First Year of Life

During your child's first year of life, remarkable changes take place. Almost daily you will notice new gestures, smiles, movements, sounds, and eye movements. Given the rapid development that happens during this time, it is not surprising that your child's musical development is beginning as well.

During the first six months there are not many observable musical behaviors that your child will show.[19] However, researchers have been able to demonstrate that certain skills are beginning to develop in your child's brain that are the foundation for a lifetime of listening and making music. As described earlier, babies who are five months old are able to differentiate music from other sounds by recognizing pitch patterns in the music. I find that the first question asked of me when I report this is how the researcher knows if the babies are recognizing music. There are a few ways. Some researchers monitor the heart rate of the babies as they listen to musical patterns. When melodies are played that have a new contour (or shape), the heart rates go up the same as they do when they encounter anything new. However, if babies hear melodies having the same or similar shape to melodies they have heard before, their heart rate does not change.

In other studies, tapes of different sounds and types of music are played and the child's attention is measured through eye movements. From this we know that children are more attracted to both instrumental music and songs with words than spoken words, drums, or sounds.

During this time, however, you, as a parent, will not be able to see many overt behaviors to show that your child is processing music. You have to trust that it is happening. It is easy to get confused because some repeated actions your baby will make, such as babbling, can *sound* like music, but these are probably not attempts by your child to actually be making music.[20]

What does this instruction look like?

Some preschool music programs offer instruction for children as early as six months old. This instruction will always include the parent and will feature many activities designed to have your baby focus on simple music. Since the goal is enculturation, the music used will have the basic patterns of music embedded in it over and over. The teachers and parents will sing, play, and move to music with the baby. The emphasis will not be on having the babies produce music (singing or playing), but instead on surrounding them with music and providing songs for the parents to sing and play around the house.

Age-appropriate Music Study Ages One to Five

For children age one until around age five, the most appropriate musical activities to be involved with are activities that have the child exploring sounds, moving to music, participating in rhythmic chants and activities, and, of course, singing. The purpose of these activities is not to produce great musical sounds. Instead, the purpose is to allow your child's brain to make sense out of music. This is very important because it appears that "musical development . . . at this age is proceeding along genuinely different paths from speech."[21] Your child is probably getting lots of verbal experience and instruction to develop that skill. Likewise, children need to have similar experiences to develop musical paths. The basic concepts (mental patterns) of different musical styles and basic musical elements start to be constructed (or not constructed) during these critical years.

How are these concepts developed? Let's first look at chants. Most children explore them as part of childhood. The common chant "This little piggy went to market, this little piggy stayed home" is always recited in a specific rhythm. This rhythm establishes the feel for some of the most basic rhythmic patterns found in music. It also establishes a sense that music is arranged in patterns with four beats each. That is why, for example, there are pauses after the word market. This puts in the fourth beat of each pattern.

This little piggy went to market (pause)
This little piggy stayed home (pause)
This little piggy had roast beef (pause)
This little piggy had none (pause)

As an adult you would probably have trouble reciting this poem without the pauses. This seems very basic to us as adults because we learned it a long time ago. It does not seem natural to the child until he or she learns it. Reciting chants helps to establish these basic rules of music without our even knowing it. If we do not learn these "rules," there is no way for our brains to make sense out of music.

Likewise, singing has the added advantage of exposing your child to the pitch patterns of music while also exposing him to rhythm patterns. Just like the rhythm patterns of the little piggy chant, most music is made up of basic patterns on pitches. We learn these pitches and use them throughout life from singing these basic songs.

At about two and a half years old, many children are able to imitate parts, or patterns, within songs.[22] They will probably start singing the repetitive parts of songs (such as "*ee-ei-ee-ei-oh*" in "Old MacDonald Had a Farm"). This will continue to expand until the child can sing the whole song around age four.

Movement to music should also be a basic part of music instruction at this age. However, the goal of the movement should be to guide the child to experience and focus on the phrases, beats, tonality, or patterns. This is the stuff of future musical growth.

One way to accomplish this would be through what is called the Dalcroze method. This method of teaching, devised by Jacques Emile Dalcroze, involves the entire body in moving to music. The goal is heightened awareness and thus music learning. It makes sense that if your children are moving to music, they are paying attention to it.

Notice that for the ages of birth to five years, no mention was made of instruments. Although it is totally natural to equate musical ability with playing an instrument, it is important to remember that the instrument is just a tool for demonstrating the musicality *within* an individual. During the early years we start to develop this musicality within children and to develop their aptitude. While simple instruments are often used during this time, they are employed as tools to help children focus on certain aspects of the music. Musical achievement will be demonstrated on an instrument later.

Still, the importance of providing music during this time is evident. At the end of a huge study involving 500 children from differing backgrounds, Moog concluded:

> Up until the age of about three we could not observe in response to music any significant difference determined by the environment; children from poorer homes reacted no differently to our test from children in upper income groups. Children who, according to their parent's reports, were inundated with music from morning till night showed little difference, in either the quantity or quality of their responses, from children who were only allowed to hear carefully weighted amounts of carefully chosen musical stimuli. . . . But, between the ages of three and four, differences in home environment begin to show their effect in the field of music. Girls and boys who are taught songs and games by their parents, brothers and sisters, or in nursery schools, have a clear advantage over other children.[23]

What does this instruction look like?

A music class geared toward preschoolers will have a great deal of variety, enthusiasm, and fun. There will be a routine repeated at every class, including moving to some aspect of the music (marching to the beat, following the melody up and down, or following the loud and soft aspects of the music). The children will move to a wide variety of music and the teacher will classify it according to its style. The children will chant and sing songs that contain basic musical patterns. And they will repeat these songs many times. Fun repetition is a characteristic of sound preschool music programs.

The lessons will not emphasize playing an instrument or note reading at this time. All songs will be learned by repeating after the music teacher. This helps the child put the songs and patterns in memory.

A word of caution: Incorrect patterns can be laid down just as easily as the correct ones at this time. Therefore, it is very important to chose instruction wisely here. Watch to see if the activities are truly tied to, and in sync with, the music. If, for example, the movement activities simply allow children to move in any manner they want, regardless of what the music is doing, they are probably not getting much musical value out of the experience.

There are many music programs for very young children. Two of the most popular and well known are called Kindermusik® and the Suzuki method. Although both provide systematic and progressive age-appropriate experiences with children, they are quite different.

The Suzuki method is based on the principle that since children learn language by listening to and repeating what they hear, they can do the same with music. A child learns to play an instrument (usually the violin, but sometimes the piano) by listening to the teacher and parent and copying what they play. The emphasis is on what is called talent education—in other words, the goal of instruction is to develop aptitude through playing.

Kindermusik® is an early childhood music and movement program begun in West Germany in the 1960s. It provides group instruction in music for children from birth until age seven. Children are divided by age into classes, with the common divisions being birth to eighteen months, eighteen months to three years, three to five years, and five to seven years. The emphasis is on having children experience music through freeform and structured activities involving movement, singing, and games. The basic philosophy of this instruction revolves around the beliefs that all children are musical, the parent is the child's most important teacher, and the home is the most important place for learning. Kindermusik® maintains a website (www.kindermusik.com) with a locator that will help you find the closest class to your home.

Although these are the two most widely available approaches, there are many others. If you live near a university with a music department, it will often sponsor a music program for children. For example, at the University of Arizona we offer a weekly class for children eighteen months to three years old. Local music schools, community centers, or YMCAs will often have programs as well. Check your local paper and bulletin boards at your child's preschool to find what is available in your area.

Age-appropriate Lessons Ages Five to Ten

Between ages five and nine your child will be ready to begin learning to play an instrument. However, it is very likely that the instrument begun at this age may not be your child's final instrument. For one thing, your son or daughter may simply choose a different instrument as he or she gets older. Also, at this age children are not physically ready to tackle some instruments, so their choices are limited. For example, they do not have the physical strength or facial muscles to hold or control a tuba. Therefore, the first instruments should be viewed as the starting point of future study.

Only a very few instruments are regularly used for early instruction: piano and string instruments such as violin, viola, and cello.[24] These instruments are easily manipulated by young fingers and are well suited for this age. A comparison of the pros and cons of each will help you decide which is best for your child.

The piano has a strong advantage over the violin in that anyone (even your pet dog) can produce a pleasant sound by simply pushing down a key. Provided the piano is in tune, the sound will be OK. This is not true of the string instruments—in fact, just the opposite occurs. I have heard beginning violin students whose music more resembled fingernails on blackboards than musical sounds.

Interestingly, this advantage would seem to favor the piano for beginning instruction. But, from a music learning standpoint, it probably favors the violin. Remember that the primary purpose of early instruction is the development of aptitude and musicality, not building achievement. We are still working to lay down certain mental skills in the child. While the piano sound is more refreshing to the listener (you!), it forces no mental energy on the part of the performer to create the right pitch; push the right key, the right pitch comes out. Research (and practical experience of thousands of piano teachers) has shown that in situations such as this, children actually concentrate so much on other things that they fail to listen to the sounds they are making.[25] The same cannot happen with string instruments. Children find the correct pitch by listening and adjusting their fingers along a continuous string. Therefore, pitch perception is practiced every time a child plays the instrument.

The strings have another advantage over the piano. One of the things that makes music sound pleasing happens when the performer plays the music in phrases that gracefully progress from note to note. These phrases are the sentences of music and, when performed appropriately, they make the music seem to flow. When done awkwardly, they break the flow of the music and make it jagged. When playing the violin, a child moves the bow in response to the musical phrases; a child is thus actively phrasing the music correctly from the very beginning.

Finally, string instruments can be constructed satisfactorily in half and three-quarter sizes without sacrificing much sound quality. Thus, the instrument can be made to be the ideal size for very young children.

Although there are advantages of violin playing, they do not make the violin a clear winner in the choice of instruments. For one thing, the child learning on the violin does not always experience the immediate success of playing music that one feels on the piano. Also, the piano has advantages for learning (and visualizing) the elements of music theory. If your child decides to get really serious about music later, he or she will have to gain some familiarity with the keyboard. Plus, the piano allows the opportunity of being able to play harmony and melody at the same time and is appropriate for playing a wider variety of musical styles than the violin. Last, piano is easier on the listeners. All these advantages are arguments in favor of the piano.

There is no right answer about which instrument is better for beginning, but both have great advantages over just about any other instrument. To help you decide which instrument is best for your child, I offer the following suggestions. First, arrange for the child to try both instruments. Second, pay close attention to your child and ask for feedback. Five year olds can be very opinionated, so let that work in your favor. Finally, consider the investment you will need to make. A violin is much less expensive than a piano. However, both can be rented for a similar monthly payment.

During this (and all later) stages of your child's development you will probably have help from a music teacher in your child's school, but do remember that the school music program is not intended to supply all the instruction needed for a truly musical child. I encourage you to be in contact with your child's school music teacher for help and advice or for choosing instruments or private teachers. By and large, you will find music teachers a dedicated and helpful group. They would like to hear from you if you have any questions.

What does this instruction look like?

The lessons at this age are probably one-on-one with the teacher. The parent is probably encouraged to attend unless it creates a distraction to the student. The focus of these lessons involves the development of the child. In other words, we are still emphasizing aptitude development over achievement of performance skills. Still, a good teacher will focus on musical development, but will also lay down the proper foundation for performance skills and your child will show progress in performance ability.

This instruction should also be characterized by a curriculum. The teacher should have a clear plan for the progression of your child. Several excellent piano and violin methods are available that introduce songs that are enjoyable and work to develop, in a systematic order, the basic musical and instrumental skills for playing the instrument. If the teacher is not following some sort of progressive curriculum with your child or does not seem to have a clear sense of direction for your child, find another teacher. Chapter 4 will help you do this.

Lessons at this age will begin introducing the basic concepts of note reading, but this will not be the primary function of the lessons. Instead, the teacher will encourage children to listen to themselves and perform musically. Too often note reading gets in the way of these important skills for young children because all their concentration goes toward learning to read notes on the page. To balance this, the teacher may encourage some rote learning of musical pieces at this time.

Age-appropriate Music Study Ages Nine to Twelve

During the upper elementary years, the focus of lessons will change from the development of aptitude toward the development of achievement on an instrument. At this time children may switch from the piano or violin to the instrument that will become their life-long instrument. They will be helped in this decision by their school music program, which will probably offer instruction on an instrument beginning in fourth or (more commonly) fifth grade. One of the most important decisions that will be made during this time will be selecting an instrument. Because an entire chapter is devoted to this topic, I will not go into the many aspects of choosing an instrument, but will instead refer you to Chapter 9.

This is also the time when your child will be expected to develop good practice habits. For this, I refer you to Chapters 6 and 7.

What does this instruction look like?

In school your child will take lessons in small groups of students (three to eight) who are playing the same or very similar instruments. The teacher will emphasize note reading and producing pleasant-sounding tones. Everything will probably be geared toward getting enough skill to play in the school band or orchestra. It is truly amazing how quickly most students progress once they begin playing a band or orchestra instrument. This is especially true if they have had a wealth of musical experiences prior to beginning.

Age-appropriate Music Study during the Teen Years

For the child interested in music, there is no substitute during the teen years for private lessons on the instrument of their choice. Group lessons will no longer provide the detailed guidance needed. Also, playing in band (while offering a great experience) does not provide the detailed growth needed at this time. If there has been a childhood of appropriate musical experiences to this point, it is not too late to begin private lessons. Interestingly, research has shown that students who start lessons on a brass or woodwind instrument at age twelve quickly catch up with students who began at age ten. They also will be more likely to continue.[26]

This research may sound contrary to the importance I have placed on early musical experiences for your child, but it really is not. These studies concern learning regular band instruments from start. In other words, what they are saying is that twelve-year-olds can catch up in one year to other twelve-year-olds who started at age ten. But all these students are still playing at a pretty basic level. The effects of all musical experiences provided to them when they were young will become evident as they become better players on their instruments and are able to demonstrate their musicality better. So, in many ways it can be argued that if there has been ample musical experience throughout childhood, the early teen years may be the appropriate time to start private lessons on most instruments.

During this time, some of the more physically challenging instruments are begun. These instruments include the oboe, French horn, baritone, and tuba.

What does this instruction look like?

The lessons at this stage are much more serious and businesslike than earlier lessons. The focus is clearly on developing skills on the instrument. Much more will be expected of your child. Also, music theory (which teaches about how music is constructed) should become an important part of the learning process. To add music theory, the teacher may use workbooks, computer programs, or lessons. If the teacher does not include theory, you should inquire why not.

In short, music instruction will become much more work than ever before. But the reward is in the accomplishments associated with achievement. Unfortunately, this increase of expectations corresponds to the age at which children begin to rebel against rules and authority figures. For many students, this combination results in the stopping of lessons. Private music teachers are very aware of this problem, and experienced teachers will do an amazing balancing act between pushing and holding back your child. The maxim that each child is different is never so true as during the teenage years. Good teachers are worth whatever they charge, because they earn it.

Summary

The answer to the question "what age should my child begin taking lessons?" is as follows. You should surround your child with music from as early an age as possible. Starting at around eighteen months, some sort of structured music activities can prove very beneficial for developing the musical aptitude that will remain with your child for life. Your child should learn to move to the expressive qualities of music, identify different styles of music, experience patterns in music, and develop basic skills, such as marching to a steady beat. These activities should not emphasize an instrument or involve music reading.

Starting around age five, it is time to consider beginning instruction on piano or strings. These instruments are wonderful tools for developing basic musical skills such as phrasing, rhythm, tempo, and dynamics. The emphasis is still on developing your child's musical aptitude.

Between the ages of ten and twelve, your child can add an instrument or switch to a wider variety of instruments, such as trumpet, saxophone, clarinet, trombone, flute, bass, guitar, and drums. This will often happen in conjunction with the school music program and lessons will most likely be in small groups. Musical achievement becomes the primary goal now.

During the teen years, more physically demanding instruments such as bassoon, double bass, French or English horn, baritone, or tuba may be started. Private lessons are necessary for the serious student. Music theory should also become a part of private instruction.

There are no absolutes, yet it should be clear that the type of lessons you provide for your child would change as the child grows. Not only will the actual instruction change, but so will the goals of the instruction. If you understand and keep the goal of the instruction as the main focus, you will probably make the right decisions at each point.

Chapter 4

Measuring Musical Talent

If you remember from Chapter 1, aptitude is the term used to describe your child's *potential* for becoming musical. Aptitude is what most people call talent. You would think it would be pretty straightforward to tell if individuals have aptitude. Simply listen to them play their instrument and, if they play well, they are talented; if they don't, they are not. End of story.

Unfortunately, it is a bit more complex than that. First, not everyone lives up to his potential. Second, something may be keeping a child from showing his potential. For example, a child may be a wonderfully talented pianist, but if she sprained a finger the day before her playing test, she would not score up to her potential. More subtle examples would be a child who was asked to perform when he was not feeling well, was distracted or upset, or simply was not used to the piano being played.

The same is true in a variety of settings. How can you spot a child with high musical potential if the child is too young to play an instrument? What if a child with high musical potential comes from a family that could not provide the opportunities to learn to play an instrument? What if the child is trying to play an instrument for which she is not well suited? All these situations would hinder the ability to identify musical talent in a child.

You may be wondering if it is important to actually measure a person's musical potential. You are not alone. Testing is a very controversial topic in music education and I will make no attempt to try to solve that controversy here.

Still, some schools do give formal music aptitude tests and many others use informal methods to identify aptitude. As a parent, knowing what these tests can and cannot determine will help you. I am not including the addresses for purchasing these tests because they are not intended for use by nontrained personnel. Instead, I offer these descriptions to help you understand the process if your child's aptitude is tested.

Why test?

The primary reason to test for musical aptitude is to identify a child who has outstanding potential so that it can be properly nurtured. Some schools test for this and place students in a gifted and talented program based on their musical, not academic, talent. The second reason is to identify children who have low potential—they will need extra attention to help them along. For the vast majority of children in the middle, I am not sure testing has much usefulness. From a teacher, parent, or student standpoint, it would not seem to help much to know you are average. In fact, it can be detrimental to a child's motivation and drive to know that he or she is average. Still, there is no way to determine who is above or below average without also identifying all the kids in the middle.

How to Use the Results of an Aptitude Test

There are many tests available that will measure musical aptitude. Regardless of the test used, you must remember that it is only one piece of the whole puzzle. No test can predict who will become a great musician because aptitude is only one ingredient. Becoming a good musician takes a combination of effort, the proper opportunities, intelligence, interest, and personality.

The primary reason to test for musical aptitude is to identify a child who has outstanding potential so that it can be properly nurtured.

This multifaceted foundation for musical skill is supported in the research literature and by common sense. Every study I have read that looks at good musicians finds that aptitude is just one ingredient.[1] Talk to accomplished musicians and they will tell you about people they have known who seem to have more musical aptitude than they do, but never became good musicians because they were not self-motivated or interested enough to practice.

Once you have the results of the aptitude test and other indicators, what you choose to do with these results varies. If your child shows high potential, you will probably want to provide every possible musical experience. However, I would hope you would do this even for a child of average ability. One thing that should never be done is to use a test to exclude a child from receiving music instruction. Every child has some degree of ability. A test can sometimes identify the child who will need extra help and experiences to reach her potential.

Many teachers feel that they do not need a test to tell if someone has musical aptitude. They can just "see" it when working privately with a student. All children are attracted to what they are good at. Therefore, a child with high musical aptitude will be drawn to playing instruments, singing, or dancing.

Still, tests can be very valuable, especially in school settings. Public school music teachers often meet with several hundred students each week. There is no possible way for them to identify the aptitude of all their students without the aid of a test. The danger is that some potentially talented child could get lost in the cracks. Therefore, tests can be a real aid to both teachers and parents.

Norms

Just about all musical aptitude tests are based on norms. To establish norms, a test is given to many students from a variety of settings and backgrounds. From these scores, it is determined what is average (and therefore what is above and below average). Usually there are different norms for different ages and different norms for boys and girls.

A test that is based on norms is called a standardized test. Every standardized test produces a variety of scores (a raw score, a *t* score, a stanine score, a percentile rank score). Perhaps the easiest score to interpret is a percentile rank. This score simply tells you what percentage of children scored below your child's score. So a percentile rank score of 65 says that 65 percent of the students scored lower. When interpreting these scores, it is important to remember that most people who take the test will be in the average range. Because there are so many people in the middle, a small difference in the score of the test could result in a large difference in percentile.

For example, consider a marathon. After the race has been under way for some time, three distinct groups will emerge: a small group way out in front, a large group in the middle, and another small group far behind. If you are in the middle group, you will have people all around you. If you run a little faster, you will pass several people, thus having more people behind you. This is like moving up in a percentile rank. But if you are in the front group, there are fewer people to pass. If you run a little faster, you will probably pass no one and so your percentile rank will not change. In other words, if you increase your speed while in the average range, you will have an increase in percentile rank because you have passed a certain percentage of the other runners. If you increase your speed exactly the same amount while running with the faster (and thus smaller) group, you might have little or no change in percentile rank because you pass fewer people.

The same is true with standardized tests. One or two answers, either right or wrong, will affect percentile rank substantially if that rank is in the average range, but may not do much if your child's score is already high or low. Therefore, I suggest concentrating on the following rule of thumb. Consider just about anything between the 35th and 65th percentile as average. Use the 65th to 80th percentile as above average. Above the 80th percentile is outstanding.

Available Tests

Several tests are commercially available. The ones described here are the most popular and will most likely be those you may encounter as a parent. For more detail on these tests, other tests, or any of the issues involved with musical testing, I direct you to the book *Measurement and Evaluation of Musical Experiences* by Boyle and Radocy.[2]

Seashore Measures of Musical Talents—as idyllic as its name implies, this test has nothing whatsoever to do with an actual seashore. Instead it is named after the test's creator, Carl Seashore. This is the oldest available test and has six sections: pitch, loudness, rhythm, time, timbre, and tonal memory. In each section the child listens to pairs of example and has to determine whether they are the same or different. This is intended for grades 4 through 12.

The *Musical Aptitude Profile* is a test intended for grades 4 through 12. This test, created by researcher Edwin Gordon, is probably the most popular test of aptitude in use today. It has three major divisions: tonal imagery, rhythm imagery, and musical sensitivity. The first two sections require the student to hear two pairs of musical phrases and determine whether they are the same or different. The last section plays short sections of music and asks the student if the second was better, the same, or worse than the first. The "correct" answer in each section was determined by trained musicians agreeing on which was better.

Offshoots of the Musical Aptitude Profile, also created by Edwin Gordon, are the *Primary Measures of Musical Audiation*, which is intended for children in kindergarten through grade 3, the *Intermediate Measures of Music Audiation*, intended to help discriminate children who do well on the primary version (above the 80th percentile), and *Audie*, a test for children ages six month to five years.

In addition to these standardized tests, there are many instrument manufacturer tests for teachers to use. One of the most popular is the Selmer test, which is marketed by the Selmer Instrument Company. These tests are very popular because they are readily available, inexpensive, and provide the music teacher with practical information. They are designed to test students' potential in music and also to help determine which instrument will be best for them. Naturally, the instrument manufacturers want every child to end up with an instrument, so it is pretty hard to score poorly on one of these tests. Still, many teachers find the results to be helpful.

Many music stores advertise that they will give a free piano lesson with a test that predicts your child's potential. These are the same types of tests as those designed for use in school, but are geared toward private lessons. They probably have some worth, but I doubt that these tests would show anybody as less than slightly above average. It would not be a great marketing technique for a music store to tell a parent "Your son's musical potential is below average. Can I interest you in renting a piano and purchasing six months worth of lessons?"

Creating a good test of a child's musical potential is difficult and time consuming. Still, many teachers devise such tests, often with surprisingly good results. Your child's teacher may have a variety of tests to help in determining your child's potential. These often involve having your child echo rhythmic clapping or echo sing a short phrase. Often teachers ask the child to attempt to play an instrument so they can check things like body and finger size as it relates to the instrument.

Such tests can be quite accurate. But they depend on the observation and experience of the teacher. As I noted earlier, an experienced music teacher can often assess a student's potential. These little tests allow them to observe your child and make a determination. Although not scientific, they are often surprisingly accurate, but can be quite off the mark as well.

In these tests, as in all tests, it is important to remember that no one test will determine your child's musical potential. Take all the information available to you, add some common sense regarding your child, and trust your gut reaction. This combination will produce the best possible results.

Chapter 5

Creating a Musical Home Environment

A music teacher I know recently asked his junior high students to write an essay about their first true memory of music. He also came to one of my graduate classes and asked my adult musician students the same question. What was fascinating was how similar the answers of both groups were.

In most cases, these "revelation" experiences had three things in common. First, the student's first *true* memory of music was around the age of four. Second, in almost every case, the experience involved a parent, usually the mother. Third, the experience usually revolved around everyday music—not some great classical piece. For example, one graduate student remembered listening to her mom singing the song "Rainy Days and Mondays" by the Carpenters and noticing how involved she was in the process. Another student was playing with toys and got distracted by his mom playing the record "Light My Fire" by the Doors; a third talked about hearing the song "Feelings" and realizing for the first time "what music was."

This points out some of the most crucial aspects of raising musical children. As a parent, you are the most significant force in your child's musical development. The groundwork will be laid when your child is very young, and you don't have to be a great or accomplished musician to have a positive effect. What you do, or do not do, will have lifetime effects. In this chapter, we will examine some of the ways you can create a musical environment for your child.

The Importance of Role Models

Like it or not, we are role models for our children. "The apple doesn't fall far from the tree" has as much relevance today as it did when it was first coined. So an important place to start is by examining *your* musical behaviors.

Notice that in the previous examples, the mothers were not doing anything that would be considered out of the ordinary with music. They were not concert artists, nor did they invite a string quartet to practice in their home. Instead, their children remembered these musical events because they were important to the parent. The Carpenter song scenario is an excellent example. The student recalled that her mom was singing along with the radio with such feeling and emotion that it caught the attention of the child. That, in turn, drew the child's attention to the music.

Children are great at figuring out what is *truly* important to adults. Your body language, verbal language, actions, or inaction toward music all speak very loudly. To make the statement "Music is important in this house" here are some suggestions.

Bathe Your Home in Music

When we go to a nice restaurant, we know that music helps add atmosphere and a humanizing effect. We can make our homes much more beautiful by adding music as well. Beyond the basic humanizing effect, there is a basic musical function inherent in playing music. The purpose of surrounding children with music is to enable them to begin learning the vocabulary of music. Children who are surrounded with language (as most children are) learn to recognize the basic rhythm patterns, sounds, and inflections of their language just by hearing it. Children who are not exposed to language at an early age can display delayed language development. A child's babbling reflects the inflections, sounds, and rhythms of the language with which they are surrounded. Chinese babies babble in Chinese sounds, English children babble in English sounds.

So too with music. As explained in the previous chapter, music is made up of basic vocabularies of rhythm patterns, pitch patterns, and timbre. These are different and unique for each style of music from country to classical to Chinese. Your child's brain will begin to recognize these patterns by repeated hearings of them. But it takes many exposures before they will begin to sink in. Having music playing in the background of your home provides an almost unconscious music lesson for your child. Just as children do not understand the conversations around them when they are young, they may not understand the music around them. This is fine. They are picking out the basic elements of music and incorporating them into their concepts.

What recordings are best? I think *any* music being played in the home is hands down better than no music. Still, I find that parents are always asking for some advice about building a good listening library for children, so at the back of the book I offer some suggestions in Appendix D.

Listen to Music with Your Child

Listening to music is quite a bit different from the first suggestion of bathing your home in music. We can have music around us all the time (and often do), but not really listen to it. Listening takes focus. Just as reading advocates suggest you read *with* your child, you should also actively listen to music with your child. How do you do this?

Pick a recording of a piece of music that you really like. Try to select something short, under three or four minutes. Listen and talk with your child about it. Talk about what you like about it, how it makes you feel, what color you think it is, what sounds you like. Let your emotion about the music be evident. Don't worry too much about right or wrong, proper musical terms, or anything. This is not a formal lesson. You are working to send the message "I love music and I want to share it with you." You are also teaching your child to focus on music.

I remember being about five years old and driving along the coast of Lake Erie with my dad. Suddenly he turned up the radio when a new song started that he obviously knew. He said: "Listen to this song. Doesn't it make you feel like you are traveling on that boat?" He pointed to a motorboat on the lake. I remember this vividly because I listened to the music intently and realized he was right. It *did* make me feel as if I was on the boat. I have no idea what the song was, something long forgotten, but I remember the lesson: Music moves my dad, music has strong powers, and it is an exciting thing. This worked because it focused me on the music and sent a strong message.

That is the point. If you are reading this book, then I suspect music is important to you. Make sure your child knows this. Actively listen and talk about music with your child. Point out things in the music such as: *That is a very pretty instrument playing; I like the mood this music creates; This music has tons of energy; This music would be good as background for a love story; This music has such a strong beat it makes me want to march*. Also, ask your child questions about the music. "Do you know what kind of music this is?" "Do you know what instrument that is?" "Do you think this music moves quickly or slowly?" "What color does this music make you think of?"

As you can see, these are not profoundly musical questions. Some do not even have a "correct" answer. The purpose of these statements and questions is to focus your child on the music. Your goal is to make children actively listen to the music and become aware of the joy it can provide in their lives.

There is one other goal of this activity. In the previous chapter, I talked about the importance of a child and young adults being able to classify music by style. Active listening activities are a great way to make sure this is done. Although this takes some musical judgment on the part of the parent, for most it is within reach. Simply ask your child, "What kind of music is this?" Or explain, "This type of music is called jazz (rock, swing, classical, Indian, etc.)." Nurture their answers into proper musical classifications just as you would if they looked at a chair and said "table" or "sit thing." Your goal with these questions is to help your child start to create proper musical concepts they can build on for life.

Active listening can happen just about anywhere. One of the best places may be the family car. You probably spend a good part of your waking hours shuttling your children around. Your car most likely has a radio, tape deck, or a CD player. This active listening can be a fun and rewarding use of commuting time.

About the only mistake I could see a parent making in regard to encouraging active listening is doing it too much (so it becomes a chore), or too little (so that it does not make an impression). There are no exact answers here, but short sessions on a very regular basis (every other day?) may be the best.

One last point. This active listening is easier now than any time during the history of humanity. The wealth of items available on CD, the Internet, television (especially cable), and videotape is excitingly overwhelming. Take advantage of this colorful musical world already at your fingertips.

Expand Your Child's (and Your) Musical Universe

Children are generally open to a wide variety of music. So the early years provide you, the parent, a great window of opportunity for introducing your child to a wide variety of music. Unfortunately, I feel this opportunity is often wasted or even undermined by most parents. It is lost by parents not willing to expand and undermined by those trying to indoctrinate their children into liking a certain type of music.

We will look at not expanding first. We are all comfortable with a certain kind of music. For many people, the style of music they surround themselves with during their teen years is a favored style for the remainder of their life.[1] This means that parents who are in their mid- to late twenties are going to be playing music related to their tastes that were formed ten to fifteen years earlier. This really represents an extremely small slice of the world of music. Having children provides a wonderful reason to expand *your* musical horizons.

Please note that I am not suggesting that you as a parent need to change your musical tastes or that there is anything wrong with the music created in the past decade or so. Instead, I am simply suggesting that there is more, much more, music that can be explored.

The other side of the coin is the parent who works to indoctrinate a child into liking a certain kind of music. While this is often done with the best of intentions, it is not in the best interest of the child's musical development.

I have met many parents who attempt at this time to expose their kids to only classical, or country, or some other style of music. I have seen grandparents trying to force Frank Sinatra on teenagers. I have known parents who allow children to listen to Christian rock only. From a musical growth standpoint, this is not appropriate. Remember that you are trying to provide your child with the experiences that will help them make sense out of this wide world of music.

Therefore, childhood should be a time for exploring the whole world of music, especially those styles that are unfamiliar to us. As you do with food, strive to have a balanced diet, including current music, bluegrass, jazz, film music, early rock and roll, folk, classical, and musicals. These can be very rousing types of music to children. Also, the many musical styles not from the Western tradition (Asian, Middle Eastern, African, Polynesian, etc.) can be exciting. Your children are still very accepting of the different sounds and rhythms (probably more than you are!) and this exposure will help them expand their concept of music. Here is one area in which you, as a parent, will also expand. Who knows—you may fall in love with a style of music you never knew existed.

Your local library is a great resource. In years past, records from libraries were always scratched, dirty, and otherwise less than acceptable. With the advent of CDs this is no longer true. Recordings from the library sound great. Just about every library will have a wide variety of music available. Explore, experiment, and check things out. The nice part is that it costs you nothing. If you really don't like something you check out, nothing is lost. If you have an active listening time with your child, even lousy music can have educational results.

Here is an important point when listening to new types of music: Don't expect one session to be enough. It takes at least five hearings for a new piece of music to grow on you.[2] Radio stations are very aware of this phenomenon and often play songs repeatedly until you like them. The same is true when exposing your child to new types of music. Many parents (and teachers) make the mistake of playing a new piece of music (whether a Beethoven symphony or a Balinese gamelan) only once. Instead, think of ways to play the piece many times. Perhaps it could be used as background for some other activity around the house several times before it becomes part of an active listening game.

Dance with Your Child

I suggest you dance with your child often. Maybe "dance" is too strong a term for what I am suggesting you do with your child. Music psychologists have noted that one seemingly universal response to music in all cultures, past and present, is that people move when they hear it. This is not always dancing. People sway, tap their feet, bounce around, and move their heads, arms, or legs. Eventually these motions lead to the more formal discipline of dance. But the root of all dance is a very human, and natural, response to music. In fact, "nearly all babies [under one year of age] make some sort of movement response [when they hear music]."[3]

Your child can participate in this activity. I see parents holding their children and swaying to music, bopping to music, and just about everything in between. This is great. Movement actively involves the child from the earliest ages in a response to music. Moving your child's hands and feet to the beat, or tapping out simple rhythms is

Dancing with your child helps the child focus on the music.

also valuable. Move hands to the ups and downs of the melody, change direction when the chords change, or change the size of the movements in relation to the volume. Make it fun. The experience of moving in response to the music is what is important. Especially for children under four or five, specific musical goals (maintaining a steady beat or rhythm pattern) are not the reason for these activities.

Make Music with Your Child

I recently heard an interview with the singer Celine Dion. She was explaining how her family would make musical bands at the dinner table by taking silverware and tapping out complementary rhythms on the glasses and tabletop. The younger children in the family kept the beat while the older children added layers of rhythms on top of it. Everybody sang.

There is absolutely no substitute for immersing your child in these types of activities. During childhood, you should strive to sing, move, and play music with your child. Actively involve your child with music on a day-to-day basis and also play a variety of music styles. Keep music in the home at this point. Remember, you are building, through experience, the basic music concepts that your children will use for the rest of their lives. Concepts will not develop without regular and extensive musical experience.

This is not as difficult as you might think. The most obvious way to make music is through singing. Choose songs that are lively with an easy melody and simple words. For a great start in finding songs, refer to the list of songs that Americans should know compiled by the Music Educators National Conference and reprinted in Appendix B.

When singing with your young child, keep the following in mind. Try to pick songs with a limited range of tones that are adjacent to one another (in other words, they don't skip around). Second, try to sing in the range in which your child can sing. Many parents sing songs in their adult range and the child cannot join in. The basic range of a young child is about middle C to G above that. If you are in doubt, just pay attention to your child's natural voice and see if you can sing along with him or her, instead of the other way around. This is especially true of fathers who will have voices much lower than their child's.

At first, children will have much trouble matching the correct pitches or will wander from key to key with only a few tones in tune. This is OK. Singing is a skill that needs to be developed over time. Also, singing is a reflection of not only the child's singing ability, but also what the child is learning about music. The process is slow, but with much repeated practice great things could be accomplished.

The second way to make music with your child is through rhythm activities. You can help your child feel the beat by encouraging him to tap or clap along with a song. You can also pick a simple rhythm pattern (such as long-short-short-long-long) that can be repeated throughout a song or piece of music. Another fun activity is to hit different parts of the body for making different sounds. Hit your knee, and it sounds different from a clap on your stomach. Simply exploring sounds can create some interesting rhythm patterns.

Another fun and educational activity is to have your child repeat rhythm patterns that you play. For example, you play long-long short-short-long and your child echoes it back. Slowly the patterns can get longer, which develops your child's musical memory.

The importance of these experiences is not to create a polished performer. Instead, they are all used to develop an awareness of pitch and rhythm patterns in music, help your child to maintain a steady rhythm or beat, and let the child experience the fun of music making. Some musical goals may be appropriate. With children under five,

Making instruments can be fun for your child and you!

helping them to maintain a steady beat throughout a variety of songs is a worthwhile goal. Some children (especially boys) will have great difficulty with this.[4] Having them repeatedly march, clap, and play instruments will help them develop this crucial musical skill.

An often overlooked resource at this age is the family of rhythm instruments. Most children's bookstores will sell highly attractive packages of rhythm instruments that are very appealing to children. These tambourines, clickers, drums, and shakers can be used to play along with favorite records or accompany family singing.

As attractive as these instruments are, it is not necessary to buy them. A fun and creative activity would be to make instruments with your child. Coffee cans with plastic lids make fine drums; new (unused) flowerpots when hung upside down and struck with a mallet make great tuned gongs. One of my favorite instruments is made by cutting two-inch diameter metal electrical conduit (available at any home improvement store) into various lengths from one to two feet long. Drill a hole through one end of each pipe and suspend them. Each piece will create a unique and pleasant-sounding pitch. The mallets for these instruments can be made by wrapping duct tape around the end of a stick. Lengths of each pipe are given in Table 5-1.

Be creative in finding sound sources. I once had a sixth-grade student who had learned to play an entire repertoire of songs by changing the speeds on a blender. The motor sound would change pitches, up or down, depending on the speed. He was extremely good at this and I had him perform, to a standing ovation, at open house. One important point needs to be mentioned. When encouraging your chil-

TABLE 5-1 LENGTHS OF ELECTRICAL CONDUIT
NEEDED TO CREATE A XYLOPHONE

PITCH	LARGE INSTRUMENT	SMALL INSTRUMENT
Low sol	22-7/16"	11-7/32"
Low la	21-1/4"	10-5/8"
Low ti	20"	10"
Do	19-1/2"	9-3/4"
Re	18-1/4"	9-1/8"
Mi	17-1/8"	8-9/16"
Fa	16-5/8"	8-5/16"
Sol	15-5/8"	7-13/16"
La	14-3/4"	7-3/8"
Ti	13-3/4"	6-7/8"
High do	13-7/16""	6-23/32"

NOTE: For a large instrument, you will need 20 feet of 1/2 electrical conduit or copper plumbing pipe (which is more expensive). For a small instrument, you will need 10 feet of the same.

When you place the lengths of pipe on the felt or Styrofoam, put the holder about one-third in on each pipe. Or you can simply make a hanging tree and suspend them horizontally by wrapping string around them (they will look like a Christmas tree).

dren to make these sounds, you should encourage them to make *musical* sounds. Many music teachers have students clap using only the first two fingers of each hand. This creates a softer sound and does not overpower the rest of the music. The same can be done with gently striking instruments. These instruments are either musical instruments or noisemakers depending on how they are played. The choice is yours.

Experience Live Music with Your Child

There is nothing like experiencing music live. While recordings are wonderful techniques for preparing for a concert and follow-up, nothing can substitute for actually attending a concert. Seeing the performers, their instruments, the audience, the lights, are all part of the event. This adds to the excitement for children.

Once your child is old enough to attend a concert without disturbing other audience members you should try to take her to concerts on a regular basis. Just about every orchestra in the country performs children's concerts throughout its season, and there are almost certainly concerts at your local high school, college, and community center. Outdoor summer concerts are especially attractive to kids. A tradition we had with our children was to go hear the Cleveland Orchestra perform the 1812 Overture every Independence Day weekend. We would sit on the grass at their outdoor performance hall. The concert always ended with real cannons and fireworks. The kids talk about it to this day.

Look for opportunities. Most major newspapers have weekly listings of activities appropriate for children. Local museums, orchestras, and schools often present regular concerts geared to children. Many regular concerts are also appropriate for children of different ages. If you have any doubts, call the box office personnel and ask. I find they usually will be very honest about whether a particular concert will be appropriate for your age child.

Make Music Yourself

This is so obvious it hardly needs mentioning. We are great role models for our children. If you played an instrument in the past, pull it out of the closet and play it; if you never learned to play an instrument, why not start now? You and your child can learn together.

When our girls were in elementary school there was a male teacher at the school who decided to learn to play piano. Every spring he would play in the school talent show. The first year he was pretty weak, far worse than many of the student piano players. But every year he got better and better. What was so amazing was the students' response. They saw him, an adult, struggling with something many of them were having difficulty with as kids. The audience would go crazy when he finished his performance. He sent a strong message not only to the kids, but also to us adults: This is important to me and I am not too old to begin. I admire him to this day.

As Your Child Gets Older
Most of the previous suggestions were intended for use when your children are young. However, most are important and appropriate throughout your child's life at home. Certainly the music will change,

but you can still bathe your home in music and actively listen to music. You can also continue making music with your child, but the roles may change. It may not be long until your son or daughter is better than you are at making music. If so, *you* can be the person keeping the beat while *they* play. Or perhaps you can play duets or put together a family band or orchestra.

Ours kids are all teenagers now. One of our favorite pastimes is to make a bonfire (or go camping) and play music around the fire. We play the banjo, guitar, mandolin, dulcimer, and, of course, we all sing. Often our kids' friends come over and we try to have some extra instruments and let them join us or sing along. We have a great time.

During the teenage years your children's music listening habits will begin to be influenced by their peers. It is important to listen to this music with an open mind. Don't condemn it because you don't like it. They probably listened to music they didn't like that you played for them at some point. Instead, try to listen actively. Change roles; let your children guide you through their music. Teenagers of all generations have claimed the music of their teen years as their identity, often for life. You probably did it and your grandchildren will do the same. Respect their ownership of their teen music, but don't try to make it yours. You could strike a deal; they leave the music of your teenage years for your memories and you will leave theirs for their memories.

You will also continue to play a supporting role. Your contribution to your child's musical lives will be driving to lessons, encouraging practice, buying instruments, going to recitals and concerts. These are all signs of support. Perform them with enthusiasm and don't underestimate the importance of your involvement. Your children may not outwardly thank you for coming to their choir concert, but from my years as a middle school music teacher I can assure you that they know you are there.

So, in summary, even as the kids get older, keep the music making and listening a part of family life. Sing, play, listen, and talk. Have fun. Do it with enthusiasm. Do it regularly.

Chapter 6

Finding a Good Private Teacher

Hang around the office of any university music department and you will be surprised at the number of parents who call on any given *day* asking for the names of college students to give private lessons to their kids. These parents can be divided into three categories. The first are the parents who are shopping all possible resources to locate a future teacher. The second are those looking for a bargain, rationalizing that college students, in need of ready cash, will teach cheaper than other musicians. Last are the ones who have no idea where to begin looking for a music teacher for their children. All these parents have found that there are few objective sources to turn to for advice when seeking a private music teacher. I can relate. Finding a really good private teacher is perhaps one of the hardest tasks you will undertake for your child's musical development.

It seems that just about anybody who plays an instrument feels qualified to teach private music lessons. This is one of the biggest myths in the profession. The ability to play an instrument well seems to have little relationship to being able to teach that instrument to beginners. When you think about this, it makes sense. A person who plays with a local symphony may be so far removed from the struggles of a beginner that he or she cannot relate at all to a child.

Now let me clarify that, for proper instruction, teachers should be quite competent on their instruments, otherwise they could be teaching the fundamental technique of the instrument incorrectly. But finding the best performer in town to teach your child is not necessarily the best way to proceed.

I am not alone in this opinion. A very interesting book by Benjamin Bloom called *Developing Talent in Young People*[1] details a research study in which he looked at the early instruction of truly outstanding musicians, athletes, mathematicians, artists, and a variety of stars in other disciplines. One factor common to all these successful people was that their first private teachers (whether in music, dance, or sports) were extremely caring, patient, and enthusiastic. These teachers tended to focus on the child, not the subject matter. In most cases, the first teachers were not great at their trade of piano, swimming, or baseball, but they were able to capture the student's imagination and attention and focus it toward the instrument.

My years of experience support what Bloom found. There are many out-of-work musicians who teach private lessons because they cannot support themselves performing. By their own admission, their instrument and their performing comes before anything. Some of them may be good teachers, yet many are not.

But how *do* you find a good private teacher for your child? Locating the right teacher has been perhaps the hardest part, personally, of raising our own kids. In this chapter, we will examine some guidelines that should help.

Where should you look for a teacher?

You can find music teachers just about anywhere. Next time you're in the grocery store, check the bulletin board as you walk in and there will almost certainly be music teachers advertised. The phone book, local newspaper, local college office, and websites will all list private teachers, most of whom will teach in their home. If you are fortunate enough to live in an area with a community music school, you will find many quality teachers there. Last, but not least, your local music store is probably providing teaching space for many private teachers

First let's examine the teachers who are advertising on bulletin boards, phone books, and newspapers. It has been my experience that the best private teachers will not be found through any of these sources. The really good teachers tend to be so popular and successful that they have all the students they can handle just through word of mouth.

Consider this: A full-time private teacher probably teaches between twenty-five and forty students per week. Now consider a piano teacher who has 60 percent of his or her students returning each year and starts with five first graders in the first year of teaching. If we assume that each student will take lessons into their high school years and the teacher accepts five new first graders each year, then after a few years, this teacher has all the students he or she can handle and cannot even accept any new first graders. The only new openings in this teacher's studio occur when someone stops taking lessons. These few openings don't need to be advertised. Instead, this teacher probably has a waiting list just due to word-of-mouth advertising.

Therefore, the teachers you find through advertising are very likely (1) beginning teachers, (2) unsuccessful teachers, (3) teachers new to town, or (4) teachers who can't find students on their own. Although some of these teachers may be excellent (especially those new to the area), the odds are against your finding a really good teacher through this method. Still, it remains that many excellent teachers teach out of their homes—but how do you find them?

I strongly suggest that you actively seek the advice of other parents, the music teacher at the local elementary or high school, or the local chapter of Music Teacher's National Association (MTNA), which will be discussed in more detail. When asking around, you will be amazed at how often the names of the really good teachers come up. Don't be surprised to hear the same recommendation from two or three sources. These teachers are the ones who are in the loop. For this reason, these teachers will usually be able to recommend other quality teachers if they don't have room for your child themselves.

Another avenue to pursue is your local music store. Usually the store will rent space to private teachers for the purpose of teaching private lessons. The store takes a percentage of the lesson fee in return for providing space, a phone contact, and the like. However, this can be somewhat hit-and-miss as well. The primary reason for many stores allowing lessons is to get traffic into their business. Parents waiting for their children are likely to shop in the store. Further, lesson materials and instruments will likely be purchased from the store. Although these are all great conveniences for both parents and teacher, the fact remains that the primary purpose of the store is sales, not instruction. While some stores take great pride in monitoring what is taught in the lessons, many do not. Therefore, the quality of instruction may be uneven, with few guarantees of quality.

Unlike the music store, the community music school is designed to be first and foremost an educational institution. My first teaching job was at the Cleveland Music School Settlement where I taught piano and music theory to youngsters ages six to sixteen every day from

3 to 9 P.M. I still remember the joy of simply being in the atmosphere of a school totally devoted to music. There was music everywhere. The feeling among faculty, staff, and students was one of supporting the learning of music. I can think of no better environment to immerse your child in.

Not every community will have a school such as this, but those that do seem to follow a common structure. Private lessons will be offered on a variety of instruments as well as enhancement classes in music theory, history, and composition. Often there are concerts to attend and musical activities, such as chamber music and ensembles, in which your child can participate. Usually the quality of teaching is assured through the administrator of the school whose responsibility it is to ensure quality teaching.

There are many different types of community music schools. Some are associated with universities or colleges (often called preparatory programs), others are for-profit schools, while still others are non-profit and supported by grants, tuition, or donations. Regardless of the structure, community music schools provide a great resource to the community.

Another great resource for private lessons may be your local public school. I know many music teachers who arrange for private teachers to come to their school and give lessons after school to interested students. Although the parent still pays for the private lesson, the music teacher assures the quality because the private teachers are hand chosen. Another advantage is that these private teachers are often in sync with the goals and curriculum of the school program, ensuring that what your child is taught in the private lesson will be reinforced in the school music program. However, because school programs tend to be band oriented, the lessons are often confined to those instruments. Some schools are also forbidden to allow private lessons because of liability concerns.

Despite these options, the fact remains that it is difficult to find a good private teacher. I suggest being one of those parents who explores options in your community before committing to one particular institution.

What should you look for in a teacher?

When you are examining at the credentials of a music teacher for your child, I would probably not be too impressed or concerned if this

*Knowing what to look for in a private
teacher is as important as knowing where
to look.*

person played with the New York Philharmonic, has a degree from
Juilliard, or won major competitions on her instrument. Instead, it
seems that the music teacher who talks of the accomplishments of his
students or explains the musical path he envisions for your child is
the better teacher. Although it is important that the teacher play an
instrument well, the person does not have to be a concert soloist or of
the caliber to play with a major symphony orchestra to be a great
teacher. So the first piece of advice is to analyze the words (written or
spoken) of a potential teacher. If the teacher focuses primarily on her
accomplishments (degrees, performances, and former teachers) instead of her students, she is probably not the right person for your
child.

It has been my experience that the best private teachers are also
involved with one of the local professional organizations of music
teachers. The largest of these for private teachers is the Music Teachers National Association (MTNA); it has local chapters in many cities
both large and small. This organization will often sponsor competitions, festivals, workshops, and will sometimes even have a suggested
curriculum outlining the skills that should be taught at each stage of
the lessons. Although this is no guarantee of quality, finding individuals involved with this type of organization will focus you on the
most serious and professional private teachers. MTNA tends to concentrate on piano teachers, the American String Teachers Association
(ASTA) focuses on string instruction, and the National Association of
Teachers of Singing (NATS) emphasizes voice training. I know of no
organization for band instruments focused on private instruction.
Information for reaching these organizations is listed in the Resources for Parents section at the end of the book. The national office
of each organization will be able to put you in touch with the local
chapter president.

Another important point is to ask for references. However, if you found this teacher through word-of-mouth referrals, you can probably skip this step. If the teacher does not have written references, ask if you can call parents of the teacher's students. While I doubt any teacher would simply turn over the names and numbers of all students, most would be willing to give you two or three numbers of parents whom they know would not mind a call or two. In these references, look for mention of the teacher's *teaching* ability, rapport, professionalism, and reliability.

Another indicator may be the type of degree the person has (assuming he or she has one). A degree in music education or pedagogy (the art or profession of teaching), while not ensuring that the person is a great teacher, will give evidence that the person is probably child centered and shows an interest in the teaching side of music.

My last suggestion is to go to the recital that most teachers will organize at the end of the year to showcase the accomplishments of their students. See how the students perform: Are their performances musical? Does it sound good? Do the students seem to be enjoying what they are playing? Listen to what they perform: Is there a variety of musical styles? A recital of all pop music or all classical music demonstrates a lack of variety. What is the rapport between teacher and students? This is a very nervous day for both. Is the teacher supportive of the students? Does he or she seem to know the students? The teacher's body language and whole mannerism during this time can tell you volumes about the teacher.

No teacher will have all the traits described here. No teacher needs all these traits. Use these guidelines to help you find evidence of a musician who takes the role of teaching children seriously and professionally.

One other point needs to be made. All this advice has been given with the idea of looking for your child's *first* private teacher. Your child may reach a level of achievement at which a true expert is needed. It is common for a talented or motivated student to reach a point when their first teacher has little more to offer musically. Often it is the teacher who will spot this and many take it as a great compliment to their teaching abilities.

When this happens, it is time to change. Probably at this point you will have help from the existing teacher or from others. You will also have a better understanding of the needs of your child. While you may know it is best for your child to change teachers, this can still be a delicate and uncomfortable situation for you and your child. At this point it would be easier to simply stay with the current teacher despite your desires. But this will only lead to frustration and lack of learning on the part of your child (and a waste of money for you). There are ways to make this situation easier. Focus on what is best for the musical development of your child. Emphasize how well the teacher has prepared your son or daughter for his or her next step.

Be aware that often the bond between student and teacher has become very strong. Try to not put your child in the middle by using comments such as "Billy feels that . . . " or "Alexis wants . . . " Instead, focus on what you want for your child: the best possible musical experience he or she can have.

What should you expect from lessons?

There are things that your common sense as a parent will tell you to expect from lessons. You should expect your child to be treated with respect, the teacher to act professionally by starting the lesson on time, and the teacher to focus on your child and the child's progress while being encouraging and enthusiastic and avoiding distractions.

Beyond these basics, you should expect other characteristics from a private lesson. First and foremost, the teacher should have a plan for your child. The music that is being taught should progress from one level to another. There are many, many series books containing pieces of music that systematically develop skills in a logical order. Your child could be following one of these or the teacher might have devised her own curriculum using individual pieces. Regardless of the approach, progress should be obvious to you and, more important, your child. If the teacher seems to be arbitrarily choosing pieces of music or, conversely, blindly progressing through a series book with little thought or care, you need to question where the instruction is headed. A good teacher will be able to tell you without hesitation.

This implies that the teacher is the person who picks the music. Although it is important for children to be able to suggest pieces they like, often a song that a child wants will be too difficult or just does not fit the instrument very well (like playing rap music on a trumpet). The teacher should definitely work to accommodate your child's tastes and likes (and good teachers will), but ultimately the final decision on music is up to the teacher.

Something else you should expect from a lesson is that there are clear goals and your child knows what is expected. A teacher should *write down* exactly what he expects. There are music assignment books available at just about every music store. Your child's teacher should write out the week's assignment in some detail. An example of one entry in an assignment book might read: "Bach Invention #2— practice measures 8–16. Concentrate on correct fingerings and keeping the beat steady. Practice these measures slowly at least five times a day with hands separate. Next Thursday try putting both hands together." Most teachers will do this automatically because it helps them as well. You will often see them looking through the book at the start of the lesson to mentally gauge the progress of your child over the past month or so. This helps them decide what needs to be done next and at what rate.

Another thing you should expect from the lessons is for the teacher to be organized and have a system for checking the progress of your child. I don't mean that the teacher should give tests, but it should be very clear to the child that there are goals. You will often hear informal comments such as "Next week I hope that we can finish off the entire first part of this piece so that we can start the second part." Or "This piece is in pretty good shape, but I want you to play it once a day so that you won't forget it before the recital next month."

You should also expect to see progress in your child's ability. Although a teacher cannot make the progress happen (that comes through practice, as explained in the next two chapters), successful lessons should still result in noticeable improvement.

What should you expect to pay?

The fees you can expect to pay for lessons vary over a wide range. My experience has been that you usually get what you pay for. Good private teachers are dedicated to their craft and act professionally. In return, they expect to be paid like a professional. Many parents are shocked at the cost of a private lesson from a good teacher. If you compare it to the hourly rate of a plumber or car mechanic, it is probably similar. Keep in mind that you are not only paying for the half-hour or hour of time. The teacher has to find music, keep track of your child's progress, purchase and maintain an instrument (in the case of piano especially), and perform a whole variety of behind-the-scenes activities.

Lessons are usually given in half-hour or hour segments. Many considerations go into determining the best length. These include the attention span of your child, the amount of time necessary to assemble and tune the instrument (a bassoon takes more prep time than a piano), and the playing ability of your child. It is safe to assume that as your child progresses, the lessons will get longer. A half-hour lesson is adequate for a young beginner, but as the music gets more challenging and your child is able to tackle more music, the lessons need to lengthen.

Your child's teacher will recommend when this lengthening should happen. Naturally, you will need to pay more, but often not double, for an hour lesson instead of a half-hour lesson.

What should the teacher expect from you?

One lesson per week will do very little for your child unless the teacher can rely on your help in a variety of ways. What private teachers seem to want the most is for you to show respect for what they do through *your* actions. For example, arrive at the lesson a few minutes early so your child has a chance to get ready for the lesson. Pick your child up when the lesson is over. A common complaint among music teachers involves the parent who drops the child off for a half-hour lesson, goes to run errands, and returns an hour later. The music teacher is not a baby-sitter. Also, many teachers have problems with payments for lessons. I suggest you pay by the month in advance or at the very least at the lesson. Don't make the teacher have to call and ask for money—ever. If you have to miss a lesson, be sure to make arrangements with the teacher in advance. I have personally sat and waited many times for private students who never show up. Later, a call comes, but I have already wasted that time.

Beyond these professional issues, the teacher can realistically expect you to monitor your child's practicing (more on this in the next chapter). Also, the teacher will expect you to provide the tools for good practicing such as a music stand, a quiet place to practice, easy-to-read music, an in-tune and quality instrument, and a whole host of other considerations such as reeds, keypads, rosin, picks, or new strings.

Lastly, the teacher will expect you to be a partner in your child's musical development. Outside of the weekly half-hour lesson, you are responsible for your child's musical development the other 167 1/2 hours per week. The teacher will expect you to be an ally in working toward this goal.

What should the teacher expect from your child?

The last, but not least, person in the partnership is your child. This is the person whom the two adults (teacher and parent) are working to help. The child has responsibilities to be respectful of the teacher, give her best effort, and trust that the teacher has a plan for her growth. It must be remembered that the child is expected to practice, but can only do so if she understands the procedure. Music lessons are more than learning an instrument; they teach the child how to practice, reach for goals, and make incremental accomplishments.

Your child should be a willing partner along this path. Truthfully, most private teachers have nothing but positive things to say about their students. They tend to live up to their part of the bargain, providing the teacher and parent both live up to theirs.

Wrapping Up

In summary, finding good private teachers is difficult and takes effort on the part of the parent, yet they are definitely out there waiting to help. Here are some of the important points of this chapter:

- Depend on word-of-mouth references from other parents and teachers.
- Check out all resources in your area, including music stores, community music schools, and colleges or universities.
- Look for a teacher who is child centered.
- Teachers involved with professional organizations are often better than teachers who are not.
- The teacher should be competent on his or her instrument.
- Lessons should be organized and show a logical progression of progress.
- Teachers should be professional and focused on your child.
- Professional teachers charge professional fees and are usually worth it.
- The private teacher has certain expectations for you and your child.

Chapter 7

Choosing the Right Instrument for Your Child to Play

For every child who is interested in music there comes a time when that child will have to choose an instrument. For some children, it will just happen. There might be a piano, guitar, or keyboard instrument in the house and the child simply begins to play. But, for most, they will have to make a conscious decision. It is for those children (and their parents) that this chapter is written.

There are few sure or easy rules regarding choosing instruments. The one unchanging rule is that instruments have personalities. Thus, not every instrument is for every child. Matching your child to the right instrument may be one of the most critical decisions you will have to help your child with.

This chapter lays out five guidelines to follow when it comes time for your child to choose an instrument. These guidelines are (1) be sure your child is physically ready to handle the instrument; (2) trust your child's instinct about an instrument; (3) guide your child to choose an instrument for musical, not social, reasons; (4) be sure you can afford to continue with the instrument, but don't let financial considerations rule you; and (5) be sure that any suggestion from a music teacher has your child's best interest in mind. These are not rules. I have seen instances in which each of these guidelines has been successfully broken. But by and large, these are the factors you should keep in mind when helping your child choose an instrument. Also keep in mind that these guidelines may be modified for your own child.

The first guideline is: *Be sure your child is physically ready to handle the instrument.* This seems so logical, yet it is sometimes easily overlooked. Instruments come in all shapes and sizes. Some, like the string bass and the sousaphone, are huge. Others, like the harmonica and piccolo, are tiny. Instruments also require a variety of muscles to operate. Many demand that the facial muscles, finger muscles, arm muscles, back muscles, and sometimes even leg muscles are all sufficiently strong and coordinated enough to work together to produce musical sounds.

A child who is too small or physically undeveloped to handle an instrument cannot be expected to perform on it. Yet this seems to happen all the time. Children are pushed to play instruments they are not ready to handle.

What happens if children try to play an instrument to which they are not physically matched? They can give up in frustration or, worse, become convinced that they cannot play music, no matter what they do. They can learn that they are helpless when it comes to making music.

The psychological literature describes a condition called learned helplessness. This is what you, as a parent, must avoid for your child. Learned helplessness was first noticed in lab animals. Dogs, rats, and pigeons were all placed in a cage with a lever that did nothing.[1] The animals were then put into uncomfortable situations. At first the animals tried hitting the lever to try to get out of the cage. However, that did nothing. Once they gave up trying, the lever was activated to either let them out of the cage or stop whatever was making them uncomfortable. A funny thing happened. The animals could not be taught to use the lever. Instead, they just gave up and did not even try. Quite literally, they had learned to be helpless.

This condition is not confined to animals; it is also a powerful force in humans. I personally feel this way about algebra. I remember well trying hard to do well in algebra—I would study for tests, do the homework assignments, and pay attention in class. When a test would come I would do poorly. When I would not study, do homework, or pay attention in class I would do just as poorly. What I learned from my years of algebra study in high school was that I was completely helpless in learning about algebra. Today when I help my kids with their homework, I can sense the learned helplessness. I understand the feeling from an intellectual standpoint, but it is still there.

I am sure everyone reading this book has experienced learned helplessness at some stage of life. There had to have been a situation when you just felt that no matter what you did you had no control to succeed. The result for most people is that they avoid those situations like the plague.

We don't want that to happen to your child with playing a musical instrument. Yet it occurs all the time. Children are given instruments that are too large for them or too difficult to physically maneuver or control. I have seen third graders given French horns to learn. This instrument requires facial muscles that are not well developed in children of this age. I have seen physically small children given full-size string basses. Their hands could not possibly move on the strings in such a way as to create a good sound. I have seen second graders given guitars with metal strings. Each of these would probably lead to a textbook example of learned helplessness in music.

But it is not only the age of the student that could lead to learned helplessness. The quality of the instrument can also be the culprit. I have seen students trying to play guitars that are of such low quality that I, a professional guitarist, am not able to push down the strings. Or I have observed students trying to learn on a guitar with a warped neck, which means that even when the correct fingerings are put down it will sound wrong.

I have seen clarinetists trying to play with reeds that are a year old. Nothing they do can overcome this reed problem. They are doomed to creating bad sounds. But even "easy" instruments can become frustrating. I remember Mark, one of my sixth-grade students, who was frustrated to the point of tears learning to play the recorder. He was seemingly doing everything right—correct fingerings, mouth position, posture, everything. Still, the sounds his recorder made were just awful. He was ready to throw the instrument away in frustration and anger. As a last ditch effort to help him, I took the recorder apart and out fell a plastic action-figure soldier. He looked up at me and said, "So that's where that went." Luckily Mark was saved from a lifetime of adverse reactions to music, but it took his getting to the point of total frustration before it became clear to me, his teacher, what was happening.

I recommend that parents be on the lookout for the signs of learned helplessness. You are in a unique situation with your children because you see them practicing. Your child's private music teacher only sees him or her in a lesson and your child's band, orchestra, or choral teacher only sees your child as one member of a large group.

Always provide your child with a quality instrument. A quality instrument will work with your child to create beautiful music. Be sure the instrument is physically appropriate. Examine the instrument in terms of finger size and body structure. And be on the lookout for unusually high levels of frustration.

So what age should a child begin playing to avoid the problem of learned helplessness? I have covered this in Chapter 3, but will review it again because it has relevance here as well. Let me remind you that each child is different, and these are simply guidelines.

In general, students can begin some instruments at a very young age. These instruments are those that do not require great physical strength or coordination to begin. The two most popular are piano and violin. With a piano, the child can get a good, in-tune sound by simply pushing down the appropriate key. This takes much of the pressure off the children and allows them to concentrate on learning to play the correct notes in rhythm. One limitation is that children really do not need to listen to themselves play. If they push down the correct key, they assume they have the right note.

The violin is another common instrument for beginners. Violins are available in small sizes (half and three-quarter) and are favored by many music teachers because the student develops musical listening skills while playing. Unlike the piano, the child must listen carefully and adjust his or her fingers to find the proper pitch. This type of listening is a good skill to develop.

For these reasons, the piano and violin are very good instruments on which to begin learning, especially in private lessons. For group instruction in schools, many teachers rely on the recorder in the early years of elementary school. Recorders have the advantage of being very inexpensive (under $10) and easy to carry. They work well in a classroom situation because each child can have his or her own instrument. If instruction is begun too young, the child will not be able to physically cover the holes. This leads to poor, or incorrect, tones, which could lead to frustration and learned helplessness. You would probably have difficulty finding a private teacher for recorder. For private lessons, stick with piano or violin.

One of the most overlooked instruments for beginning instruction is the singing voice. Yes, the voice is an instrument. Good, accurate singing at this age has many of the same musical benefits as playing an instrument. But the singing and learning of songs must be systematic and not casual. Although private lessons in voice for very young children are rare, a good children's chorus experience can lay a wonderful musical foundation for your child. In these choruses children are taught to sing in tune, in harmony, and with a healthy tone.

When is it appropriate to learn band instruments? Here is an area in which I will get disagreement from most music teachers. So I am going to rely on research to back me up. Finding the best starting age for learning band instruments is one of the most studied areas in music education. Dissertations and studies by university faculty have been conducted for at least the last twenty years. They all seem to support the same conclusion, but for some reason it is completely overlooked by most schools. I will put it simply. The most appropriate age to start a band instrument is in the sixth or seventh grade.[2] Interestingly, most schools begin instruments in fifth grade and many as young as fourth grade. Yet the research does not back this up.

Let's look at four hypothetical students. They all begin trumpet instruction in school with equally good teachers. Mary begins in fourth grade, John in fifth grade, Joe in sixth grade, and Jane in seventh grade. In ninth grade, who will be the best trumpet player? The answer: whoever practices the most. The starting grade makes little difference. But of those four students, who will be most likely to still be playing in ninth grade? Joe and Jane, the students who started the latest. Research shows that students who start in sixth or seventh grade are less likely to drop out. This is probably due to the fact that they do not experience learned helplessness by beginning too young.

Again, this is not my opinion. This is based on the results of research. Unfortunately, this is a hard guideline for parents to follow. If the school starts lessons in fifth grade, then the parent has little choice but to follow along. All your child's friends will join at that time. If you wait until sixth grade, the student will be behind the others and cannot catch up because, from day one, the teacher is ahead of them. The solution would be to go to a class with younger students, but this would create confusion in the classroom and has negative social implications as well. Another solution would be for the school to have beginning lessons in several grades, but most schools do not have the financial resources to do this.

Let me add one other caveat to this statement. I am not suggesting that students begin *music* study in sixth or seventh grade. They should be having structured music activities throughout their childhood. But the switch to a band instrument should probably be held off until age twelve or so.

Is the parent helpless in this matter? No. Simply being aware of the potential for a learned helplessness response if your child begins early can go a long way to avoiding it. Watch for signs of this in your children and help them understand that they need to be patient. Don't rely on the music teacher from school to spot this. Symptoms of learned helplessness are subtle. The music teacher is seeing your child in a group with other children once a week. He or she is probably unable to spot the symptoms under these circumstances. Watching for this is your responsibility as a parent.

The second guideline is: *Trust your child's instinct about an instrument.* Most people don't realize this, but instruments seem to have personalities. Children, of course, have personalities too. Matching the two is of prime importance.

This is an area in which many stereotypes about instruments and the type of people who play them seem to flourish. Drummers are usually stereotyped as being cool and fun at parties, but not real musicians. Violinists are considered prima donnas who wouldn't talk to a drummer if their life depended on it. Violists are felt to be musicians who weren't good enough to play violin. Brass players are thought to be outgoing and crass. Flutists are wimps. As with most stereotypes, there is about 1 percent of truth to these—but that is enough to keep them alive. As a parent, try to concentrate on the other 99 percent, but be aware that the remaining 1 percent is very powerful to an adolescent choosing an instrument.

Gender issues further compound these stereotypes. In this area girls are more fortunate than boys. Today a girl can choose any instrument she wants. But look at the flute section of the school band and see how many boys you find. Basically, the flute section and, to some extent, the clarinet section are off limits to boys. In days past, the trumpet and percussion section were off limits to girls, but those days are gone.

Is there any basis to these stereotypes? It seems that there are no musical or physical reasons, only social ones. Over the past twenty

Instruments have personalities just like your child. Matching them up is important.

years, numerous research studies have examined both the social and gender stereotypes of instruments.[3] By and large they have concluded that, yes, these stereotypes hold true in schools. Interestingly, these same stereotypes seem to disappear in professional bands and orchestras among adults (although not completely). The studies also show that the stereotypes are changing, especially among girls. Unlike the 1960s and 1970s, when girls were confined to the flute and clarinet sections, girls today are clearly choosing (and succeeding) in all sections of the band and orchestra.

A large body of research also shows that a child's personality type, when measured in terms of such factors as introvert and extrovert, does not help or hinder the learning of certain instruments.[4] This personality stereotype is also ungrounded. In short, from a purely objective standpoint, the bottom line is that as long as your child can physically handle the instrument, your child could play it.

But this is not to say that it doesn't matter which instrument your child chooses to play. Instead, it gets us back to the idea of instrument personalities. Certain instruments will attract certain children. In college I had to learn to play literally every band and orchestra instrument to some extent. It became clear to me that I love the strings— classical guitar, bass, harp, and cello. I do not like to play reed instruments; in fact, I totally dislike them as well as the brass instruments. Although I thought the percussion instruments were OK, it became obvious to me that I was a string person.

This attraction is related to both the feel of the instrument and the actual sound that the instrument produces. In one longitudinal study, students were asked to choose sounds they liked from hearing a tape.[5] Later they were given the opportunity to select instruments. Students who chose instruments that corresponded with the preferences on the tape were more likely to be still playing the instrument several years later when compared with those who picked different instruments.

Ideally, your school will have a time when students and parents can come to explore the different instruments. This is usually in the evening near the beginning of fifth grade. Your child will be allowed to try an instrument from each of the families of instruments. This is a great opportunity for you and your child.

During this meeting, watch your children's reaction. For example, if they seem uncomfortable putting the mouthpiece of a clarinet in their mouth, then trust their first reaction. If they appear truly attracted to one instrument, then encourage them to proceed with it. Also watch their reaction to the sound of the instrument when others are playing it. If they instinctively cover their ears when a drum or trumpet is played, it is probably not the instrument for them.

Try to be aware of the social pressures they will be feeling. A good friend may decide on flute and want your son or daughter to play so they can sit together. Fight this at all costs. Your son or daughter has to find his or her instrument. Likewise, if your son is truly attracted to the flute, be aware that the peer pressure might make him hesitant about this. Point out that perhaps the most two most famous flutists (James Galway, classical flutist, and Ian Anderson from Jethro Tull) are both guys.

Lastly, watch yourself and your biases and preferences. Don't limit your child's choices to the instruments you prefer. When encouraging your child to choose an instrument, be aware of *your* motivations as well.

After you choose, monitor the choice. If it's clearly a mismatch, let the child switch. I am a firm believer in allowing children to change instruments (once or at most twice) in the first year or two of study. After that they will fall too far behind their peers. Just be careful to not let them switch simply because it is getting more difficult. Every instrument becomes more difficult as you progress. In that, all instruments are pretty equal.

The third guideline is: *Guide your child to choose an instrument for musical, not social, reasons.* This is closely related to the last guideline, but still deserves mention.

Musical instruments are closely aligned with many preteen and teen social institutions. The entire music industry depends on this for its basic survival. Teens are expected to identify with rock stars. Manufactures of instruments invest to ensure that marching band instruments and uniforms are attractive to students. Therefore, it is probably unlikely that this will not affect your child in some manner. This is not necessarily negative. The music industry is one of the largest in the country and works hard to assure that it is reaching as many children as possible. But in attempting to reach every child there are also some potential pitfalls.

No hard and fast rules exist here. For example, my main reason for learning to play the bass was to be like Paul McCartney. My daughter Madeline took up the harp to emulate Harpo Marx. I remember having a student named Alice join choir to be able to sing like Janet Jackson. Likewise, there was a sixth grader named Gary who wanted to learn to play trumpet solely because he admired a ninth grader who just happened to play trumpet (interestingly the ninth grader hated playing the trumpet and I suspect only did it because his parents made him). What do all these people have in common? They started for nonmusical social reasons, but all went on to be successful players. The social aspects of instruments are hard to ignore and can be strong motivations to succeed.

However, peer aspects can be just as strong and often detrimental. A child can feel peer pressure to take, or not take, a certain instrument. This too can be a strong motivation—but usually in a negative sense. A child might really want to play the clarinet, but watches first to see what the cool kids in class choose. Another child may avoid orchestra because it is uncool. A third may avoid band so as not to be called a band nerd.

The bottom line here is to be aware *and accept* that there are social aspects to just about all instruments your child may choose. Being tuned into this and perhaps exploring it with your child is important. You know your child better than anyone. Respect her choice, but see if her reasons have any musical merit. Ultimately, if I did not like the bass guitar, no amount of social motivation would have me playing that instrument today.

The fourth guideline is: *Be sure you can afford to continue with the instrument, but don't let financial considerations rule you.* Most likely when your child begins studying an instrument, the cost of the instrument will not be a big factor. Many children start their musical study on the piano. Although pianos are expensive, this has not been a problem because few parents would start their kids on piano if they did not first own a piano, have one available, or could rent one. However, there is another issue here that is a more recent problem. Today, electronic keyboards are inexpensive and readily available at just about any type of store. Therefore, it may be tempting to begin piano lessons with the thought that your child can practice on the keyboard. Unfortunately, while the keyboards look the same, they feel totally different. If your child continues playing the piano, an investment in an acoustic (nonelectronic) piano is almost certainly in your future.

In the upper elementary grades, your child will be offered the opportunity to learn to play a band or orchestra instrument. In this area cost will not be a factor because most beginning instruments can be (and should be) rented from a local music store. And while the monthly rental fee is related to the overall cost of the instrument, usually the differences in prices are minimal.

Many parents make the mistake of purchasing an instrument at this point. Sometimes an instrument is found at a garage sale or the parents are simply so excited about an instrument that they want to own it from the start. Try to avoid both situations for two reasons. First, children should be allowed to change instruments if they find they really dislike the one they choose. If you have made an investment in owning the instrument, this becomes less likely. Second, the instrument your child begins on should be a beginning model of that instrument. If the child continues, he will need to purchase a better quality instrument. Resale on beginning instruments is extremely poor, which is why they are so common at garage sales. Why not purchase that inexpensive instrument at the garage sale? This is advisable only if you know something about instruments. Too often the instrument has been sitting in a closet for years, is out of alignment, broken, or in disrepair in some other way. You or your child will not realize that the problem is the instrument and not the player, and you will be in a classic learned helplessness loop.

Even though the initial instrument will be rented, there should still be some eye toward the future. Some instruments (harp, tuba, or bassoon) are more expensive than others (trumpet, clarinet, or flute). A harp or grand piano, for example, costs more than many new cars. It is wise to think about this at the start. However, it should not dictate a decision. In reality, *all* quality instruments are expensive. If your child continues to perform, you will need to make an investment in some instrument at some point.

One last note on costs. Many incidental expenses are involved with learning to play an instrument. Reeds, music stands, sheet music, and strings all add up. Remember these are the maintenance items involved.

The fifth guideline is: *Be sure that any suggestion from a music teacher has your child's best interest in mind.* In many ways, I am sorry I have to include this. I was a junior high and high school music teacher for several years. In my current position I work with music teachers on a daily basis. I firmly believe that these individuals are the hardest working, most dedicated, and usually the best trained teachers in the schools. They have to be. Their students' accomplishments are on display for the entire world to see, whether it is at the Friday night football half-time show or at the community winter concert or at a Rotary luncheon.

The constant pressure to have excellent performances is also something that can lead music teachers to make decisions for the good of the group and not necessarily in the best interest of the individual child. For example, let's imagine your son or daughter really wants to play saxophone. The music teacher has a gazillion students already playing saxophone. What he or she really needs is a good oboe player. Intentionally or not, that director will be hoping your child would consider the oboe. I have seen this done with outright statements: "Sorry, we have all the saxophones we need" to something more subtle: "Since you come from such a musical family, you can probably try something more challenging like the oboe."

Sometimes this works out. Many oboists and bassoonists might never have even tried the instrument if they were not encouraged to do so. The important point is that is a delicate balance exists between the teacher's big picture and the best interests of your child. You know your child better than anybody. Be sure to monitor this situation.

I want to emphasize again that all these statements are guidelines and not rules. To show you how important it is to modify these guidelines to your child, I will tell a story about one of my children. I play bass guitar in a band that performs in bars around town. When Nathan was very young I would often pick him up from school and go to set up my equipment for an evening job. He would help me with my amplifier, microphone, and sound system. By the time he was in third grade he wanted to be like me and play the guitar. If any other parent had asked me if a third grader should play the guitar I would have said "no." Children are not physically ready for playing a guitar at that age. But Nathan was determined, I was flattered (like father, like son), and so we began.

I bought him a half-size guitar and some guitar books and we began. He made great progress. In fact, he was good enough to accompany the school choir on a song in the spring concert. But it was totally frustrating to him. His hands were not big enough, nor strong enough, to push the strings. He played, but he was constantly fighting the instrument. He quit in frustration before beginning fourth grade. This was a classic example of learned helplessness. I was sure he would never play an instrument again. I was mad at myself for not following what I knew was best.

In sixth grade he started playing the drums in school. After about one month on the snare drum he wanted to move to a full drum set. I said "no." I was afraid he would become frustrated once again by having to coordinate two hands and two feet simultaneously. Every music teacher I knew said he was too young for a full drum set. Fortunately for him, he had a paper route at the time and had saved up $200. He read the classified papers everyday until he found a drum set for $200. I still said "no."

He persisted, and we went to just look at the set. It was a *great* deal, so I let him buy it, but we agreed that he would have to put it away until he was ready to play. We got the drums home and set them up to make sure everything worked. The drums stayed up and the rest is history. Today he plays in a rock band that performs around town and recently went into a recording studio to record six original songs.

What went wrong here? Well, nothing really because it had a happy ending. But Nathan could have been lost to music forever. In the first case, he was doomed to failure because, as much as he wanted to succeed, he could not overcome the physical barriers that were put in front of him. Further, he was choosing to play the guitar to be like me—not because he liked the guitar. It was not *his* instrument.

In the second case, I overreacted. He was probably just on the edge of development and could have handled the drums. That is when his motivation completely overcame this limitation. But I wanted to play it safe a second time and tried to overcompensate. I did not realize that the drums were *his* instrument (not mine) and that his motivation would overcome the small amount of mismatch between his abilities and the demands of the instrument.

Here is my advice, parent to parent: There are no easy answers. The key is to listen, really listen, to your child. Be willing to admit mistakes and be ready to begin again.

What instruments are available?

There is almost no limit to the number and variety of instruments available. There are the traditional instruments of bands and orchestras, the instruments of pop music, as well as a wealth of folk and ethnic instruments.

Sometimes the availability of certain instruments will depend on your family. I have had many students who have played unusual instruments because their family encouraged that. For example, some students played bagpipe, panpipe, and Indian drums. In each case the student knew much more about the instrument than I did.

All instruments can be categorized according to the way in which they produce their sounds. For example, instruments that create their sounds by means of vibrating strings are called string instruments. The variety in this area is extreme, ranging from violins to electric guitars to zithers.

There are four traditional categories or *families* of instruments:

strings, woodwinds, brass, and percussion. The traditional instruments in these families are taught in the schools.

Instruments Taught in the Schools
The String Instruments

The string family consists of violin, viola, cello, and bass. These instruments are all played with a bow and produce their sound by pulling the bow across the string and causing it to vibrate. Placing the left-hand fingers on the appropriate place on the string changes individual pitches. Pushing down on the string at certain locations has the effect of lengthening or shortening the amount of string that can vibrate. The shorter the string the higher the pitch. Thus, the location of the fingers determines the pitch.

Some string instruments, such as the guitar, have metal bands across the neck called frets that help to show where to place the fingers. Others, like the violin, viola, cello, and string bass, do not.

The Brass Instruments

Brass instruments produce their sound by means of the lips vibrating on a metal mouthpiece. The individual pitches are produced by changing the tension of the lips in combination with pushing keys (or sliding a slide in the case of the trombone). Most people are surprised to see that brass instruments have very few keys (usually three or four). This is because each key can be combined with any other key and then combined with different amounts of tension on the lips to produce all needed pitches. As you can imagine, a huge number of combinations are possible (keys two and three plus medium lip tension, etc.). Fortunately, this is not as complex as it might seem.

The sound produced at the mouthpiece is then amplified and refined by traveling through the long metal tubing. This tubing is bent in a circular manner so that the instrument will not be several feet long. Brass instruments are trumpet, trombone, euphonium, tuba, and horn. (Note that the saxophone is not a brass instrument even though it is made out of brass.)

The Woodwind Instruments

The oboe, bassoon, flute, saxophone, and clarinet are all instruments in the woodwind family. With the exception of the flute, these instruments produce their sound by means of a cane reed that is attached to the instrument and vibrated by pushing air over it. The flute produces its sound much like blowing across the top of a soda pop bottle. To change pitches, all the woodwind instruments have a variety of keys that alter the pitch. Like the brass family, the sound produced near the mouth is refined and amplified by traveling, and resonating, through the body of the instrument.

The Percussion Instruments

The percussion instruments include just about anything that produces sound by striking the instrument. This includes drums, cymbals, xylophones, brake drums (literally), gongs, and chimes. Most people are surprised to find that this family also includes the piano. It is included because there are hammers that actually strike the string when the keys are depressed.

Students often sign up for percussion, hoping to learn to play the drum set the way they see rock and country stars play. Yet this is not what they will learn to play. Instead they will learn the keyboard or Mallet percussion instruments as well as the concert instruments of snare and bass drum. The reasons for this are fairly simple. The goal of school music programs is to go beyond teaching students to play an instrument. The teacher wants students to understand some music theory as well as some history. The percussionists need to learn how to read pitches in order to understand theory. The mallet instruments such as bells and xylophone allow them to do this. With a drum set, only one student can play at a time, whereas with the individual instruments more students can participate. Although these are sound educational reasons for not teaching the drum set, this is still a source of disappointment for many students.

The Voice

When dealing with the voice, we have to differentiate before and after a child's voice changes. You can expect your son or daughter's voice to change during adolescence. Before voices change there is little difference in the singing range of boys and girls.

After the change, voices fall into one of four ranges. Girls will be divided into sopranos (highest) and altos. Boys will be divided into tenors (highest) and basses. This assignment is based solely on the natural singing range of your child. I have had many parents over the years ask questions like "If Suzy tries harder, can she become a soprano?" Or "If Laura takes voice lessons, will you move her up to soprano?" I have never understood these questions, but it is a common misunderstanding that the sopranos are the best part. Not true.

In fact, sopranos usually sing the melody in a choir, so if it is a tossup for a girl between soprano and alto, and she is a really good musician, most choir directors would put her in the alto part where the singing is often more challenging.

Instruments Not Taught in Schools

Several popular instruments are not commonly taught in schools. The reasons for this are threefold: (1) tradition, (2) they do not lend themselves to large group performance, and (3) most school music is written without these instruments.

This is one area that will most likely change over the years, and there is evidence that it is already starting to. Still, until music is written that can accommodate six or eight guitars (the way band music can accommodate trumpets), it probably will not become widespread just because of logistics and economics.

The following instruments may be of interest to your child, but most likely will not be available in school.

Piano

The piano produces its sound from hammers hitting strings when the keys of the piano are depressed. This is probably the most common musical instrument of all. Anyone who decides to study music in college will have to learn some piano at some point. The reason for its centrality in most music study is that it is one of the few instruments on which a person can play more than one pitch at a time. Because of this, both the melody and the harmony can be played at the same time. This is extremely valuable for singers, conductors, and just about all musicians. Music theory is also much easier to visualize on a piano keyboard than almost any other instrument.

Keyboards

Since the invention of synthesizers, the electronic keyboard has become a dominant instrument for many people. It has all the advantages of the piano from a learning standpoint, but without the drawbacks of needing to be tuned and being very expensive. It also has the advantage of being portable.

There are huge differences in the types of keyboards available. Many of the low-cost ones that are found in department stores have very inferior sound. For just a bit more money you can often get a keyboard with truly good sounds. Let your ear be your guide here. Interestingly, the actual computer chips in synthesizers are all fairly similar between models and brands. The difference in sound is often due to the quality of the built-in amplifier and speakers.

Two types of keyboards are also available. One has weighted keys and the other does not. Weighted keys are much better, but usually cost considerably more. With weighted keys you can control the volume of the note by how hard you push the key. Nonweighted keys simply turn the sound on or off like a switch. You have infinitely more musical control with weighted keys.

Guitars

It is surprising that guitars have not gained a higher presence in the schools. It is still the unusual school that will offer guitar despite its being an excellent instructional material for teaching.

There are four basic types of guitars: electric, folk acoustic, classical acoustic, and bass. The electric and folk acoustic guitars are played in the same manner. They differ in how their sound is produced. Electric guitars need an amplifier to take the electronic signal from the strings and amplify it. Acoustic guitars use the body of the guitar to resonate and amplify the sound. Although they both use metal strings, the amplification process results in different sounds for the two types of guitars.

On the classical guitar, the strings are farther apart than on the other two. This is to ease the playing of individual notes, as is often done in classical guitar style. Classical guitars use nylon strings, which are easier on the fingers, but do not stand up well to guitar picks. For this reason, classical guitars should always be plucked with the fingers, not a pick.

The bass guitar has four strings and sounds an octave lower than the other guitars. The bass plays individual notes (not chords) and is played with either the fingers or a pick. Most need an amplifier to be heard.

I prefer all students to begin instruction on an acoustic guitar— either the classical or the folk. This will allow them to learn to play without also having to deal with learning how an amplifier works. The nylon string guitars are easier for beginners, but not using a pick will frustrate many. For this reason, I prefer the folk acoustic for beginners.

Realize that this advice is going against the grain a bit. There is peer pressure to play the electric guitar and electric guitars are usually less expensive than comparable quality acoustic guitars. Thus, you can purchase an inexpensive electric guitar that will look great and probably please your child. Unfortunately, the sound will probably be poor, it will have metal strings that will be hard to play, and an amplifier will be needed. This is the perfect formula for a guitar whose owner will never learn to play it.

Purchasing an Instrument

I have mentioned the importance of getting a quality instrument for your child. This does not mean that you must choose a professional quality instrument or even an expensive one. It simply means that you need to buy an instrument that is of the appropriate quality for your child's playing ability.

One of the biggest frustrations I have had as a teacher is seeing students come to school with an instrument they received as a birthday or Christmas present that is almost unplayable. Far too often, the parents could have spent about the same amount of money for a quality instrument if they had known what to look for.

How can you avoid this problem? First, always buy from a reputable music dealer who will let your child try the instrument, will suggest several brands, and will involve the student in the choice. Avoid catalog stores (because you can't try it) and department stores (because the sales staff probably does not know about instruments).

I am impressed by how much most music stores will truly try to recommend the best instrument for a beginner. But a few may try to sell you something that they cannot sell to someone else or will try to oversell you—attempting to sell a professional quality instrument for a beginner.

Buying from a reputable dealer can be a bit confusing. One store may not be good for all instruments. Often music stores specialize in certain types of instruments. For example, they may be experts in band instruments, but fairly unknowledgeable about guitars and keyboards (this is very common). Conversely, a store may cater to the rock/pop clientele and know little about school band instruments. Still another type of store specializes in selling music and giving lessons. Selling instruments is more of a sideline. Also, stores are basically franchises for certain brand names, much like car dealerships. Very few stores are large enough to carry all brands of instruments. Therefore, you will have to visit several stores to see different brands.

Unfortunately, these stores all look pretty similar to the customer. And since they all technically do all these things, and all carry certain brands, it can become very confusing. The best way to make sense of all of this is to go shopping with someone who knows about instruments. Even the parent of an older child who plays the same instrument might be knowledgeable about that particular instrument (it is amazing how much you will learn about your child's instrument over the years). Your child's music teacher is also a great resource. He or she wants what is best for you and your child. However, you might have to read between the lines of what the teacher is saying. Recent lawsuits and the general politics of teaching have made it difficult for music teachers to recommend one local store over another. When I hand out a list of stores in my class, I am always careful to include all of them. However, I will talk about certain stores, or say that a certain one carries a brand of instrument that I like. Listen carefully.

I am also a strong believer in name brands. Although I have played some really nice instruments made by companies I had never heard of, by and large it was hit or miss. On the other hand, I have rarely played an instrument by a major company that was outright bad. These companies have a reputation to maintain and are careful about that reputation. I also find that price really does make a difference. Most instruments are somewhat expensive to make, and basically a cheap instrument will play and sound like a cheap instrument.

If you can't have someone accompany you, my advice is to stay with a name-brand instrument, but in that company's less expensive end. You will probably get more value than with any instrument of an unknown company regardless of price.

Aids to Help You Decide

I am a fairly firm believer in trusting instincts and natural attractions when choosing instruments. Still, there are some more formal measures that can be helpful in making the decision.

The first is the playing tests devised by several instrument manufacturers. Your child's music teacher will likely have access to these. In these tests, the student is asked to produce a sound on several instruments (brass, woodwind, percussion, and strings). The teacher notes the ease with which the student can produce the sound, looks for physical characteristics that might favor (or hinder) success on certain instruments, and allows the student to feel and hear the instrument while playing it. These are not highly scientific tests, but they do offer some guidance in choosing an instrument.

GIA Publications sells a timbre-preference test for helping children decide what instrument to play. On this test the child listens to a variety of sounds and chooses the ones he or she likes the best. These sounds are artificially produced so that the child cannot really recognize them as any specific instrument. Based on their choices, certain instruments are recommended.

In one extensive study, students who selected the instrument recommended by the test were more likely to still be active in band three years after beginning than students who chose an instrument that was not the recommended one.[6] This would seem to indicate that the test is indeed helpful in choosing an instrument. Despite this, the test has not gained popular appeal and is rarely used. Perhaps the fact that it has to be purchased is a detriment. Still, it could probably prove useful if your child is having difficulty picking an instrument.

The most common aid will be the test or procedure your child's music teacher has devised to help students decide. Although these tests are neither scientific nor proven, they are probably very reliable because they involve the knowledgeable teacher one-on-one with your child. As I stated earlier, watching your child during this process and then listening to what she has to say is probably the best way to choose an instrument. My experience is that children seem to know themselves better than anybody else when it comes to selecting instruments. Trust them.

Conclusion

Helping your child choose an instrument to play is one of the most important musical decisions you will make. There are no hard and fast rules, but I think you need to trust your instincts while watching and listening to your child try several types of instruments. The basic guidelines to follow are these:

- Be sure your child is physically ready to handle the instrument.
- Trust your child's instinct about an instrument.
- Guide your child to choose an instrument for musical, not social, reasons.
- Be sure you can afford to continue with the instrument.
- Be sure that any suggestion from a music teacher has your child's best interest first.

Keep these in mind while you help your child decide. Then stay involved in the decision and keep a keen eye on the progress.

Chapter 8

Getting Kids to Practice

If you played an instrument as a child, you probably have many memories, and some of them may be less than pleasurable. For example, you may see yourself sitting at the piano while the rest of the neighborhood is outside playing baseball. Even if you have never played an instrument you may remember that your friend's mom always made her practice right when you were trying to get a game started. Either way, these are not positive images.

Therefore, we may have some foundations to build or repair before we go further. Let's start by establishing three basic premises: Most kids don't like to practice; good practicing is hard work; and a child will never play an instrument well without practicing.

Let's examine the first premise: *Most kids don't like to practice.* Many of my friends and colleagues in music would violently disagree with this statement because they love to practice and have forgotten what it was like when they were eight years old.

Actually, there is a good reason why my musician friends love to practice and children don't. For the skilled musician, the act of practicing is fulfilling in and of itself. For most children, however, this level of reward for practicing is about as remote as a trip to Saturn. Therefore, in this chapter our *goal* will be to get children to the level of practicing that is rewarding in and of itself, ideally by the early teen years. But how do we get them to that point?

Let's examine our second basic premise: *Good practicing is hard work.* Although I see many teachers and parents who work to make practicing fun, I think their efforts are misplaced. Practice should *never* be severe or harsh, yet it rarely will be fun (in the way that playing a game or going to a party can be fun). If we are always trying to make the experience fun, we will lose the child as soon as the going gets rough.

Instead, we should worry less about *fun* and concentrate more on *rewarding*. A feeling of reward only comes through accomplishment and accomplishment in music only comes through practicing. Thus, we have a classical example of a vicious circle.

We also have the need for a third premise: *A child will never play an instrument well without practicing.* This seems obvious, but I am shocked at how many kids and parents don't believe this. They expect to be able to make beautiful music almost immediately. When they can't, they give up, using the excuse that they, or their kids, must not have enough talent. It cannot be emphasized enough that if we want our children to be good musicians we need to have some way to get them to practice when they would rather be watching television.

Thus, this chapter is based on these three premises. To be sure, it is a pretty discouraging set of premises, but that is where we need to start. By the end of this chapter, you should understand some concrete ways to help your child through this entanglement.

Getting Your Kids to Practice

One of the problems we face when trying to encourage children to practice is that they never see other people practice. The *process* of music making is completely invisible to most people. They will see the final product as the concert, music video, or CD, but good performers make playing seem so effortless that many people jump to the conclusion that making music is fun and easy. We watch these people make it look so easy, but then we try and it is hard. The conclusion we come to is that "it is easy for others but not for me, therefore I have no talent." In fact, very few people can play music without a lot of behind-the-scenes practicing. Unfortunately, we always say we *play* music but *work* at our jobs. This gives the wrong impression.

For that reason, practicing will never be automatic for children. Instead, some sort of intervention is necessary. Sadly, the interventions most people come up with are not the most effective. To show what I mean, I will start with a true story. When I pass a pay phone, I can rarely resist the urge to check the coin-return slot. I will even go out of my way to do this. For me, this is the equivalent of playing the slot machines in Las Vegas. And it has really paid off. After thirty

I always check the coin slot but rarely find any money.

years I am at least a dollar richer than if I had never checked once. Obviously, the number of times I have actually found coins in the slot is relatively low.

Now let's consider another scenario. If I knew that every time I reached into the slot I would find a nickel, I would probably not look as often as I do now. Instead I would rationalize, "Is a nickel worth stopping for?" "Do I want nickels in my pocket?" "Do I need an extra nickel right now?" Many times the answer to these questions would be "no" and I would walk right by.

Obviously, the financial rewards of checking those slots are not what is driving my behavior. It is something about the uncertainty of the rewards, both "Will I get one" and "How much will it be," that keeps me going. This illustrates an important principle that relates to practicing a musical instrument. Some sort of a reward system needs to be in place, but this is not as easy as simply giving a reward every time a child practices. Reward systems are complex: some work, some don't; some work sometimes and not others. Fortunately, research has shown which types of reward systems work and which ones don't.

To really step back and understand these principles, it helps to look at research done with laboratory animals. It is important to know that educational researchers in working in classrooms have received exactly the same results as researchers working in laboratories with pigeons or mice. I am sure these same principles apply to adults too. They do to me.

Pigeons will do all sorts of things to get a pellet of food.[1] They don't think about it, they just learn certain habits. If a pigeon is put in a cage and taught to hit a button every time it wants a pellet of food, it will learn to hit the button. However, if the pigeon gets a pellet every time it pushes the button, an interesting thing will happen. At first it will push the button often. But after a while the amount of pushing will fall off. This is pretty much like my checking the coin-return slot if I knew there was always a nickel in it. Sometimes I don't want a nickel; sometimes the pigeon does not want a pellet of food.

This is also what will happen if a reward is given each time a child practices. For example, if children are given a candy bar every time they finish practicing, or allowed to go outside and play, they will practice a lot at first. After a short while, however, they will begin to ask themselves "Do I really want a candy bar?" "Do I really want to go out and play?" If the answer is "no," then the child will not practice. Even if they want to go out and play, it may not be a strong enough incentive for them to have to practice first. Therefore, they will choose to do something else. What would happen if we alter this reward scenario?

Let's say a pigeon is given a pellet of food only on the first time it pecks after a certain time interval, for example, five minutes. The behavior will be quite different. In this case, the pigeon will learn to start pecking at the button just before the time interval is up. So in this case the pigeon does no pecking for four and half minutes and then begins frantically pecking until the reward comes at five minutes. Then the pecking drops off to nothing. (This is true—they *really* do learn this). Psychologists refer to this type of system as a *fixed-interval* reinforcement schedule.

To anybody who has ever taken music lessons this should sound

The reward has to be strong enough to make your child choose to practice.

pretty familiar. Let's say your lesson is on Wednesday. You come home from your lesson and do not practice. Thursday arrives and maybe you practice a bit. The weekend hits and you completely forget about your lesson and relax. Now it is Monday and the reality strikes you that you have a lesson on Wednesday. Still no panic, you practice. On Tuesday you realize that you don't know your lesson well enough so you practice frantically. The same is true of Wednesday. I firmly believe that most practicing for the entire week is done in the twenty-four hours preceding the lesson. On the way to the lesson you promise yourself you will not do this again. After the lesson, you come home and don't practice. The cycle starts over.

What's going on here? We are smarter than that, aren't we? Well, we can learn something from the pigeons. Most music lessons are set up on a fixed-interval reinforcement schedule. We get no reinforcement for our efforts until a certain amount of time has passed. The usual interval is one week. Regardless of what we do, or do not do, during that week the reinforcement (praise from the teacher or not being yelled at for being unprepared) will always come at the designated time (i.e., Wednesday at 4:30). This will result in a practice pattern very much like the one shown below.

As you can see, it looks much like the pigeons that are pecking for

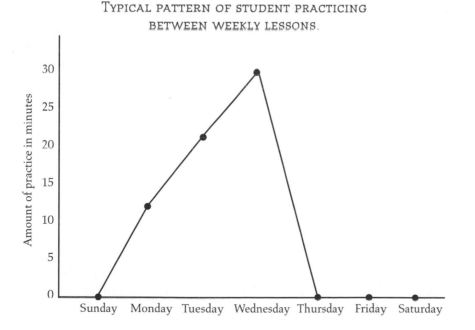

TYPICAL PATTERN OF STUDENT PRACTICING
BETWEEN WEEKLY LESSONS.

the food when they know it will only come at a certain time. In the case of practicing, the most important day is the one right after the lesson (Thursday), because the instructions and suggestions of the teacher are still fresh in your child's mind. Yet, in this system, that is one of the days with the least amount of practice. It should be apparent that this system is not going to work without some help. Clearly, you as a parent need to get involved. You are the only one around between lessons.

Most parents address this problem by rewarding the child for a certain amount of practicing per day—usually half an hour. This is unquestionably the most common system used. But all this does is to add *another* fixed-interval system on top of the one that is not working. After a half-hour, regardless of the amount of practicing (pecking?) that is done, a reward (stopping) is given. So now we have two fixed-interval systems. The end result is certainly better than doing nothing, but it still is not the most effective. Let's look at some other possibilities.

Another way of reinforcing practicing would be to forget about time completely and only reward accomplishment. For your child it will mean that he or she is given daily goals to accomplish. If your child can complete them in ten minutes they are done. On the other hand, if the child takes forty minutes, then that is how long it will take. This kind of practicing is called fixed-ratio reinforcement schedule.

In this type of practicing, a reward is given after a certain number of goals are accomplished. For example, if your child has an assignment similar to that shown in the chart below, then your child must make some progress on each of the goals every day. This in itself will create an interesting outcome. In the first practice sessions after the weekly lesson, it will take your child longer to get through the list because everything is new. As the week progresses, the practice time will become shorter. Thus, this one change will completely turn around the practice pattern created by a fixed interval schedule. It eliminates the problem of not practicing immediately after the lesson. Of great importance, it will also build in a reward system for learning the lesson. Children will have to practice less as the week goes on because they know the lesson better.

It is surprising that this system is so rarely used in music. Because music is so results oriented (concerts, recitals, etc.) it would seem logical that this system would be the most common. But it isn't. Instead, the earlier time-based practicing seems to be more popular.

As a parent, you are responsible for helping your child decide how

---

A TYPICAL GOAL-ORIENTED ASSIGNMENT

STUDENT: Peggy
ASSIGNMENT FOR THE WEEK OF: February 19th

1. Play C, G, and F scales with no stops or hesitations.
2. Begin work on Prelude 1. Learn to play first 8 measures slowly but steadily.
3. Fix wrong notes at Measure 18 in Sonata 2.
4. Continue work on Sonata 1. Add dynamics on page 2.
5. Memorize Sonata 8.

---

much is appropriate for each day's practice. The immediate reward is that the child will get to end the practicing when the list is completed. The longer reward is a feeling of accomplishment that comes from meeting goals. This type of reward does not result from a time system. (How much reward do you feel from putting in a half-hour of time on something compared to accomplishing something?)

The fixed-ratio system is an improvement over a typical fixed-interval system. But it can be improved even more. Think back to the telephone story I told earlier. If I knew that every eighth time I checked the coin slot I would receive a reward, it would not be that much different from some of the other reward systems. What keeps me coming back for more is that I never know when a reward will be found. The same can be said of practicing.

What is happening with the telephone is that there is a *variable-ratio* system in place. This is the most rewarding type of system. Las Vegas wouldn't exist if this were not true. In this type of system, children are never completely sure when they will receive a reward—but it will come in response to their actions.

The parent must *plan* this out to be sure it works. The parent should know that after working on something a certain number of times, a reward will come. The child should not know. Using the previous example, the parent might decide that after practicing the scales a reward will be given after three times, then two times, then four times, or whatever. The same will be true of each part of the lesson. The reason the parent must plan this is to ensure that it will be done. If it is left to chance one of three things will happen: (1) the parent will forget, (2) the parent will overreward, or (3) the parent will reward when the child gets discouraged (because parents never like to see their children discouraged). In the long run, this last situation will actually reward (and thus encourage) being discouraged!

A WEEKLY PRACTICE CHART AT THE BEGINNING OF THE WEEK

	Thursday	Friday	Saturday	Sunday	Monday	Tuesday	Wednesday
C Scale	*Twice*	*Twice*	*Twice*	*Twice*	*Twice*	*Twice*	*Twice*
G Scale	*Twice*	*Twice*	*Twice*	*Twice*	*Twice*	*Twice*	*Twice*
F Scale	*Twice*	*Twice*	*Twice*	*Twice*	*Twice*	*Twice*	*Twice*
Prelude 1	*Sight-read measures 1–4.*	*Play measures 1–4.*	*Sight-read measures 5–8. Play 1–4.*	*Play measures 1–8.*	*Sight-read measures 9–12. Play 1–8.*	*Play measures 1–12.*	*Play measures 1–12.*
Sonata 2: Measures 12–24	*Play measures 17–19.*		*Play measures 17–19.*	*Play measures 12–24.*			*Play measures 12–24.*
Sonata 1		*Work on page 2.*		*Work on page 2.*		*Work on page 2.*	
Sonata 8	*Play page 1. Try from memory.*	*Play page 1 from memory, then open book and fix mistakes.*	*Play page 1 from memory and go as far as you can onto page 2. Correct mistakes from music.*	*Work on pages 1 & 2 from memory rest of time.*			

After the child's lesson, you can take the teacher's assignment and make a chart like the one above. Once you create it, you must follow it. Each day your child should cross out each block as it is completed it. In this way, progress will be concrete and obvious. A feeling of accomplishment will emerge.

All this might sound pretty calculated; to be effective it must be. Let me remind you that practicing is a skill to be learned; it is hard work. Your child will need this type of encouragement until he or she reaches the point that it is no longer necessary. If you think it is impersonal, consider this: What happens to your child's self-esteem when week after week he shows up for a lesson unprepared? I assure you, it won't improve. Your child needs your help. After several weeks of being prepared for lessons and feeling accomplishment, your

A WEEKLY PRACTICE CHART AT THE END OF THE WEEK

	Thursday	Friday	Saturday	Sunday	Monday	Tuesday	Wednesday
C Scale	Twice	Twice	Twice	Twice	Twice	Twice	Twice
G Scale	Twice	Twice	Twice	Twice	Twice	Twice	Twice
F Scale	Twice	Twice	Twice	Twice	Twice	Twice	Twice
Prelude 1	Sight-read measures 1–4.	Play measures 1–4.	Sight-read measures 5–8. Play 1–4.	Play measures 1–8.	Sight-read measures 9–12. Play 1–8.	Play measures 1–12.	Play measures 1–12.
Sonata 2: Measures 12–24	Play measures 17–19.		Play measures 17–19.	Play measures 12–24.			Play measures 12–24.
Sonata 1		Work on page 2		Work on page 2		Work on page 2.	
Sonata 8	Play page 1. Try from memory.	Play page 1 from memory, then open book and fix mistakes.	Play page 1 from memory and go as far as you can onto page 2. Correct mistakes from music.	Work on pages 1 & 2 from memory rest of time.			

child's self-image in this area should start to improve. Then, perhaps, you can become a bit less calculated. Speaking of the future, there is another important point that comes from educational research concerning practice: Intermittently reinforced responses are more long lasting than continuously rewarded responses. In other words, your child will practice even as he or she gets older after the rewards are removed.

Still, this plan may not be for every child. If your son or daughter can't wait to practice every day, works through the entire assignment, and is always prepared for the next lesson, then this method is not for you. For the rest of our children, these suggestions should make a big difference.

In summary: Two types of reward systems can be used. One is an interval system that rewards a child's response after a given time interval. The other is a ratio system that rewards a child after a certain number of responses. Music lessons are set up on time-interval systems. Research shows that ratio systems produce better results. Further, a ratio system with a varying rate is the best. Parents can establish a variable-ratio system in addition to the time-interval system already in place.

What we haven't talked about are the types of rewards that are appropriate for good practicing. We will now turn our attention there.

What are appropriate rewards?

It is hot today in Tucson, Arizona, where I am writing this—106 degrees to be exact. My kids are in the pool and I want to be with them. I have just finished writing the section on variable-ratio reward systems. Swimming would be a great reward. But instead of telling myself, *"I will write for another half-hour and then I will join them,"* I am thinking, *"I will join them when I finish this introduction to the section on appropriate rewards."* I am now completely results oriented and typing (and thinking) much faster than I would had I given myself the time reward.

So swimming with my kids will be my reward. That reward works today, but probably would not in December. That is the funny thing about rewards—what today is a reward might not be one tomorrow. Further, what is a reward for your child may not be one for you. Finding appropriate rewards is hard. To address that, we need to understand what makes something a reward.

Researchers in this area define a reward as anything that will make people do the thing that you want them to do. That helps, doesn't it?! In other words, just about *anything* can be a reward.

Consider this: I want to be swimming today. A punishment would be for me to have to stand out in the sun for a couple of hours in this heat. A friend from the neighborhood, Alexis, was over earlier. She *loves* softball and could not wait to go and play a softball game this afternoon. She is standing out in a field right now in 106-degree heat playing a doubleheader. A softball game is not my idea of a reward, but for Alexis it was a big reward. What would be a punishment for me is a reward for Alexis. I probably could have gotten her to wash and wax my car in return for a ride to the ballfield.

Obviously, rewards come in all shapes and sizes. Yet there are some consistencies. All rewards can be put into one of the following types:

intrinsic (true to the task) or extrinsic (not related to the task). An intrinsic reward for playing the piano could be the musical joy received from performing a piece that was well prepared. An extrinsic reward could be to get a new outfit for school. Each type of reward can be further divided into categories such as social, personal, or material.

All rewards have their strengths and weaknesses, so we will examine each in turn. Now that I have completed the introduction to this section, I am going swimming. I will receive the extrinsic reward of jumping in the pool only twenty-seven minutes after I set the goal. I am sure I wrote more than if I had set a goal of writing for thirty minutes. See how well it works?

Intrinsic versus Extrinsic Rewards

There are basically two broad categories of rewards: intrinsic and extrinsic. Intrinsic rewards come from *within* the task—doing something because you like doing it. Extrinsic rewards come from *outside* the task—going to work to receive a paycheck.

These two types are pretty easy to keep straight if you remember that intrinsic rewards are the ones we would like to use and receive. (Wouldn't we all love to go to work each day just for the sheer enjoyment of it?) The extrinsic rewards are the ones we usually use and receive. (Would you still go if you won the lottery?) Everyone would like to be able to use only intrinsic rewards. We want our children to practice the piano because of the joy and feeling of satisfaction they receive from playing. That is certainly the long-term goal of any reward system, but to get started we need to offer some extrinsic rewards.

When I was young my parents wanted me to play the accordion, which I hated. The Beatles were raging, and I wanted to play the bass guitar like Paul McCartney. My parents did an interesting thing. They told me that if I would practice the accordion, they would reward me by letting me practice the bass. I don't suggest making your child play an instrument they hate in hopes that they will want to practice an instrument they like. This worked for me, but not because of any love for the instrument. Although I liked the bass, the real reason I wanted to play had nothing to do with the instrument. The truth of the matter was that I wanted to play the bass to be as famous and cool as the Beatles. Today, while I am certainly as cool as Paul McCartney, the fame thing has eluded me and will probably continue to do so. Still, I continue to play and regard it as a very important part of my life. I play because the act of playing the bass has

Intrinsic rewards such as the joy of playing are better than extrinsic rewards such as money or fame.

become its own reward. I *love* playing the bass. This took years to happen.

I point this out to emphasize that at the beginning your child will almost certainly need extrinsic rewards. But I also offer a note of caution: All extrinsic rewards are not created equal and it is important to know which ones work in the long run and which don't.

Researchers divide extrinsic rewards into two additional categories: social and material. So far we have talked about material rewards, but not the social ones. Although they both work, the social ones seem to work better (and are much cheaper) in the long run.

In a social reward system, the child is rewarded by social approval. We all respond well to this type of approval. When we are given an award, recognition, or simply a pat on the back, it works to make us want to do the activity again. This may come in many forms.

One of my graduate students did an interesting research project. She was a piano teacher who taught about forty students a week in private lessons. One of her requirements was for every student to be able to play all twelve major scales, up and down, without a mistake. This was always a problem requirement, because many students don't like to practice scales. In the past, most students waited until the last few weeks of the entire year and then tried to play them all at once to get them checked off.

She had tried to use a reward system that gave the students an attractive sticker every time they completed a scale. She would put this on a chart in the back of the student's folder. This material reward (a sticker) seemed to work for a few students, but not the majority. She then decided to do something different. She chose half of her students (at random) and put their names on a poster board. Next to each name were twelve spaces, one for each scale. She put this poster board on a stand that was on top of the piano. Whenever a student whose name was on the poster was having a lesson, the poster was standing up so it could be seen. When a student whose name was not on the poster had a lesson, the poster was put face down so it could not be seen.

When any student finished a scale, the child was given a sticker and told to either place it on the poster (if the child's name was there), or in the child's assignment book. No mention was made of the poster or the other students. Thus, all students got the same stickers and all were equally aware of their progress. The only difference was that half of the students' results were on display.

Have you guessed what happened? The students whose names were on the poster for all to see were done with their scales *months* before the other students—*every one of them*. The fact that they had been given a social reward (the public display of accomplishment) seemed to have made the entire difference.

I especially like this example because the reward was closely tied to accomplishment on the piano. It was not a bribe in any sense of the word. The social approval came from an accomplishment on the piano.

Contrast these examples with the teacher who says that if you finish all your scales, we will have a party at one of your lessons or the parent who says, "If you practice all week, we can go to Pizza Hut on Friday." Common rewards such as money, candy, a new baseball mitt, and going outside to play have nothing to do with playing an instrument. These types of rewards will work to increase practice time, but they are not the most effective in the long run because they do little to make the act of playing a reward.

Thus, extrinsic rewards (both social and material) should be related to the act of playing the instrument. For example, a reward for practicing could be a book containing your child's favorite songs. A parent recently told me she bought a book that had songs from *Les Misérables* as a reward for her son's finishing an entire series book of piano pieces. Finishing the pieces had been his goal and the book became the musical reward for practicing and achieving a musical goal.

Therefore, when you choose extrinsic rewards, you must be creative. Examples of material rewards that could relate to playing the

MATERIAL   SOCIAL

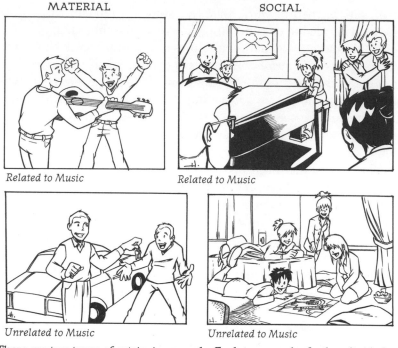

Related to Music   *Related to Music*

Unrelated to Music   *Unrelated to Music*

There are two types of extrinsic rewards. Each type can be further divided.

instrument would be a new reed for the instrument, a better music stand, a light for the music stand, a box to store straps and other instrument paraphernalia, a bottle of polish for the instrument, a new set of drumsticks, a CD or tape of music for your child's instrument, a lapel pin of the instrument, and so on. The list could be almost endless. Some catalogs specialize in accessories specifically for musicians and you can buy charms, key chains, and tie tacks in the shapes of instruments, stationery with notes, pencils in the shape of treble clefs, stickers with instruments, and just about any item you could imagine. Your child's music teacher can probably supply you with such a catalog or you might simply browse in your local music store for ideas. Some of these catalog stores are listed in the Resources for Parents section at the end of the book.

Social rewards could be performances for the entire family. At a designated time, the family (mom, dad, and any siblings) will sit and listen to your child perform. At the end, your child should stand and bow and everyone then applaud. A less formal reward would simply be to tell a grandparent or family friend how proud you are of the child's progress at a time when your child is present. There are many opportunities for social rewards. You only need to be aware of them and take advantage of them. What is important to remember is that the reward is tied to the child's playing the instrument, which creates a chain reaction that in turn creates more interest in playing the instrument. Although these rewards are extrinsic to the joy of playing music, they work to enhance and reinforce the fact that your child is a musician.

Even though extrinsic rewards are very valuable and effective, the long-term goals of a reward system should be to establish intrinsic rewards. In other words, the joy of playing the instrument and creating music becomes its own reward. The joy of attaining musical goals can also be as self-rewarding as performing in a successful concert or recital.

These are the ultimate goals of playing music. But they come slowly, much more slowly than the ones previously described. Therefore, the recommendation is to use extrinsic social or appropriate material rewards always with an eye to replacing them with intrinsic rewards. So what are these intrinsic rewards? They are harder to explain and use, and many of them are fairly intangible but certainly real. There are two intrinsic rewards, however, that I feel can be developed or nurtured in young musicians. These are the rewards of reaching personal goals and playing music you love. The parent (and teacher) can have an active role in nurturing these rewards

Many years ago, my wife and I purchased a nineteenth-century home. As romantic as this sounds, the house was in pretty bad shape. Our goal was to restore it into something beautiful. I was a public school music teacher at the time and had the entire summer to work on it. We took possession of the house in early June just as the school year was ending. I woke up every morning and worked all day long on the house. I worked hard, but after a few weeks became very discouraged. For all my work, it just didn't seem like anything was getting done. It was then that I learned the power of goals as rewards. We sat down and made a list of projects. Each was put on a sheet and broken down into the steps needed for the project to be completed. These sheets were then placed on the refrigerator. When I completed something, I would go to the refrigerator and check it off.

I remember having a major revelation one day as I ran to the refrigerator to cross something off the list. I couldn't wait to do it. The act of getting the task done *and then crossing it off the list* had become self-motivating. I could see my progress and knew where I was headed. I was not working any harder, but I sure felt like I was making more progress and was certainly enjoying the whole process more.

This also works with practicing. Far too often the goals for practicing are vague or too distant. The ultimate goal may be to play better (this is vague) or to perform at the spring recital (this is far off to a child, even in February) while the short-term goal is to learn that week's song (this is really boring). So the chance of your child's feeling accomplishment or sensing that she is getting anywhere is pretty low.

Instead, the act of reaching musical goals can be very rewarding. For this to happen, however, these goals must be specific, concrete, and clear to your child. If you remember the research project my student did where she put a sticker on a board for every scale performed correctly, you will see that one of the things that made this work was that the students had a series of short, attainable goals (the individual scales). These short goals added up to a larger goal (knowing all the scales). All instruction should be this goal oriented.

This seems quite logical and I can't think of any music teacher who would not agree with this. The problem is that while most teachers have similar goals for their students (actually all *good* teachers do), they are sometimes not communicated. The teacher just assumes the students know where they are going. The teacher has been on this path many times before with countless other students and knows what lies right around the next corner, but often forgets to tell students what is coming or where they are. Progress is obvious to the teacher, but not to the child.

Just like my list of small house repair tasks that led up to large accomplishment, so too must we offer this opportunity for our children with some sort of systematic program. It is important that they see their goals and accomplishments regularly.

Perhaps the best intrinsic reward is being able to play a piece of music you love. This may sound lofty or unrealistic, but it truly is the most motivating factor I have seen for any musician. But it is not as easy or simplistic as it sounds.

Recently, my daughter Melanie heard Für Elise by Beethoven and fell in love with it. It seemed well beyond her ability, but, thanks to her perceptive teacher, Anne, it was used to motivate her beyond her current playing level. First Anne found a simplified version of the piece. Because it was not simple enough for Melanie, Anne explored the Internet and located a series of three books called *The Road to Für Elise*. These books had collections of pieces that develop certain skills required to play Für Elise. However, Melanie wanted to play the actual piece, so it became her summer goal to learn it. She struggled for three months on the piece. But eventually she got it. It was the music that motivated her to push like this.

But how does that happen? This is where it gets difficult. Children know the music they hear on the radio. Most of it is so rhythmically complex that they could not possibly read it. Further, they hear it with a full band or orchestra. It never sounds the same when it's played on a solo sax or even piano. For this reason, the popular music they hear may not work well on their instrument. Even if it did, it is often way out of reach.

You, the parent, and the teacher have to be on the lookout for pieces that your child likes but that also will work on your child's particular instrument. Usually the child and parent do not know enough about the instrument to be sure what will work, but the teacher will. Perhaps the best way is for you (and your child) to suggest particular pieces to the teacher.

But there is more. Melanie would never have heard Für Elise if she had not been at a piano recital. So it is important to let children hear music written specifically for their instrument. This can be accomplished through CDs or live performances.

As with most rewards, there are no simple answers when it comes to using music as a reward. A piece one child likes may do nothing for another. A piece a child admires may not work on that child's instrument. A piece your child loves may be way too difficult. So the best thing for a parent to do is to be sensitive to this phenomenon. I am not sure you can make it happen, but you can certainly set up an environment in which an opportunity would not be missed.

What is the message of this chapter on rewards? The best way to get your kids to practice is by setting up a system of intrinsic rewards using short- and long-term goals (such as the chart shown earlier, along with recitals) and music they love. Combine this with some sort of extrinsic reward system. The reward system should reinforce your child often and at times when it isn't expected. Further, you should use both material and social extrinsic rewards that are closely tied to the act of playing music.

Some Additional Thoughts on Practicing

There are some further hints for practicing that do not fall neatly into a category and don't need much explanation

Eliminate unimportant decisions for your child

You want to eliminate as many decisions as possible for your child and allow him to concentrate on musical decisions. One good idea is establish a specific time for practicing. This eliminates the decision of when to practice. If it is set up that the child will practice every day at 4:00, then the decision of when will be avoided. Without an established time it is too easy to simply say "later."

Associate a specific place with practicing

If a specific place can be set aside for practicing and only practicing, then that location tends to trigger the practice response. This is easy if your child plays an instrument like the piano, harp, or drums. These stationary instruments demand a place in the home that cannot be used for other purposes. But it is not as easy if the instrument is a flute or trumpet. Therefore, if a designated place could be devised for practicing, it will become more automatic. It also eliminates another decision: Where can I practice?

Associate practicing with pleasurable activities or times

Try to link things your children enjoy doing to practicing, and avoid combining practicing with things they don't like. If your child hates practicing, but enjoys doing activities with you as a parent, perhaps the practicing can be is done together. The child cannot like and dislike something at the same time.

If your children are tired and grumpy when they get home from school, then this is not a good time for practicing. Instead, find a period when they are generally happy (this will vary child by child, even within a family). This is the time to set up their practice interval. You may ask, "But won't that ruin their happiness?" My experience is that it won't. They cannot be happy and sad at the same time. Their natural tendencies and biorhythms will win out.

Summary

Here are the highlights of this chapter:

•There are three basic premises: (1) Most kids don't like to practice; (2) Good practicing is hard work; and (3) A child will never play an instrument well without practicing.

- Rewards (reinforcements) can be used to encourage good practice habits.
- There are two types of reward schedules, interval and ratio. Most practicing is set up around an interval system, but a ratio system works better.
- A ratio system with a variable rate of reward is the best type of reward system.
- Many things can act as rewards and they will be different for each child.
- There are two types of rewards: intrinsic and extrinsic. We use extrinsic rewards for the end goal of arriving at intrinsic rewards.
- Extrinsic rewards can be further divided into two types: material and social. Both are effective, but should be tied to the act of making music.
- One of the most effective rewards is the feeling of reaching tangible goals. Good practicing should have goals.

Chapter 9

What Is Good Practicing?

The previous chapter provided some ideas on how to encourage your child to spend time practicing. Unfortunately, that is only half the battle. Although it is true that a relationship exists between the amount of time spent practicing and a child's performance ability, it is a surprisingly weak relationship.[1] In other words, it is not just a matter of how much time a child spends practicing, but what the child does with that time. The old saying "Practice makes perfect" is only true if the practice is good practice.

Knowing how to practice is very important. Practicing is actually self-teaching that happens for the entire week between lessons. This is very different from how your child learns in other subjects. For example, math is taught daily in your child's school. When homework is given, it's usually a focused assignment due the next day. Long-term projects in which the student is expected to be self-motivated and self-regulated are usually not assigned until upper elementary or more likely middle and high school.

Music lessons are the exact opposite. Children will receive lessons once a week and between those lessons are expected to practice on their own and know how to do it. Other outside activities, such as sports, usually have more than one meeting per week. Music lessons are unique in their approach.

Practicing is difficult for most students because they are not taught *how* to practice. Even among university music majors, 60 percent say that they were never taught how to practice.[2] Instead of the quality of the practice time, many teachers concentrate on the amount of time a student has practiced. As a parent, you probably will be required to sign a practice sheet each week that verifies the *amount* of practice time done. Rarely will a parent be asked to account for the quality of that time.

But the quality of the practice is what is important. Not only will good practicing make the use of time more efficient, it will avoid the potential problem of learning musical passages incorrectly. If the child has misunderstood something from the lesson or reads something wrong from the musical notation, it is very likely she will spend the week learning something wrong. In this case, the student has to then spend time *unlearning* something the next week.

Fortunately, you, as a parent, can do some simple things to help your child practice.

Planning the Practice Time

What happens during the time set aside for practicing is simply a matter of time management. As simple as that sounds, it is something all of us struggle with. The first key to successful practicing is to have a routine. In one study, music students who were given written instructions about how to practice performed better than students who were not given such instructions.[3] For professional performers the actual routine does not seem to matter as much as just having one. Professional performers have routines that they use while practicing, but each routine is different.[4]

Until your child is experienced enough to develop an individual routine, it is best to start with a standard structure. Most routines will begin with some sort of warm-up. There is a twofold purpose to the warm-up. First, the warm-up gets the muscles that will be used in the practice ready to go. This is exactly like an athlete warming up. The second purpose is to prepare your child mentally for the practice. It is a warm-up to concentration—we can't just jump into concentration, we have to work up to it.

The warm-up should consist of either some exercises, such as scales or etudes, or a piece that is already known. The warm-up should probably take about 10 to 15 percent of the rehearsal time (three to five minutes in a thirty-minute practice session).

After the warm-up, the practice can proceed to a piece that is in progress. This is a piece that has been worked on, but needs further practice and polish. This piece should be approached in what is referred to as the synthesis/analysis/synthesis approach. First, your child plays through the entire piece (synthesis). This will refresh the child's memory of the piece and also to help him to remember where the trouble spots are. The next step is to pick two or three spots that need work and then work on these isolated spots until some progress is made (analysis). The last step involves playing through the entire piece again to put the improvements into the larger context (synthesis). This entire procedure can be repeated for several pieces that are in progress.

At this point, your child is probably halfway to two-thirds through a typical practice time. Now is the time to tackle a new piece or one that still needs much work. Learning a new piece is perhaps the hardest part of a lesson. It can seem overwhelming to a student to have to transfer a new piece from notation into music. The rewards of actually playing the piece are far in the future and so this is the step children will most often avoid. Specific hints on working through this stage are presented in a later section.

The last part of the practice should be something that is enjoyable and less work for the child. It should be a piece that reinforces why your child is playing an instrument in the first place—because it is enjoyable. For that reason, the practice should end with the playing of something that your child really likes—this could be a just about anything. In some ways, this is the cool-down of the practice.

A typical practice session looks like this:

- Warm-up
- Synthesis/analysis/synthesis of a work in progress
- Synthesis/analysis/synthesis of another work in progress
- Work on a new piece
- Cool-down

Naturally, many variations of this are possible. I suggest this plan as a good starting point—there is nothing sacred about it. Based on your son or daughter's personality, it can be varied accordingly.

Fixing a Specific Mistake

I find that the process of fixing a specific mistake is rarely understood among music teachers mainly because it is not often given much thought. I believe that the ideas of the learning theorist Edwin Guthrie have much to offer us in this regard.[5] Guthrie's theories have become standard practice among therapists who are working with individuals to break unwanted habits such as smoking, fear of public speaking or heights, or what have you. To apply this procedure we have to consider a mistake as a kind of unwanted habit. We also have to consider it a physical (or motor, as it would be termed in the psychological literature) mistake. In other words, an incorrect physical response has been learned in reaction to something else.

The mistake is viewed as just one link in a chain. For example, if you were playing racquetball and missed a return volley, you would have to analyze the chain of physical movements you did that led up to your missing the ball. This chain probably starts the instant you see the ball hit by the other player. Unless you practice correcting the whole chain (not just the actual hitting of the ball), you will not do any better the next time you are in that situation.

In music, the chain idea is critical. To explain this, I need to use an example that is very common among beginning music students. This is one of the few places in the book that I will have to assume you have some basic knowledge of music.

Your son Billy is playing a piece of music in the key of F. In the key of F the note B is always played as a B♭. Since this is always the case, the flat is put at the beginning of the piece (in the key signature), and performers are supposed to remember that every time they see the note B it is to be played as a B♭. Beginning students like Billy might not remember this and play it as a B natural.

On the left of Figure 9-1 is a passage that Billy is trying learn with the pitches F-G-A-B♭-C. But Billy plays F-G-A-B-C as it is written on the right of the figure (can you find the difference?).

As soon as Billy hears the B he knows something is wrong, so he quickly corrects it to become a B♭. This is also how many teachers teach. They stop the students when they hit the wrong note and have them correct it. But let's think about this in terms of a chain. The mistake actually happened *before* Billy played the incorrect note. The mistake occurs as soon as the fingers start to go to the incorrect note. This is before the incorrect note actually is heard. It is after the A, but before the B, as shown in Figure 9-2. By correcting it after the incorrect note is sounded, the correction is between the B and the B♭. This

FIGURE 9-1: *A passage of music as written and as Billy plays it.*

FIGURE 9-2: *The mistake actually happens when the fingers first start to move to the note. This is before the note sounds.*

addresses the memory part of the mistake, but not the physical part. In fact, it makes the physical problem worse because now the fingers have played A-B-B♭, which is more wrong than the initial mistake! The problem arises the next time Billy plays the piece. He may mentally remember it to be a B♭, but his fingers have already gone to the wrong note.

To avoid this, you should not correct the mistake after it has been made. Instead, when you hear a mistake, point it out, then have your child go back to the start of the chain and correct it. In this case, the chain starts on the F.

The next way to fix a mistake is to slow it down. Often a student understands what is supposed to be done, but cannot physically do it. The idea of chaining comes in handy again. Learn the chain of muscle commands at a slower speed and then gradually speed it up. Here it is critical that the entire chain is played at the speed at which the hard part can be successfully completed. If your daughter plays part of the chain faster and slows down when she gets to the hard part, she has in essence practiced the chain wrong since timing is part of what the muscles are learning.

To effectively use slow practice, your child should back up to several measures before the problem note. Begin there *at the slow speed at which the child can successfully play the problem passage*. The child should then continue a measure or two *beyond* the problem passage without speeding up. This keeps the timing relationships between the notes constant across the entire passage and avoids the fairly common problem of sometime hearing a problem measure played exactly half as fast as the rest of the piece. A child performing this way has learned the timing of the passage in an incorrect relationship to the rest of the music.

How slow should your child practice? As slow as necessary to ensure that he can play the problem area successfully. When your child can play the passage successfully two or three times at this slow speed, the speed can gradually be increased. Your child then practices at this speed until two or three successful attempts in a row.

How many times this can be repeated in one practice session depends on many factors, such as the age of the child, the difficulty of the passage, and the ability of the child. It is rare that a child can get up to speed on the entire passage in one practice session.

I don't know what famous pianist said this, but when asked how he practiced he replied, "I practice everything many times very slowly, only then am I able to play it again . . . slowly." I would add to this, slowly and in a consistent rhythm.

Specific mistakes take specific correction techniques. Your child's teacher will handle those. But these two rules can be applied to most mistakes your child will encounter.

Whole versus Parts

The idea of fixing a specific mistake brings us to the important issue of practicing all or parts of a piece to actually learn it. The research on this topic is contradictory and offers little help.[6] So, we need to turn to common sense and experience.

Fixing a mistake or learning a new section of music takes much work. The temptation will always be for your child to play the piece from the beginning until reaching the hard spot in the music, then stop and start over. Children will never learn the whole piece this way. They must, at some point, use a technique like the one previously described.

But—and this is very important—the small part worked on must at some point be brought back into the whole of the piece. Although this sounds logical, it is not as easy as it seems. After a mistake is fixed in a part, it must be practiced in the whole to make sure it can be played at the same speed and with the same sound as the rest of the piece.

One way to do this is to divide the piece into logical sections. Listen for a place in the music where a new section seems to be starting and mark it. Often music will already have these so-called rehearsal sections marked with letters in the printed music. Use these to practice whole sections once the mistakes have been worked out. This type of practice has another advantage if your child is working to memorize a piece of music. Let's say your son has a memory slip during a performance. He can jump back to the start of a section and begin again. Since he has started at the point before on several occasions during practice sessions, his probability of success is much higher.

Starting a New Piece

Starting to learn a new piece will be one of the greatest challenges for your child. If the child is really excited about the piece, there may be motivation to start, but, even then, it seems to quickly wear off. This is not surprising since learning a new piece from scratch is really hard work and the payoff (the piece being learned) seems very far away.

Two things will help. First, having a time for new pieces within the practice routine (as suggested earlier) makes it harder to avoid. If your child knows that 25 percent of the practice time is devoted to this, then it becomes much more palatable.

Also, it is important to set specific goals. I talked about this in the previous chapter, but it is still bears reiterating. When approaching a new piece, your child must break it down into manageable parts. These parts could be an entire section, a short passage, or a few measures. Each piece will be divided up differently, but just about any piece of music can be sectioned off like this. Perhaps the initial goal will be to only work on the "A" section or the first verse, or the introduction. After a week of that, we move on to the next section. This will help immensely.

Mental Practice

Not all practice involves actually playing music. There are other valuable uses of practice time and one is called mental practice. In mental practice your child works to hear the music in his head while actually moving his fingers on the instrument (or pretending to have the instrument). The key is that your child has to actually concentrate on hearing the music. This is somewhat hard to monitor as a parent because no one outside your child's head knows if it is happening or not.

People are often surprised to learn that this type of practice can be very effective. Students who divided their time between mental and physical practice did at least as well (and sometimes better) than students who spent the entire time with physical practice.[7] A big advantage of mental practice is that it adds variety to the practice time, which is always a plus. However, these same studies point out that mental practice by itself is not as beneficial as physical practice. However, this might be better than doing nothing when your child forgets her instrument at school or it is in the shop for repairs.

There are many different types of practicing. Sometimes it is hard to tell the difference.

Modeling

It is pretty hard for children to perform a piece of music if they don't know what it is supposed to sound like. Very often a teacher will play through a piece during the lesson, but it is difficult to remember this for the entire week. Therefore, try tape recording the teacher at the lesson with a portable tape recorder or if your child is sufficiently advanced that the music he is performing is available on CD, use that. Your child can then listen to the piece while following the music several times during the week.

Does this help? *Definitely*. Several researchers have investigated using tapes and recordings in this way and the general conclusion is that it benefits just about all students.[8] Hearing the piece will not only help your child with learning the actual piece of music, it will also assist them in learning to make the instrument have a good tone. For example, if your child plays the saxophone and has never heard a really good saxophone tone, she will not know what she should be striving toward.

Some teachers will disagree with this approach. They claim that if children hear the piece of music, they will never learn to read notation. That is like saying if children hear a person speak, they can never learn to read. Instead, I think just the opposite is true. Could you imagine learning to read aloud if you had never heard the language you were trying to read?

Still, it is true that some children are so good at modeling what they hear that they never learn to read notation. This playing by ear is a valuable skill to have and develop, yet it can greatly hinder the need to read music. Therefore, some teachers may be warranted in using modeling with caution for certain students, but, for most, hearing a model and learning to read notation can go hand-in-hand. Hearing what they are to be playing will help, not hinder, their reading ability.

Learning to Hear Your Own Mistakes

When children are practicing, they may be so intently concentrating on reading the music, getting a good sound, sitting up straight, that it is very possible they will not have much concentration left to actually listen to themselves. Research has shown that middle and high school students do not hear their own mistakes when they make them, but can hear them easily when they are not playing.[9] One way to encourage your child to check her own mistakes is to tape record her performance and let her listen to herself. Research has shown that this can be an effective means of improving musical performance.[10]

To do this, have your son listen to a tape of his playing while watching the printed music. Have him indicate (by nodding, pointing, or any other means) when he hears something he wants to talk about. Make a mark in the music at that point. When the tape is over, or when there are several items to discuss, stop the tape and talk about each point. Work with him to find ways to correct or improve each highlighted area. When you are doing this, don't forget to also talk about overall issues such as tone, speed, and smoothness. Also be sure to point out things that were done correctly as well as incorrectly—you do not want your child thinking his performance is just mistake after mistake.

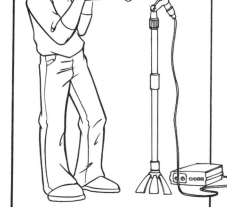

One way to encourage your child to check his own mistakes is to tape record his performance and let him listen to himself.

Another way is to focus your child's attention on listening with questions such as "Did you think that your saxophone sound is the right sound for that piece?" "Did you hear a place in the piece where you hesitated between notes?" "Did you notice a place in the piece that you played softer than other places?" The questions are not as important as the fact that you are focusing your child on listening to her performance.

Get Rid of Distractions

One of the best things you can do for your child is to take it upon yourself to remove as many distractions from the practice time as possible. In this era of electronic communication gadgets, our homes are no longer peaceful places. Televisions, stereos, telephones, computers, video games, e-mail all compete for our attention. You can act as a shield to keep these from interrupting your child's practice time.

Good practice takes concentration. Concentration, once broken, is hard to regain. Therefore, if your child receives a phone call during this time, take a message or use the answering machine. If you or other members of the family *must* watch television or play computer games, be sure your activity is far enough away from the practicing child. A little common sense combined with the awareness of the importance of concentration in practice can go a long way.

The Role of the Parent

Your role in your child's practice time is very important. It is also quite complex and involves a balance that will depend on your child's age, personality, and degree of playing ability.

In Japan, there is a popular approach to learning to play an instrument called the Suzuki method. A fundamental part of this approach is that the parent attends the lesson with the child and then practices *with* the child during the week. Although this approach has been quite successful in Japan, attempts to import it to the United States have been mixed. Perhaps the biggest limitation is that American parents don't seem to have the time (or perhaps the desire) to practice with their children.

Regardless of the reason, it does point out the importance of parental involvement with the lesson. In looking at the research literature on this point, I located ten separate studies that examined the role of parents in student practicing.[11] All ten showed that students whose parents monitored their practice did better than students whose parents did not. Interestingly, parents do not need to be completely involved as in the Suzuki method. Simple attention to the child's practice on the part of the parent was found to make a difference in student playing ability.

It is very important for you to realize that you do not have to be a musician yourself to help your child. Your role could simply involve being available to answer questions, keeping your child on task, or listening to the lesson and pointing out obvious mistakes (don't worry, you'll hear them!). Your role will be dictated, in large part, by the relationship you and your child have at other times. If you are a parent who helps with homework, you will probably be a parent who helps with practice.

Until your child learns how to practice, you need to be involved. If your child always goes to his room, closes the door, and practices without any monitoring or feedback from you, most likely the practice time will not be used as wisely as it could.

Using a Metronome

A metronome is a small, clocklike device providing a "tick-tock" sound in a variety of speeds. It is used to help students play pieces at the right speed and with a steady beat. Many student do not enjoy playing with a metronome. I myself really dislike the experience. But it is a valuable tool. In fact, my band practices occasionally with a metronome to make sure we are getting the speed right for the dancers.

You should have a metronome and encourage your child to use it if the child is having difficulty with timing in a piece of music. Your child's teacher can instruct you about the appropriate times and ways to use it.

Using an Accompaniment Tape or Computer

There are audiotapes and CDs available that have accompaniments for many of the pieces your child will be learning. There are also computer programs that will actually follow your child while she plays and add an accompaniment (see Chapter 15 for more on this). Either of these can be very motivating for your child. These tapes can also help your child to practice in a constant tempo, much as a metronome will. Check the front of your child's music book or ask your child's teacher if these tapes are available.

Breaking Practice into Small Units Throughout the Day

Some children may benefit from several smaller practice sessions during the day instead of one longer period. This is extremely easy to do if the practice time is being organized around goals instead of time. Research shows that two or three practice times within a day are more productive than one long period.[12] However, this research was done with advanced students who were practicing several hours per day.

Still, this may work just fine. The biggest drawback I can see is that you are going to have to get your child to practice several times each day.

Fitting in Music Theory

Ideally, your child will have some music theory as part of his lessons, usually involving some paper-and-pencil tasks. I find that this does not fit in very well with the actual practice time. For one thing, if your child plays an instrument such as a trombone, it will physically get in the way of writing. If the child is at the piano, it is more fun to play than to do the paper-and-pencil work.

I have found the most successful way to incorporate theory is to schedule an extra time for it. If your child has seven playing goals a day, perhaps at a different time he can complete one theory goal each day until the assignment is done (which is normally going to be just two or three days).

Summary

Time itself is not enough to turn your child into a good musician. That time must be spent wisely. You as a parent can help by doing the following:

- Establish a routine.
- Help children learn how to practice by having specific tools for fixing mistakes. These include mental practice, listening to models, taping themselves, and note-fixing strategies.
- Help avoid the temptation of simply playing through the parts of pieces your child already knows.
- Get rid of distractions
- Assist children in listening to themselves while practicing.
- Be involved with their practicing.
- Remember, practice does not make perfect. Only *good* practicing makes perfect.

Chapter 10

Music in the Public Schools

In the United States, we are fortunate to have ambitious and extensive public school music programs in many communities throughout the country. The basic tenet of school music is "every child for music and music for every child," which reflects the democratic nature of our society. In many other countries, music instruction is provided outside of the school environment or reserved for the musically or economically gifted person.

Still, it is amazing how many parents don't take full advantage of this resource. I think part of the reason is that they really don't understand what is available and, more important, what to expect from a public school music program. This is especially true if the parent did not participate in school music as a child. To the uninformed (or even the informed) parent, school music programs will often seem like an endless maze of classes, performances, contests, expectations, and costs.

I was a middle and high school music teacher for several years. Since then, I have worked with training music teachers and find myself frequently observing student teachers or working with teachers on projects. Yet, when our own kids entered the school music program, I was amazed at how different a school music program looks to a parent. Waiting to pick up one or another child after an afternoon or evening rehearsal, I often talked with other parents. I found that they really did not understand the reasoning behind much of what was being done.

In this and the next two chapters, I will offer you an insiders' view of school music programs while adding a parent perspective highlighting the differences between the many programs within the public school system. I will explain the history of school music programs, how they are structured, what they are trying to accomplish, and what parents can expect from their local school music program. I have deliberately excluded private and parochial schools from this discussion because I find that the diversity of music programs in such schools ranges from the extensive to nonexistent and with such little commonality that a general discussion would be exceedingly difficult at best and inaccurate at worst.

Short History of Music Teaching in the United States

When the Puritans landed at Plymouth in the 1600s, there was little time for music making or learning.[1] Survival was paramount, and any music available occurred in the Protestant churches. Even the church music was minimal and reduced to the singing of a few well-known hymns. Because organs or pianos would have been an inconceivable luxury then, all singing was done in a call-and-response manner. A song leader would sing a line of the hymn and the congregation would echo it. The result was that the singing in the churches, in time, diminished to the singing of a few familiar hymns.

Some music schools did open up in Boston during colonial times, but these were primarily for individual instruction on instruments such as strings, trumpet, flute, or harpsichord. They were also intended for those who could afford both the cost and time inherent in learning an instrument.

By and large, the general population received no musical training or experience. By the early 1700s, this lack of musical skill among most people was becoming quite noticeable, especially to the clergy. Many observed how poorly their congregations were singing and how the entire repertoire had been reduced to a select handful of hymns. From this state of affairs came what could be regarded as the first large-scale attempt to make music instruction available to everyone. This very American idea (that music was not just for the rich or noble classes) was manifested in the creation of the New England singing schools of the mid-1700s.

These were hardly schools as we think of them, but they were an important first step to where we are today. Some of the schools were held in church basements or other temporary facilities. Some traveled the countryside like shows. The teacher would announce that he would be coming to a town for a given week and church leaders would encourage their congregations to attend. The goal of this movement was to improve the quality of singing in the churches. These schools were much like what we would label workshops today.

They were so popular and so successful that in the late 1700s singing societies were created. These clubs were organized to perform large vocal works such as Handel's Messiah. Soon, every major city had singing societies and some still exist today—for example, one in Stoughton, Massachusetts, has been in existence since 1786.

Even with the success of singing schools and singing societies, a feeling still prevailed that music instruction was for those who sought it out, instead of being for every citizen. Cities such as Chicago, Cincinnati, Philadelphia, and Boston began experimenting with starting music groups in schools. Choirs and orchestras were formed for students who wanted to participate. Often these were organized as clubs. Other times they were set up to provide moral development for children or as a break from the rigors of studying academics.

In 1832, a turning point occurred. A teacher/businessman named Lowell Mason convinced the Boston school board that every child could succeed in music and that music instruction should be included as a subject along with math, reading, and science. He argued that children who studied music would create better homes, be better citizens, and become happier human beings. He was so persuasive that the Boston school board agreed to let him try to teach singing to all children in the school system. Of course, they also agreed not to pay him for his services. Thus, Lowell Mason became the first full-time public school music teacher in America, perhaps in the world. He also started the tradition of music teachers working long hours with little or no pay. His legacy lives on in both accomplishments.

Lowell Mason was a success. The next year he was permanently hired and soon all major cities included music instruction in the schools. Parents liked it, administrators liked it, and children loved it.

Throughout the 1800s, school music programs continued to grow, expanding into vocal and orchestral groups. Because the United States did not (and still doesn't) have a nationwide, or even a statewide, mandated curriculum, the growth was school-by-school across the nation. By the end of the 1800s, the study of vocal music was the accepted norm in the schools. Because some students were taking lessons on instruments outside the schools, it seemed natural to bring those children together to perform in an ensemble. Thus, schools started to form orchestras because string instruments were so popular. These orchestras were composed of whatever instruments were played by the students in the school. They were different from vocal music classes in that they were usually arranged as clubs and met before or after school, but not normally during the school day. From these beginnings, the idea of music education as part of a public school education was well on its way to becoming a reality.

During the 1900s, some major changes took place in music instruction. All can be traced to political or technological events. In the first part of the twentieth century, the United States entered World War I. The effect of this event on music education is interesting and unexpected. The fifty or so years between the Civil War and World War I saw the emergence of a great interest in the military-style band. Patrick Gilmore, John Philip Sousa, and others toured the countryside performing concerts and becoming modern-day performance stars.

World War I heightened this interest. When the war ended, the returning soldiers needed employment. Many of the former military bandsmen were hired to teach band music in the public schools. Thus, the band movement, unquestionably the mainstay of public school music today, can be traced directly to a war. Band programs of the late twentieth century have expanded beyond their military band roots, but the football marching band, that uniquely American invention, is a direct descendant of these early bands.

In the mid-twentieth century, the phonograph became a household commodity. This new technological wonder made music available to all people. School music programs responded by adding a component previously unheard of: listening skills. For the first time in history, there was the real possibility that most people would become listeners to music, not performers. Music teachers responded by adding the creation of listening skills to their music programs. Today, instruction in listening constitutes a large part of music instruction, especially at the elementary level. Music appreciation courses in middle school and high school are fairly common and the result of the phonograph's invention.

In the late 1950s, another technological event had a direct effect on music teaching. In 1957, the Russians launched the first manmade earth satellite, *Sputnik*. The following uproar about the need for improved education in America was a rallying cry of the cold war. During the 1960s, the federal government infused large sums of money into public education for experimental programs. The result was that many methods of science, math, and English and even music were tested and subsequently adopted in our schools. Many of these approaches to teaching music, such as Orff, Kodály, and Dalcroze, have become the backbone of teaching music today.

As we begin the twenty-first century, all educators are watching the computer and Internet revolution for ways in which they will change and alter music instruction. Another basic trend is toward national standards. For the first time in our history, there is an attempt to have a basic set of music skills and knowledge that all students, regardless of state, city, or school, should possess. No one knows how these influences will affect music teaching. Based on past history, music teaching will respond; however, it remains to be seen in what manner.

How Music Programs Are Structured

As you have seen, the history of teaching music in the schools has resulted in a unique system. Because each school system in the country decides its own needs and curricula, there is great variety in how music programs have evolved. Still, surprising consistency exists among programs in certain basic formats. The arrangement in your child's school will probably resemble the format described in Table 10-1, but will most likely not follow it exactly.

What should be taught in a school music program?

There are differing opinions about what should be taught in school music programs at all levels. Unlike other subjects, such as math or English, for which several teachers need to coordinate what is being taught, music teachers often work alone. Normally, there is only one music teacher at an elementary school; in secondary school there is usually more than one teacher, but there still may be only one choral teacher, one band teacher, and one orchestra teacher. The result of this is that the curricula become very teacher specific.

Nonetheless, most educators agree on basic content and specific skills that should be taught. These can be found in several places and all are available to parents if they ask. As a starting point, every school system is usually required to have a written curriculum for each subject. In my experience, many music teachers have never seen this or ignore it in favor of what they believe the students need. The teachers may have a point here. Writing a curriculum for an entire subject is difficult, time-consuming work and few schools are able to hire

Grades	Type of Music Instruction	General Goals	Who Receives Instruction
K–8	General Music	General knowledge of music, basic music reading skills, singing, listening, and appreciation	All students
4–6	String Instruction	Private or small group beginning instruction in violin, viola, cello, and brass	Available to all students on a voluntary basis; meets during school day
5–6	Wind and Percussion Instruction	Private or small group beginning instruction in brass, woodwind, and percussion instruments	Available to all students on a voluntary basis; meets during school day
7–12	Band	To increase student musical ability and knowledge, to expose students to quality musical literature, and to provide an ensemble experience	Available to all students; meets during the school day; students receive credit for participation
7–12	Orchestra		
7–12	Choir		
9–12	Music Theory	To develop an introductory knowledge of music theory and ear training	Elective credit
9–12	Music History	To acquaint students with the basic historical periods and types of classical music	Elective credit
9–12	Specialized Ensembles (steel band, mariachi, madrigals, folk groups, etc.)	To develop independent and more advanced skills among capable students	Elective credit or extra-curricular activity

TABLE 10:1 *Depending on the instrument your child plays, he or she will have differing opportunities to perform alone or in a group. Both types of performing are important to musical development.*

experts to do it. The result often is that the music curricula at the school or system level are poorly written and hard to understand.

A better resource for finding what should be taught is probably the state or national guidelines. Every state will have specific goals for music instruction at each grade level. These are usually carefully prepared and in a format that is easy to understand. They will never tell a teacher *how* a skill should be taught, but they will recommend *what* should be taught at each level. These guidelines are available from your state's Department of Education, usually for a small fee.

The national music standards are available from the Music Educators National Conference in print form or on their website at www.menc.org. These standards were formulated in the early 1990s by educators from across the United States under the auspices of the National Association of Music Educators. These standards are not mandates, but represent the consensus of educators about what should be taught at each grade level. For example, one goal is that "by grade four, students should be able to read whole, half, dotted half, and eighth note rests in 2/4, 3/4, and 4/4 meter signatures." The national standards highlight broad goals, but will go a long way toward focusing a program if they are followed. A summary of these standards appears in Appendix C.

To see how well your music program is working toward these goals, you should request a copy of the national, state, and local guidelines or curricula. There will probably be a cost involved because the guidelines often run 100 or 200 pages in length.

The writing in these documents will be highly specific. Although they may not be enjoyable bedtime reading, they will provide very specific information about what your child should be learning in music in every grade.

How do I know if the school program is any good?

It is very difficult to come up with one measure of what constitutes a quality music program in a school. Very often programs are judged by the community on how many awards the ensembles have won, or how large the marching band is, or the general reputation of the program.

None of these, by themselves, are an accurate measure of the quality of the program. Further, they may not be reflective of the entire music program. It is not unusual for a school to have an excellent orchestra but a mediocre-sounding band or choir. Likewise, I have seen schools with vibrant band programs and a choral program that hardly existed.

To help you evaluate, there are some resources that could help. I have already discussed the national standards that give some guidelines on what the curricula in the elementary, middle, and high schools should be aspiring toward. A publication entitled *School Music Programs: Descriptions and Standards* is also available from the Music Educators National Conference; it describes what both a regular and exceptional music program should offer your child. It suggests the amount of time certain classes should meet, how often they should meet, and what types of classes should be available. It also tells the minimum training the teachers should have in each music area and the type of materials (instruments, music library, rehearsal rooms) that the school should have.

Another way is to compare both the quality of ensembles as well as the extensiveness of opportunities to other similar schools in your area. These schools will have the same state support and will probably have similar local support. Differences in facilities, materials, offerings, and teacher qualifications may be more a reflection of administrative or parental priorities than anything else.

If you are interested in knowing how the actual facilities measure up, or if your school is building a new building or addition, a helpful book (also from MENC) is *Music Facilities: Building, Equipping, and Renovating*. It describes details of the design of music rooms to provide both good educational space as well as a safe environment. For example, it gives the number of square feet necessary per band musician so each is both comfortable and not at risk for hearing loss. Building materials, type of electronic equipment, and lighting are all covered.

These resources will be helpful, but I want to emphasize that I have seen what I regard as excellent programs in physical conditions that were totally inadequate. Likewise, I have seen poor programs in beautiful new schools. It all comes down to what types and quality of musical experiences are being offered to your child. Without doubt, the teacher/musician working with your child daily is the most important ingredient in a quality program.

School Programs Are Based on Making Music in Groups—Does my child also need solo experiences?

School music programs are based around group performance. In large part this is because one teacher is responsible for the musical development of a large number of students in the public schools. But beyond these obvious reason of practicality there are very strong musical reasons for children to perform in an ensemble.

In an ensemble, the young musician needs to be able to maintain a steady tempo that is determined by the conductor. The child cannot stop to fix a mistake and must learn to continue playing. While performing, every member of the group must listen to the other musicians and match the tone of his instrument or voice with theirs. Likewise, the volume at which each musician needs to perform has to be in balance with the rest of the group. By playing in an ensemble, musicians must time their playing, often to the fraction of a second, with all those around them. Through practice in the group, children learn an almost unbelievable set of useful skills in timing, listening, watching (the conductor and the music), and adapting to everything going on around them.

However, many parents get confused when the public school teacher recommends that their child participate in private lessons or a solo competition in addition to playing in the ensemble. Why would a child need both? The ensemble experience is really not enough for a serious music student. When musicians perform alone, they are allowed to take many liberties with the music. In fact, one major difference between what experts call an excellent, as opposed to a good, performance is that performers take great liberties with the beat: they speed up here, and slow down there, to match the expressive quality of the music. In an ensemble this is impossible for an individual to do. However, in solo performance, your child can, and will, take these liberties. This is where your child's creativity can shine.

The best performers have a balance of both types of performance experiences. The amount of of experience your child will get is directly related to the instrument she chooses to play. Pianists, classical guitarists, and harpists rarely get enough ensemble experience when growing up. Singers, clarinetists, drummers, and oboists rarely get enough solo experience. As a parent, you should encourage a balance of solo and group opportunities for your child.

What is missing from a school music program?

Relative to world standards, school music programs in the United States are very good. Ignore what you read in the media—no other country on earth does what we do with music. While you may hear of an excellent orchestra from a high school from another country, you must remember that this is often a select group of students. American schools have attempted to make music instruction accessible to all children during their public school lives.

But attempting to reach every child comes at a cost. School programs are not designed to provide everything needed by the serious young musician. Private lessons are necessary for anyone planning on pursuing music as a career. Further, the school cannot supply the quality of instrument needed for the serious student. The family of the child must provide these embellishments.

Many opportunities are also available for making music outside school and these should be encouraged. There are community and regional bands, choruses, and orchestras. Many universities sponsor summer music camps and honor programs throughout the school year. For example, many children sing in auditioned community children's choruses such as the Tucson Girl's Chorus or the Seattle Children's Chorus in addition to their own school choirs. Such children experience the joy of singing with other dedicated and excellent singers. Other children play in community bands of all varieties, others perform in regional orchestras. In summer, many schools and community-based music groups offer summer arts programs including art, drama, music, and dance.

These community and regional organizations augment the basic curriculum offered to all children in the public schools. They should not be viewed as being in competition with what the schools are attempting to achieve. In fact, most teachers encourage their musically talented students to participate in these organizations. Chapter 14 explores these opportunities in more detail.

Public school music should provide an excellent foundation for the musical child. The rest is up to the child and the parent. I have provided a listing of useful resources including professional associations, summer camps, and the like in the resource for parents at the end of the book to direct you to some of the musical opportunities available that can augment the experiences your child is receiving in the public school. The next two chapters will look at music programs in more detail in both elementary and secondary schools.

Chapter 11

Music in the Elementary School

If you have children in elementary school, they probably go to a music class taught by a music teacher. If they are in the upper grades, they may also sing in a choir or take lessons on a band or orchestra instrument. These are the three basic ways music is taught during the elementary school years: general music, choir, and instrumental music.

General Music

The general music class is the one class that all children will attend; it is not voluntary, like instrumental or choral music. This class meets for shorter periods (20–30 minutes) in the younger grades and expands to about an hour in the upper grades. Music classes usually meet two or three times per week.

Until the 1960s and 1970s, this class was commonly called vocal music because of its emphasis on singing. Today it is called general music because the curriculum has been expanded to include playing instruments, listening skills, music reading, composition, movement, music history, and a host of other aspects of music learning.

General music is a major arm of the music teaching profession. There are journals, materials, and conventions designed specifically for the general music teacher. In some schools there are very carefully planned curriculum guides and goals for elementary general music. In other schools, general music seems much more random.

Beyond a common title, there is great variety in what goes on in a class from community to community or even school to school. One of the reasons is that there are many different teaching methodologies or philosophies regarding the teaching of general music. Some, such as Orff, Dalcroze, Kodaly, and Gordon, are named after the originator of the approach to teaching. Each of these approaches has a professional organization that supports it. Most have their own conventions, publications, and materials.

In addition to these approaches, there are two major publishing companies that produce teaching series books with a sequential curriculum often incorporating the major teaching methodologies.

Most likely the teacher (or teachers) in your child's school will be an advocate of one or more of these methods and use one of the series books. Some teachers mix and match aspects of each to create something totally new. So that you can understand the method chosen by your child's school, I will give a brief overview of each. These overviews are extremely concise; each method has volumes written about its goals and methods. Therefore, these are only thumbnail sketches and they are not intended to fully explain each system.

Orff

This approach was created by composer Carl Orff as a means of developing musicality in children. This is done through the use of a sequential curriculum designed around activities children enjoy such as singing, chanting, clapping, and moving.

A very unique aspect of this instruction is the use of Orff instruments. Orff devised a series of instruments designed specifically for the method. These instruments are primarily from the wooden xylophone and metal glockenspiel families, which means they are made up of tuned metal or wooden bars that are hit with a mallet. They are unique in that the pitches not used in a song or accompaniment can be removed from the instrument, thus eliminating the possibility of the child's playing the wrong note. Thus, the child is free to concentrate on playing in rhythm and enjoying making music as part of a group.

The group, or ensemble, experience is an important ingredient of this approach. By performing within an ensemble, your child experiences, at a very young age, the joy of making music with others. If your child is in a school that follows the Orff approach, you will hear and see your child performing in these ensembles at school performances. Your child will be playing one of a variety of Orff instruments.

Orff and a colleague, Gunild Keetman, wrote several books of music to be performed with singing, Orff instruments, recorders, and percussion instruments. In addition to this music, imitation and improvisation are frequently used. In imitation, the teacher plays a short musical phrase on an instrument and the student repeats it. The purpose of this is to develop the child's musical memory. Improvisation involves making up a musical part, much like when a guitarist or saxophonist takes a solo during a song. This is intended to encourage musical creativity among children.

In this approach, children learn to make music before they learn to read music, much the way we learn to speak words before we learn to read them. They will also learn to internalize music by moving to music and rhythmic speech.

You can find out more about the Orff approach from the American Orff-Schulwerk Association at www.aosa.org.

Kodály

Like the Orff approach, the Kodály approach was conceived by a composer, Zoltán Kodály. In this approach, much emphasis is placed on developing the pure singing voice of children through the singing of traditional folk songs from the children's culture. A typical Kodály class is characterized by a great deal of singing. The goal of this singing is both proper singing production and learning to read music.

To teach pitches and rhythms, the instructor uses systems of solfege and rhythm syllables. The solfege system employs the syllables of "do-re-mi-fa-sol-la-ti" (think: "Doe a Deer" from *The Sound of Music*) to teach children how to sing and read music at the same time. Children learn to sing patterns by either copying the teacher's model, looking at music notation, or following hand signs that are a type of sign language telling which pitch to sing.

Children learn rhythm patterns by seeing each type of note designated by a syllable. For example, *tah* is used for a quarter note and *ti* for an eighth note. Thus, it would be common to hear a class reciting "*tah ti-ti ti-ti tah*" to practice rhythms.

Fundamental to the Kodály approach is the use of folk songs. Teachers wishing to become certified as Kodály educators are required to conduct folk song research related to their region or culture. These songs are chosen for their musical integrity as well as their appropriateness for the age of the singer.

You can learn more about Kodály by visiting the website of the Organization of American Kodály Educators at www.oake.org.

Dalcroze Eurhythmics

This is still another approach named for its originator and the oldest of the approaches used today. Started by Emile Jacques-Dalcroze, this program utilizes movement activities for developing musical skills. It is not dance, but instead the development of expressive movement to music. This approach is useful for all ages. I have seen kindergarten Dalcroze classes as well as college classes for music majors. All students seem to benefit from it.

The Dalcroze approach utilizes three branches. First, eurhythmics is the movement branch that trains your child's body to respond to rhythm and dynamics. Solfege, which was described as part of the Kodály method, trains your child's ear and voice. Improvisation, described in the Orff approach, brings all learning together.

Dalcroze works because it involves the learners' entire body in the learning of music. By actively involving the learner at all these different levels, the child is able to internalize the musical learning in a substantive manner.

Gordon—Jump Right In

This method was created by American Edward Gordon during the 1960s, 1970s, and 1980s. He is still actively developing the approach today.

A basic tenet of this approach is that everyone is born with a certain degree of musical aptitude. For the optimal development of this aptitude, musical training begins early, especially during preschool and early elementary school.

Gordon's approach is based on cognitive psychology. The goal of this teaching is to have students learn the basic building blocks of musical sound so that they can mentally interpret what they hear. Therefore, the child is exposed to the basic pitch and rhythm patterns of Western music early and repeatedly. The teacher will sing or play patterns that the student repeats. Gordon believes that this repeated exposure to aural patterns provides the child with a greater understanding of music when it is heard later in life.

Gordon has created a sequential curriculum utilizing this approach that he calls "Jump Right In." Here the basic patterns of music are arranged in order of complexity and systematically drilled. Evaluative measurements, or tests, are built into the program. "Jump Right In" also has a corresponding method for learning instrumental music in the upper elementary grades.

You can find out more about Jump Right In at Gordon's website at www.unm.edu/~audiate/gordon.htm.

Education Through Music (ETM)

This method was developed by educator Mary Helen Richards and is promoted by the Richards' Institute in California. The program is a well-designed and planned curriculum that has a healthy balance of singing, listening, and experiencing music. "Song experience games" are designed to help your child in both music and reading literacy. Unlike other music approaches, ETM is designed for teachers of any subject matter, not just music teachers. It uses music to teach a variety of both academic and social skills.

Through the use of listening maps, your children are guided into focusing on music as they listen. These are designed to build on children's natural curiosity to lead them to the aesthetic, which they describe as learning's friend because it connects emotion with the mind to stimulate meaningful learning.

Find out more about ETM at www.educationthroughmusic.com.

Integration

Integration has become one of the major approaches of recent years. With it, the music teacher tries to integrate music learning with learning in other subjects. For example, if the history teacher is teaching a unit on the Civil War, then the music teacher may teach songs from that era. Although this approach can work, it often does not. The music program often is held hostage to what the other subjects are working on. Many music programs are reduced to a class in which students sing songs about a particular subject based not on a song's usefulness to teach a musical skill or the song's musical qualities, but instead because the words fit in with what another teacher was planning. This approach may make the music teacher popular with other teachers, yet it will rarely result in a systematic curriculum for teaching musical skills to your child.

Series Books

Two major publishers produce correlated grade level books for use with music: Silver-Burdett Ginn/Scott Foresman and Macmillan/McGraw-Hill. Both publish excellent series books with accompanying CDs and other teaching aids. Each book series has strengths and weaknesses as well as a personality all its own. Which series is chosen for your school will depend in large part on the personality of the teachers involved, the goals of the music program, and the adoption policy of the school district. These books are so expensive (a typical school can spend tens of thousands of dollars to adopt a series) that, once adopted, they are used for at least eight to ten years. Therefore, it is likely that your child will be studying from the same music series throughout the elementary grades.

As I mentioned, both books are excellent. Unfortunately, many music teachers are placed in situations in which they are unable to take advantage of the carefully planned sequences of learning that are presented in these books. Many schools do not schedule music classes often enough or regularly enough for the books to be used the way they are intended. It has been interesting being a parent and seeing my children come home with a science or history book from these same companies. The teacher starts at the beginning and teaches through the book. This is how it is in a regular classroom where students and teacher are together every day. But because the music class is not a daily activity, and sometimes only a weekly event, this sense of continuity is often lost. Thus, one of the strongest aspects of the series book is lost.

Still, as a parent, you should ask which series is being used and how it is used. Both companies maintain websites that describe the series and their goals and objectives in detail. The McGraw-Hill website provides areas for both parents and students. In the student section, children can learn more about everything from the elements of music to careers in music. In the parents section, there are suggestions on how to enhance the music lessons your child is getting at school.

The websites can be found at www.sbgmusic.com for Silver-Burdett Ginn and www.mmhschool.com for McGraw-Hill.

As an aside, if you are lucky enough to have a child in elementary school when it is time to adopt a new music textbook, volunteer to be a parent representative on the committee. You can be a great help and learn a lot about music teaching in the process.

How often should they have music and in what grades?

Just as elementary school music programs vary greatly in approach, they also vary greatly in how often, how long, and what grades receive instruction. For a parent, it is sometimes impossible to determine whether the school is providing the right amount of instruction. To help, the Music Educators National Conference (www.menc.org) publishes guidelines on how often instruction should take place and how long this instruction should last. These guidelines are published in a paperback book entitled *The School Music Program: Description and Standards*.[1] This is a valuable resource for parents to ensure that their school system is providing a quality music program for their children.

These guidelines are very specific. For example, here are the guidelines for a basic elementary school music program:

1. At least 7 percent of the total instructional time, or not fewer than 100 minutes per week, whichever is greater, is allocated to general music.
2. Each child, K-6, receives music instruction in school at least three times weekly.
3. Classes in general music are no larger than classes in other academic subjects in the school.
4. Instruction in recorder is offered beginning not later than grade 4.
5. Elective classes of string and wind instruments are provided, meeting at least twice each week for at least 35 minutes per session.
6. String instrument instruction begins not later than grade 5, and wind instrument instruction not later than grade 6.

The guidelines also list the minimum standards for maintaining a quality program. There are specific standards for each grade level, preschool through high school. They even suggest teacher-to-student ratios and the proper musical equipment needed to have this program.

Choral Music in the Elementary School

If your school has been actively developing your child's voice through the general music classes, it will often offer a separate choir experience during the upper elementary grades (and a few even earlier). To provide this, many schools offer fifth- and sixth-grade chorus programs. These may be given during the school day, but more typically they meet before or after school or perhaps during lunch. Children who are good singers and enjoy singing will benefit greatly from a chorus. They will learn to sing their part while another part is being sung in harmony and will further their ability to read music and develop a good tone. They will also begin the important process of learning to blend with other singers.

Instrumental Music in the Elementary School

Many schools begin some type of instrumental music instruction in the upper elementary grades. The exact year that this is started varies widely, but a survey of state supervisors of music done a few years ago revealed that the most common pattern was to begin string instruction in the fourth grade and wind and percussion in the fifth grade.[2] As with most aspects of music education, this varies widely.

The reason string instruments are generally started earlier than wind and percussion instruments is threefold. First, the students can physically produce the required sounds on a string instrument at an earlier age. Wind instruments require coordination and strength in the mouth area that may not be developed in fourth grade. Second, string instruments are generally regarded as being more difficult to master than other instruments. Therefore, starting a year earlier will enable string players to perform at the same level as the band in later years. Third, to some children string instruments are generally not as attractive as band instruments. To counter this, many string teachers want to try enticing the students to try a string instrument before having to compete with the shinier (brass), louder (percussion), and more readily heard and recognized instruments such as the saxophone.

Assuming that your school follows this common pattern, your child should be given the opportunity to begin instruction on a string instrument in the fourth grade. Most likely the music teacher will arrange for some older students (middle school or high school age) to come and perform for the students. Your child will then be introduced to the four major string instruments: violin, viola, cello, and bass. Children will then be allowed to choose an instrument that they would like to learn to play.

Most likely, the music teacher will confine instruction to the violin, viola, and maybe the cello. This is due mainly to the fact that students may not be physically large enough to play the string bass. Even as it is, your child will probably not begin instruction on a full-sized instrument. Instead, he or she may play a three-quarter size violin or viola or half-size cello or bass. As your child grows she will be switched to a full-size instrument or may be encouraged to switch to cello or bass.

Once your child has chosen an instrument, he will be given a group lesson at least once a week. Such lessons generally include anywhere from four to twelve students in a lesson and there is no additional

Probably the best system is one that offers all students the opportunity for group lessons in school, but still provides after-school private lessons for those who choose.

charge. There may be a concert at the end of this first year, but that is not the goal of the instruction. Instead, the goal is for the student to learn about music and how to play the instrument.

In fifth grade, your child will be given the opportunity to learn to play a wind or percussion instrument. Just as in the strings, these lessons will often be in small groups, usually with only one or two different instruments represented in the group. Some schools will attempt to teach the instruments all together in a band setting, but this is usually less successful.

Another new trend is to abandon the idea of lessons during the day. Some school districts will arrange for local teachers to teach in the school building before and after school. In this case, the parents pay a fee directly to the private teacher. Although this trend has the advantage of saving the school system money, it does not further the goal of providing music instruction to all children and often competes with bus schedules and extracurricular activities. Probably the best system is one that offers all students the opportunity for group lessons in school, but still provides after-school private lessons for those who choose.

Regardless of whether your child chooses a string, wind, or percussion instrument, there will probably be no charge for the actual lessons if given during the day. The school provides the teacher whose job is to teach these lessons. Parents are often asked, however, to rent an instrument for their child. The school usually arranges this through local music dealers. Twenty or thirty years ago, it was common for the music store to give a percentage of the rental fee back to the school music program. This was done both to support the program and also encourage loyalty to one store among music teachers, but it sometimes led to abuses. Therefore, this practice has all but vanished from school music. Instead, the music teacher should provide a list of several dealers from whom rental programs are available.

Should I rent or buy an instrument for my child?

I have seen many enthusiastic parents purchase an instrument as soon as their child shows an interest in music. I strongly discourage this for several reasons. First, your child is exploring possibilities. Many students switch instruments after only one year, and many others discontinue playing after one or two years. There is a poor resale market for beginning quality instruments and therefore you may be stuck with an instrument you don't need. Worse, your child may feel obligated to stay with an instrument he really is not cut out to play or doesn't like. In the case of string instruments, your child will probably start on an instrument that is not full-size and will outgrow that instrument fairly quickly. I strongly suggest renting an instrument at first. Once a child finds the perfect instrument, going with the parents to purchase it or receiving it as a gift can be one of the most memorable experiences of childhood.

Won't children fall behind in their studies if they leave for music lessons?

Many parents worry that their child will fall behind in the so-called academic subjects if the child is dismissed from the class for an instrumental music lesson. There seems to be little reason for concern here.

I spend much of my time visiting elementary schools as a consultant or to observe student teachers. During these visits I often see teachers dealing with children leaving for lessons. There is no doubt that it is disruptive to the regular classroom teacher. These teachers should be commended for allowing this disruption that enables students to participate in the instrumental music program. This aside, the most common way for teachers to deal with this disruption is to schedule activities during this time that are perhaps enhancement or elaboration. When the music students are gone for their lesson, many teachers spend the time working with students who need the extra time or attention. Based on this observation, it would appear that there is little, if any, loss of instruction time for students who choose to study an instrument.

Research supports this observation. Three extensive studies have been conducted to address the question of whether instrumental lessons negatively affect student learning in other areas. Edward Kvet conducted one of the largest studies in 1985.[3] His study involved over 2,000 sixth-grade students in twenty-six schools in four school districts. Students who studied instrumental music were matched with those who did not by the following variables: sex, race, IQ, cumulative achievement, school attended, and classroom teacher. Kvet found that there was no difference in the reading, language, and math achievement between students who were excused for instrumental music instruction and those who were not. Further, this held true among schools of different size, setting, socioeconomic level, and racial composition.

Another researcher, Brandon Friedman[4] divided fifth-grade students from four schools into control and experimental groups. The two groups were matched by sex, intelligence, and age. The students in the experimental group were given instrumental music instruction during the school day. At the conclusion of the study, the arithmetic and reading sections of the Stanford achievement test were administered. Friedman found no differences between the two groups in any of the scores: arithmetic reasoning, arithmetic computation, word meaning, or paragraph meaning.

A third study[5] compared the academic achievement of sixth-grade students in West Hartford, Connecticut, who were excused from class once or twice per week to study instrumental music. The research compared the overall academic ability of students by using the scores from the Iowa Tests of Basic Skills. After matching instrumental and noninstrumental students by sex, age, and IQ, no difference was found between the two groups on any aspect of the Iowa tests.

These three studies, individually and in tandem, support my observation that removing elementary students from their regular classes to study instrumental music does not detract from their academic achievement. This is true regardless of the type of school, racial makeup, grade, or school district. Thus, as a parent, you can feel very comfortable that your child is not missing important nonmusical information.

As a parent, you may also be surprised that the scores of the music students were not actually higher than the nonmusicians. Recent media reports all seem to indicate that students who study music will do better on academic tests. These studies do not contradict that finding; they were not designed to study the effect of studying music on the students' academic scores. Instead, they were designed to measure the effect of leaving class to take music lessons. Although this might seem a minor technical difference, it in fact changes the way the entire research would be conducted. For example, it is very likely that some children who did not take group lessons were taking private lessons outside of school. Any child playing piano, guitar, singing in a choir, or even taking dance lessons would be getting music instruction, but might not go to a group trumpet lesson.

I dedicated more space to this issue than perhaps I needed to and worked to support my observation with research. It seems that whenever a school system is having problems with their students' not achieving well on standardized tests, a common scapegoat made by many superintendents is the instrumental music program. Providing free lessons to all these students may be a financial hardship for these schools, but it is clear that it is not an academic hardship. When administrators blame instrumental music for a school's academic problems, perhaps they have a vision of the district budget in their heads, not a vision of a child's future.

Summary

The elementary school music program will be influenced heavily by the philosophy of music for every child, every child for music. Therefore, it will work to develop wide-ranging basic skills in music. How this is achieved will be influenced by the particular methodology chosen by the music teachers.

Classroom music, or general music, will probably begin in kindergarten and continue throughout the elementary years. The class will normally meet several times per week. Starting around fourth grade, string instruction will begin, followed the next year by instruction in band instruments. Chorus may also start in fifth grade. Although every school is different, these are guidelines and seem to be the most popular arrangements. Your children will probably experience a program that is close to one of these if they are enrolled a public school.

Chapter 12

Music in the Secondary School

When your child enters junior high or middle school, he or she will be entering a whole new world of musical opportunities. In high school, the opportunities will often increase still further. Depending on the school, there will probably be a wealth of ways to be involved in music. Most of these opportunities will be based in performance, while a few will be in more theoretical and historical sides of music.

A comprehensive school program is one that allows for the participation of as many students as possible at many different levels. But also note that music performance starts becoming more and more selective, especially during high school. Although there should be musical opportunities for all students, not all students will be able to participate in all activities. Auditions, chair placements, and a variety of other musical factors will start to determine to a large degree the nature of your child's musical experiences. Time commitments in other, nonmusical activities (work, school functions, love life, driving) will also play a large role in the musical commitment your son or daughter is able to make.

New opportunities for parents will also arise. You may be asked to join a music boosters club, work at football concession stands, chaperone band trips, and will probably find yourself buying more than your share of candy bars, pizzas, wrapping paper, and what have you. Truly, secondary school music programs touch the whole family.

Band in the Secondary School

When your child enters middle or junior high school, the format of wind and percussion studies changes. The small-group or private lessons will disappear. In place of this, your child will sign up for band class. Most middle and junior high schools have several bands. These are arranged in one of two fashions. One is to simply have a band for each of the three grades: a sixth-grade band, a seventh-grade band, and an eighth-grade band. This arrangement was the norm in the 1960s and 1970s, but has been slowly replaced in many schools with bands arranged by ability level. The advantage of the ability arrangement is that students are performing and learning with students of similar playing ability. This arrangement allows the director to choose music that is challenging for the majority of the group without being frustrating to lesser players. This challenge is a key to the success of any group. For this reason, the idea of ability-ranked ensembles is probably the better of the two designs.

Some parents (and teachers) object to the idea of auditions to get into groups when they are as young as sixth or seventh grade. This is a valid concern and most directors are sensitive to it. I think the most important factor at this point is the manner in which the band director handles the situation. In the middle grades, most directors will downplay the sense of audition. Instead, students will take part in placement exams. These playing tests are treated as a chance for the director to ascertain what group *is best for your child*. If auditions are presented this way, it should be relatively easy for your child to handle the procedure.

Some directors may not agree with this idea. Sometimes they

Most directors will approach auditions and seating placement in a fair, nonthreatening manner.

argue that auditions are a part of the life of a musician and the student must get used to it. They will use the threat of audition as a way to motivate students to practice, saying such things as: "If you don't practice, you'll be dropped down to the next group." The result is that some students will practice simply out of fear and learn to fear and dread the auditions.

Although this scheme can yield results (increased practice), it has no place in the school music program. Yes, *professional* musicians do have to deal with the pressure of auditions, and the music world is often cruel and heartless. But there is time to prepare for this later. No child needs this added pressure during the early teen years.

Most directors will approach auditions and seating placement in a fair, nonthreatening manner. If not, it is probably time to bring it up in a private meeting with him or her. If the director tells you that "that is how it is done everywhere," don't believe it. The majority of successful programs do not threaten students.

In addition to the large school band, another standard ensemble in many junior highs and middle schools is the jazz ensemble. This group is smaller than the concert bands (usually under twenty members) and is made up primarily of trumpets, trombones, instruments from the saxophone family, and a rhythm section composed of a drum set, bass, guitar, and piano. It should be emphasized that any instrument can play jazz, but these are the instruments that traditionally perform it.

Jazz bands play music from the big band era to the present day. This is a different style of music and involves improvisation or playing solos. In this style, your child will learn to make up solos and melodies—an extremely challenging, yet valuable skill for any musician. For this reason alone, you should encourage your child to participate in jazz band whether or not she likes jazz music. The style of music is a vehicle for teaching important musical skills.

The band and jazz band will probably represent the wind and percussion offerings at most middle schools. Some schools at this level start marching bands, but this should be viewed with caution. Young musicians are still learning important playing habits and should probably be concentrating on those and not the added skill of marching. Still, if done in the proper spirit and purpose, this can be a fun addition to the program. The same is true of pep bands for indoor sports events. Although pep bands sometimes have minimal musical value (due to the quality of the music and casualness of the performance), they do provide additional experiences for children to perform with a group as well as increased playing time. The musical value of the pep band depends completely on the director. It is very hard to make any generalizations here.

The school probably will not provide private lessons, so the director will encourage your child to take them. I have met many parents who do not understand this. They wonder why their children need private lessons in addition to playing every day in band. Lessons are necessary for your child to continue to grow as a musician. Although playing in band is excellent for learning musical concepts and ensemble-playing skills, your child still needs the individual attention that can only be provided by a private lesson. The lessons will develop the playing skills well beyond the ability level required for most band compositions. In addition, the instruction will be custom-tailored to your child, not to the ability level of the entire group.

Many schools arrange for private music teachers to use the school building after school hours to provide lessons for interested students. These are often slightly less expensive than lessons at a music store and are much more convenient for parents. Your local school is usually much more centrally located than a music store and your child can simply go earlier or stay later at school. For these reasons, more students will take private lessons in schools offering this service. This, in turn, increases the quality of the band, which benefits every student. If your school does not offer a program like this, it might be good to suggest it. It costs the school nothing, but does take additional organization on the part of the music teacher and/or booster group. This would be an excellent project for a parent's group to sponsor and organize.

I have seen middle and junior high schools with active chamber music programs. Chamber music refers to music specifically written to be performed by a small group of performers, usually two to six. It is called chamber music because it was originally intended for performance in homes or small chambers. Playing this music is a challenging and rewarding experience because usually there is only one musician on a part. This means that if your daughter plays the flute in a chamber music ensemble, she will be the only person playing that part. In a larger band, several children would be playing the exact same part. Therefore, in chamber music, your daughter would have much more responsibility as an independent musician. Further, chamber music is performed without a conductor. The individual musicians in the group have to musically interact and react. This depends on eye contact, listening, and intense attention between performers.

In schools with an ongoing chamber music program, these groups of players rehearse on a regular basis throughout the year (not just before solo and ensemble contest). This is a wonderful musical opportunity for your child, if your school is lucky enough to have such a program. If your local school does not, you might want to work through the music teacher to see if you can help establish such a program. It is usually a matter of lack of time on the part of the music teacher because each group needs some guidance and coaching. The school can hire part-time musicians to help with this coaching or reduce the music teacher's teaching load to accommodate the program.

Once your child moves into high school band, things change considerably. When our son Nathan entered the high school band program even I was not prepared for what happened. Most of these changes affected our entire family. I found that when I viewed the program as a parent, it was hard to believe I was seeing the same thing I had experienced as a teacher.

In high school there will be a variety of bands for your child—marching band, wind ensemble, concert band, and jazz band at the very least. There may be more ensembles for specific instruments like percussion ensemble, brass choir, flute choir, and an almost endless variety of potential classes.

Marching Band

We will start with the most visible: marching band. Everyone likes marching bands. They have great uniforms, do snazzy shows, and generally enjoy great crowd appeal. They also consume a major part of your child's (and your) time during football season. Do not be surprised if your child is expected to spend a week before school begins in band camp. In addition to daily rehearsals during school, your child will be expected to attend at least one extended rehearsal on a school night for three to four hours. He or she will play at all home football games during the regular season (and perhaps playoffs) and may play at all away games as well. This means a commitment of every Friday night for several months. In addition to this, the band will probably travel to three or four competitions or invitationals on Saturdays and they may march in one or two parades. This is a lot of time! It may interfere with family time on weekends and even during the week. So be prepared.

For a typical marching band season, I estimate that the students contributed about 130 hours to the show. Since the band does the same show for the entire season, these hours were spent learning just three pieces of music. That is a lot of time, much more than is needed to learn the music. The vast majority of the time is spent on learning to march and perfecting the movements, not on developing musical skills.

Just about every year I get a call or two from parents asking if what their child's band director is doing is typical. They usually have a son or daughter who plays an instrument such as bassoon, oboe, electric bass, piano, or guitar. The director switches them to the drum line or guard positions (flags, rifle, or poms). The director's view is that the woodwind instruments do not project well from the field to the stands and thus this change is justified. The underlying reason, however, is not musical, but an administrative one on the part of the director. Many schools require all students who are involved in the instrumental music program to participate in marching band as well. Therefore, despite the time and financial investment you made in a bassoon for your daughter, if she is not willing to carry a flag, pompom, or cymbal in the marching band, she will be excluded from the other musical groups of the school.

Obviously, this is not a student-centered or even a musically centered policy. The director just wants a bigger marching band. Some students may not be willing, or may be unable, to make the enormous time commitment necessary for the marching band. I have heard of students who have had to choose between marching band and a regional symphony. If they choose the symphony, they are essentially banned from participating in any musical activities in the school. I have met many disappointed students who were banned from jazz band because the director insisted that everybody must also be in the marching band. To take both classes would use two school periods and tie up major amounts of nonschool time. If you are in such a school and are questioning this policy, you are right to do so.

I wish I could offer some winning strategies to parents to counter this situation. I can't. I recently posed this question to about thirty high school band directors in Tennessee. They unanimously agreed that there is so much pressure on them from administrators and parent to produce a good marching band that they cannot do anything that might weaken this group. Most felt that they could lose their jobs if the marching band did not win awards or be as good as the rival school's band.

They were sympathetic, but felt helpless. This is one area in which you, as a parent, have more ability to change things than any other

Marching bands are sometimes more about showmanship and team spirit than musicianship. There is nothing wrong with this as long as your child is getting a quality musical experience outside the group.

person does. Perhaps organizing like-minded parents to meet with the director and principal could result in a compromise situation. Be sensitive to the awkward place the band director is in—most whom I have spoken to feel they are between a rock and a hard place on this issue.

For all these reasons, many parents (and a surprising number of band directors) question the musical worth of marching bands. In truth, marching bands have much more to do with marching and showmanship than with music. Still, your child can have a great time taking trips and learning about commitment, hard work, and team spirit. For these reasons, kids love the group. So, from a nonmusical standpoint, the time is well spent for your child's overall development. From a musical standpoint, all those hours of practicing marching could probably be better used.

Concert Band

The core of the band program is the concert band, which can go under a variety of names, including symphonic band or wind ensemble. This group is the one that probably prepares the highest quality music of the entire band program. They will work on and perform music written specifically for the concert band, transcriptions of famous symphonic works, and arrangements of popular tunes or movie soundtracks.

There will often be more than one concert band. Enrollment in the top ensemble will be determined not so much by grade, but by audition. For some students, four years in the second band may be appropriate; for others, three years in the top band might be right. This will totally depend on your child's playing ability and commitment. For those involved in multiple school activities, staying in the second band might make much more sense. It often is not a matter of failure to remain in these groups, but one of mature decisions about where your child wishes to place time and energy priorities.

The music will be challenging in these groups and you can expect to see your child grow as a musician. This growth will not only be in playing ability, but in the overall understanding of music. The music children are hearing now will create a foundation for their listening and appreciation for the rest of their life.

Normally, these groups will rehearse every day for one period or its equivalent if the school has a block-scheduling system. Credit for these classes will count toward the overall GPA and toward graduation. In other words, these groups are not extracurricular in any sense of the word.

If your child is serious about wind or percussion music as a career, he must be in this group. A word of caution: these groups usually do not have guitars, synthesizers, electric bass, or drum sets. If your child plays one of these instruments, she probably will not be able to perform in that group because composers who write for these groups normally do not include parts for these instruments. This may change in time, but it will probably happen slowly, if at all. If your child plays one of these instruments, it is important that you find musical opportunities in other school or out-of-school ensembles.

Jazz Band

Most schools now have a jazz band program. When these were introduced in the 1950s and 1960s, they were highly controversial. Jazz was not considered proper music to be played in a school and the playing style was deemed inferior. That has changed. Today jazz bands are acknowledged as being a way to learn important musical skills, especially improvisation. Improvisation is the skill of being able to make up a solo on your instrument while the rest of the group is providing backup. It is a highly creative and difficult skill to learn and perfect for many students. It is also an essential skill for all musicians, especially the saxophonist, trumpeter, trombonist, keyboard player, guitar and bass player, and drummer. Improvisation can only be learned with much practice and experimentation, so the jazz band provides a perfect environment.

The jazz band also develops another important component of being a musician. Members of the jazz band are encouraged to feel the music. You will notice that once the director starts the band he will often walk to the side of the stage. This forces the band to feel the music and listen to one another to stay together. This is an invaluable skill that is learned best through ensembles such as the jazz band or chamber music groups.

Pep Band

Pep bands are loads of fun for the student. They normally are groups that perform at basketball games and other indoor sports. They add excitement to the game and provide fun for the players. The music tends to be easy and the environment is one of extreme casualness. For these reasons, the pep band is often not all that much of a musical adventure, but can be a great social outlet for your child.

Ultimately, your child should try to take advantage of as many opportunities as possible. However, something like the pep band is certainly an add-on type of experience and should not be at the core of your child's musical development.

Other Instrumental Ensembles

Most high schools have a variety of other instrumental ensembles. The possibilities are almost endless, and some of the more popular include percussion ensemble, steel drum bands, mariachi groups, and drum line percussion. These provide a great opportunity for children to learn to play their instrument in a new style of music. Such groups may meet during the school day or outside it. You should encourage participation in these ensembles as time, interest, and ability allow.

Orchestra in the Secondary School

Many, but certainly not all, middle schools and high schools have an orchestra. It is interesting that when school music was first growing at the end of the nineteenth century, school orchestras were the most common types of school instrumental ensemble. The twentieth century has seen the school band become the predominant ensemble yet the school orchestra movement is still alive and flourishing in many schools.

Four families of strings are the core of the orchestra: violins, violas, cellos, and basses. Winds and percussion are an important part of the ensemble, but often just the string members of the orchestra will rehearse on a daily basis. This occurs for a variety of reasons. First, the strings have unique challenges that are not inherent in other instruments, such as bowing patterns and finger placement. Second, the music written for string orchestra features the strings, and thus requires more work than the other parts. Therefore, in some schools the string students practice daily while the wind and percussion students come once a week or are added in as the concert approaches. These students are often borrowed from the wind ensemble.

Over the years I have probably gotten more calls from parents asking questions about orchestra than almost any other ensemble. These calls are always from parents of nonstring players who are in orchestra but not band. They want to know why their son or daughter does not play more often or why the child has study hall three times a week instead of playing. This relates to what I said previously. The strings have unique problems that take a great deal of time to address; other members of the orchestra do not need the attention that strings do. Music teachers are not showing favoritism (the common complaint) to string players. Instead, they are spending the time where it is needed for the entire group to succeed.

For this reason, I prefer a format in which only string players sign up for orchestra and other members are borrowed as needed for concerts. There are scheduling problems inherent in this design, but it seems that most directors and students are able to work around them. In schools with multiple orchestras, the top group may be a full orchestra and the wind and percussion are integral to that group. In these cases, this format will not apply. But for many school programs it is a workable option.

As in the band area, an important part of orchestra programs involves the playing of chamber music. Although it is more common to find chamber music in the string area than in the band area, these groups will still almost always meet outside the school day. Rehearsal takes place before or after school or during lunch or study hall. Because of all the musical benefits of this experience, the time invested is well worth any inconvenience.

Choir in the Secondary School

There will be many opportunities for children to sing if voice is what they choose for their primary instrument. Although choral programs have basically declined in popularity and size in most schools over the past forty years, many schools still maintain world-class choral programs.

The choir director will test your child's voice and determine the range of pitches he can comfortably sing. Your child will then be assigned to a voice part. Soprano is the highest female part, with altos being lower. Tenors are the higher male part and basses the lowest. Each of these parts can be further divided into firsts and seconds; all these divisions relate to range only. First sopranos are not better than second sopranos, or sopranos superior to altos. In most cases, you can trust the director to know what is best for your child's voice. In a few situations, however, a director may allow students to choose their voice part or even change which part they sing depending on the piece of music. This is not only a disservice, but can be harmful to your child's vocal health.

All singers, especially those whose voices are developing, should sing in their natural range. This range can, and should, be expanded, but it is important that this is done while engaging the proper vocal techniques. To do otherwise, or to constantly sing in a range that is uncomfortable, can cause vocal problems or even permanent damage to the vocal cords.

Again, most choir directors are experts in this area. However, a disturbing practice in some schools is to have the band director, orchestra director, or teachers from another discipline conduct the choir. Although a great many instrumental directors have the skills necessary to conduct a choir (or the sense to seek additional training), a good number do not. As a parent, you need to pay close attention to who is conducting the choir and the practices that person is using. Ideally, a director should be trained in both choral directing and voice.

Most high school choirs will be SATB, which stands for soprano, alto, tenor, bass. However, other combinations are possible, depending on the size of the program. For example, many schools have an SAB or other combination choir.

Choirs will usually perform music from the traditional choral literature as well as more contemporary works and some popular music. Many people wonder why choirs don't perform more popular songs. One of the reasons is that popular songs rarely convert well to choral arrangements. Too often they are interesting for one group of singers (say, the sopranos) but not for the other parts, which usually are left singing "oo's" or "ah's." Popular music has become very solo-oriented. With few exceptions, choral singing is not a part of most current pop music.

Another question many parent ask is why choirs often sing without piano accompaniment. This type of singing, referred to as a cappella, puts more emphasis on the singers' need to stay in tune and blend with other members. Piano accompaniment often makes the sound more enjoyable or interesting to the audience, but from a singing and learning standpoint it can become a crutch. Many choral pieces are written to be performed without accompaniment to highlight the beauty of the choral sound, and therefore most directors will regularly perform at least some of their selections without accompaniment.

It has been increasingly difficult for choral directors to choose music. Much of the standard literature is of a religious nature. During the Renaissance and throughout the eighteenth and nineteenth centuries, choirs were primarily ensembles found in Christian churches. Debates over the appropriateness of sacred music in the schools are often heated on both sides. The fact remains that if a choir does not perform this music, it is forced to ignore much of what was written for choir prior to 1900. For example, almost all of Bach's choral music is sacred. If choral students are to perform any of Bach's music, it will almost certainly be sacred. If they do not perform any of these pieces, they miss the opportunity to experience some of the greatest music of all time. Therefore, most choirs have taken the route of trying to balance their programs, performing music of different styles and religions. The choir director would certainly appreciate any support you can offer—or perhaps just the offer of understanding.

Concert Choir
Usually there will be one top choir in the school that is composed of mainly juniors and seniors and perhaps a select group of sophomores. This group is restricted to these ages because there is a large difference in the maturity of a child's voice from the start of high school until the end. Grouping in this way allows a director to choose music that is a challenge to the singers without being inappropriate for their vocal development. This choir will have many possible names including a cappella choir, symphonic choir, mixed chorus, or simply Chorus.

Freshman Choir
Again, this choir may go under a variety of names, but it basically refers to an entry-level choir at a high school. As I've mentioned, there is a vast difference between the maturity of a voice at the beginning and the end of high school. In a good choral program, there should also be a vast difference in music reading, sight-reading, and

musical knowledge between a freshman and a senior. Therefore it is important to have a choir that can be used as a training ground for the more advanced choir in the school.

In this choir, the emphasis will be on developing vocal ability, choral blend, in-tune singing (intonation), and sight-reading. These essential skills will be needed in the more advanced choir.

Girls' and Boys' Chorus
As might be expected, girls' and boys' voices develop differently. Boys will go through a substantial voice change sometime in late middle school or early high school. During this stage, boys may have a singing range of just a few pitches. After the voice change is complete, a boy will have to exercise his voice to be able to expand that range.

It comes as a surprise to many that girls also experience a voice change. Theirs is much less drastic than boys', but during puberty they too have a general lowering of the voice.

The changing voice (sometimes called cambiata) requires much attention and care. For this reason, many directors prefer to separate boys' and girls' choruses. This allows them to devote attention to the specific needs of the singers. Because of equal rights laws, some schools now call these choruses treble and bass choirs. Because the needs of the singer are extremely gender specific, this may be one area in which the terms boys' and girls' choruses describe true differences in needs based on gender, yet are not discriminatory because of gender.

Madrigal Choir
This term originally referred to a small ensemble that would sing music from the Renaissance. A madrigal is actually a specific type of music that resembles a short song sung in four or five parts and often characterized by "fa-la-las" (as in the carol "Deck the Halls"). Although the term madrigal choir continues today, selections of music played in such a choir have expanded to include just about any type of music appropriate for a small choral group. There are also many other names for this group.

Membership in this ensemble is almost always based on an audition, because the demands in this group are high. Usually only two to four voices sing each part, demanding much skill of the performer. Sometimes each part is divided into sections (such as first and second soprano), which results in even fewer voices per part. The madrigal group is close to the vocal equivalent of an instrumental chamber group. Therefore, it has all the advantages of performing chamber music described earlier.

These groups usually meet before or after school and typically do not result in academic credit. Instead, they are provided as an educational service to outstanding singers. Groups such as these provide excellent experience for the serious singers. You should encourage your son or daughter to participate for that reason.

Jazz Choir

Jazz choirs are not as common as the other types of groups. It is my experience that whether your school has a jazz choir will depend on where it is located in the country. For example, in the northwestern part of the United States jazz choirs are very common, but much less so in the Southeast.

A jazz choir performs jazz classics in a be-bop style. This includes vocal slides, pitch bends, and improvisation. This choir performs specific styles of music and teaches a singer to use a more popular style and with great independence. The learning of improvisation (often called scat singing) is a valuable vocal skill for any singer to have. If your school has a jazz choir, you should consider yourself fortunate and encourage your child to participate.

Show Choir

Show choirs are often confused with jazz choirs, but they differ greatly. In a show choir, singers will perform choreography while singing and usually will also wear fancy costumes. They have great audience appeal. There is great debate among music teachers about the musical value of such a group. Often the music performed, while fun and attractive, is very easy. Students are usually more challenged by learning the dance steps than by the music.

Although it could be argued that moving and singing are valuable skills to have in certain musical professions (which is true), nothing will replace a firm foundation in proper singing. A show choir can be a significant and appropriate part of a well-rounded choral program, but if it is the centerpiece of a choral program (as it is in many schools), the students are almost certainly not getting the musical education they deserve. They may receive loud applause at each concert, but when the concert is over, they are often left with only the memories and no useful musical skills.

In many ways, the show choir has become the vocal equivalent of the instrumental marching band with the directors under great pressure from administrators and some parents to increase the entertainment value of the music program, often at the expense of its educational value. There is also an important difference. It has been my experience that some choir directors switch to a show choir format because they do not possess the vocal or choral skills necessary to build a strong choral program. I have never seen this happen in a marching band program. In these instances, it is often the case of an unqualified person being put in the position of high school choir director. As mentioned earlier, for a variety of reasons, some schools assign choir to the instrumental teacher or another teacher in the school. Without a firm foundation in choral singing, these teachers can find instant success in the show choir, relying much more on costumes and showmanship than singing ability.

To demonstrate how extreme this can become, in one nearby school the only choir program in the school devotes two rehearsals per week to sewing costumes. They also repeat the same show every three years so they can use the sets they already own and spend their class time enhancing them. I have gone to watch these performances and will admit that the audiences seem to enjoy them, but I have great difficulty understanding the musical goals of such a program.

Gospel Choirs

Gospel choirs are becoming very popular in many schools. The gospel choir grew out of American black churches and performs music of a soulful nature. This music tends to be a combination of spirituals, gospel music, blues, and soul.

It is interesting to note that even if a school does not have a specific gospel choir, this movement will probably influence it. Gospel music has become so popular in the choral field that much of it has become a mainstay of all choirs. To program at least one gospel piece has become the norm at all-state choir festivals across the United States. This, in turn, has influenced many local concerts as well.

All-State Music Festivals

Most states have what is called an all-state music festival for students at the high school level. In these festivals, the best student musicians from throughout the state are chosen to create a band, orchestra, and chorus. Entrance into these groups is by taped or live audition that is organized and submitted by high school music teachers within the state. The students chosen will go to a site somewhere in the state for two or three days. They will have extensive rehearsals and will perform for the public at the end of this time. Almost always, the state will hire nationally known directors to rehearse and conduct these groups.

This is a great musical opportunity. It will give your child the chance to perform in a group with the best musicians in the state as well as the opportunity to play music that is probably out of the reach of most individual high school groups. In addition, being able to work with one of the best conductors in the country will show them the musical standard expected at the professional level. Be sure that your child's music teacher is aware of these festivals.

Nonperformance Music Classes in the Secondary School

Many high schools offer nonperformance classes in addition to the conventional performance classes. Many possibilities exist, but the most common are music theory, music history, composition, piano class, and guitar.

In a music theory class, the basic understanding of how music works will be taught. Students will learn about scales, key signatures, meter signature, chords, rhythms, and musical form. They may even do some composition. A crucial part of most music theory classes is what is called ear training. This refers to the act of being able to hear a melody or rhythm and write it down in notation. This is a time-consuming skill to attain, but it develops the critical listening skills necessary for good musicianship. A high school music theory class is a necessity for anyone planning to major in music in college.

Music history classes review the history of Western art music and maybe even world musics. Such courses will examine the basic periods of music (Classical, Baroque, Renaissance, etc.) to provide an understanding of the roots of today's music and also to acquaint the student with the great masterpieces of the past.

Some schools combine music history study with the study of the visual arts. This is a very strong approach. Many of the movements in one art form are evident in the other and a greater understanding of both visual and musical arts is usually the result.

Guitar instruction is often offered in a group setting. More often than not, this class is intended for the student who is not in a performance ensemble or who wants to learn to play an instrument for the first time. This is a great resource for a student coming late to music or whose interests lie outside the traditional band, orchestra, chorus format (rock bands, blues, country, ethnic, or folk).

Most professional musicians have some piano skill because the piano keyboard is necessary to fully understand music theory. For this reason, most colleges require piano lessons of all music majors, regardless of their primary instrument. A piano class at the high school level will give students a jump on this. If the school does not offer piano, it is still advisable that serious students pursue some piano instruction.

Booster Organizations

Music programs are expensive; music teachers are dedicated and over-worked. For these reasons, parents in many high schools have formed music booster clubs to support the music program in any way they can. Usually this support is in terms of fund-raising. The group will have a variety of activities to raise money that is then used to purchase instruments, pay for tours, or buy equipment such as choir risers for the school. If your school has a music booster club, I encourage you to join it or at the very least support their fund-raising activities.

Expenses and Fund-Raising

You will learn quickly that being a musician is a costly proposition. Instruments are expensive to buy and that is only the beginning. Strings, reeds, minor repairs, slide oil, mutes—all add up. In addition, private lessons and printed music for those lessons are ongoing expenses.

Within the school program, parents will be expected to pay uniform cleaning fees, participation fees, food fees for trips, transportation costs for some trips, and a host of other fees. For this reason, many bands have fund-raisers of one type or another. Often band students are encouraged or required to sell candy, wrapping paper, candles, fruit, or just about anything the mind can imagine. If you were to go to a convention for music teachers, you would be shocked to see that half the exhibits are for fund-raising opportunities. The remaining half is devoted to spending the money raised on instruments, uniforms, trips, and so on.

Not all programs require students to become salespeople. For example, some high school programs undertake projects in which they accept books, software, and games as donations throughout the year. These are then sold periodically or taken to local used bookstores to be sold. Other projects include play-a-thons at which students get pledges for how long their band can play on a given weekend. A related idea builds on the dreams of a surprising number of people—that of being a conductor. For a set price, individuals from the community can conduct the band or choir in an open concert. These events often take place on Saturday afternoons in connection with the play-a-thon. This is a fun way to get people to donate to the program.

Booster clubs usually oversee this fund-raising. If you have a philosophical problem with students selling items to raise money, I encourage you to get involved with this organization and offer alternative ideas. Programs need money to flourish and be open to all students, but there are many ways to raise money.

In an ideal world, school programs would be funded at the level they require. A popular bumper sticker says: *"Wouldn't it be nice if the schools got all the money they needed and the Pentagon had to have a bake sale to buy a new fighter plane?"* I can't see this happening in my lifetime, but the sentiment is a nice one. Perhaps it is time to fully fund educational programs that are the envy of the rest of the world and leave our children more time to devote to learning.

Summary

In high school, music programs will expand to provide a wealth of experiences for your children. You should encourage them to participate in as many as possible. I don't think a musician can ever have too much experience in ensembles. When we admit a music major to our university, we look at the ensemble in which the individual has participated. Usually our best students are the ones who have played or sung in a wide variety and number of ensembles.

Chapter 13

Musical Competitions

There is probably no topic within the music profession more controversial than the area of competitions for musicians. Professional journals are filled with articles both supporting and bashing competitions. As you might expect, valid arguments exist on both sides. Regardless of how you personally feel about your son or daughter participating in a competition, one thing is certain: If your child participates in music for any length of time, he or she will be involved in competitions of some sort.

There are many types of competitions. One aspect they all have in common is that they are expensive to organize because of the high costs of judges, prizes, promotion, and facilities. For this reason, I think the best way to examine them is to group them according to who is financially supporting them. Most competitions can be grouped into support from one of three sources: professional organizations, corporate sponsorship, and foundation/individual sponsorship.

Profession-supported Competitions

I have mentioned elsewhere that every state has a professional organization of music teachers. In most states, it is called the X Music Education Association with the "X" being replaced with the name of the state (e.g., the Pennsylvania Music Education Association or simply the PMEA). These associations usually sponsor contests or festivals that fall into three types: the solo and ensemble contest, large ensemble contest, and marching band festivals. One common factor in all these competitions is that the performer will receive a rating. In most states, a four- or five-point rating scale is used with a rating of "1" reserved for the best performances. More important, judges will provide detailed comments and suggestions for improvement on each performance. Although human nature will make us interested in the final rating, it is the comments that provide the most educational feedback for the student. Often they will offer specific suggestions for improvement and frequently words of encouragement.

Another thing competitions all have in common is that performances will be in arranged in classes. Usually the competition will have Class A, B, and C. This relates to the difficulty of the music chosen for the solo and ensemble competition and the size of the school for the large ensemble competition. Most of these competitions start with a regional competition, with the highest-ranking musicians progressing to the state-level competition.

Solo and Ensemble Contests

The solo and small ensemble contests are for students playing solo works or in small groups, usually no larger than twelve. The majority of the pieces performed will be solos, duets, or trios, with only a few being larger. Music for these competitions will be chosen from an approved list. Depending on the difficulty of the music, the student will then be arranged in a class. Your child's school director or private teacher will determine the class in which the student should compete.

These events provide a wonderful opportunity for a student who has developed a certain level of skill. Not every student who participates in band, orchestra, or choir will be asked (or allowed) to participate. Instead, this will be reserved for the students who have worked hard and developed a level of skill that will allow them to perform as a soloist.

Large Ensemble Contests

The large ensemble contest is just like the solo and ensemble contest except that it is arranged for groups with more than twenty-four members. Your son or daughter's band, orchestra, or chorus will probably participate in this type of contest in high school and maybe even in middle school.

All the groups will receive a rating and comments based on their performance at the competition. For each group, there will usually be three judges (as opposed to just one for solos), each of whom will provide comments and a rating. A composite rating is then given based on the three individual ratings.

Marching Band Competitions

Marching band competitions are similar in some ways, but very different in others. In marching band competitions, a percentage of the score is based on nonmusical elements such as marching, flags, and show design. Further, the emphasis is often much more on the competition than the event's educational value. The reason for the emphasis on winning these competitions probably lies in the fact that the marching band is so closely aligned with football teams and the winning mentality then permeates everything. Although not necessarily bad, putting winning a competition before the educational value can lead to negative consequences.

Corporate-sponsored Competitions

It is very difficult to make generalized statements about corporate-sponsored competitions. Some are truly attempts to support young musicians and others are lightly veiled opportunities to make money off student groups. On the surface it can be very difficult to tell the difference and regardless of the ultimate motive there is always at least some potential educational benefit for the students involved.

Most corporate-sponsored competitions involve large ensembles such as band, choir, or orchestra. They often also involve a visit to the corporate business. For example, many theme parks sponsor competitions. Students perform at the theme park (e.g., Six Flags, Disneyland, or King's Island), but also get to enjoy the park (and pay the entrance fee, buy food, etc.). These events can be great rewards for a year of hard work in an ensemble and provide an educational component to an otherwise fun and rewarding day. Because of this, it is often easier for a director to arrange for students to miss a day of school since it can be listed as an educational field trip. Such events are great as long as they are understood for what they are—a fun day at a park with an educational experience tagged on.

Foundation-sponsored Competitions

Some nonprofit organizations sponsor competitions. In fact, it is a little known fact that the Olympic games at the beginning of the twentieth century included piano and composition events. Today, private foundations or individuals sponsor some of the most prestigious awards.

These competitions are for the most advanced and skilled performers and usually involve a cash award of some magnitude. The prestige accompanying some of these competitions will launch a lucrative performance career for the winners. Although it is unlikely your child will be involved in this type of competition until he or she is no longer a child, I include this explanation here because you may hear about such events or read about them in the papers.

Are competitions reliable?

For several years, I hosted an annual solo and ensemble contest in northern Ohio. In two days, 2,000 middle and high school students would play before one of twenty-five judges. As a host, one of my jobs was scheduling each of the 2,000 students to a specific eight-minute time spot to play for a specific judge.

Every year I would get calls such as "My daughter's teacher said that judge X starts grading harder just before lunch. Could you please schedule her to avoid that time?" Or, "My son's piano teacher says that Judge Y doesn't like her and always scores her students lower than other teachers. Can you list my son as studying with another teacher?" I heard comments such as these so often that I started to wonder if there was any truth to this folklore. This was a very interesting question that intrigued several of my graduate students. Over the years, I have advised three separate research studies that examined this question. In two different studies,[1] the students examined judges' scores and related them to time of day to see if fatigue (or any other factor) in any way correlated with the scores. The result was that there was no relationship. In another study, the researcher had students dress in different ways (sloppy, neat, appropriately, inappropriately) and perform for different judges to test their consistency in rating the musical performance.[2] The result was that the judges graded the music quite consistently, overlooking how students dressed with one exception: A poor performer who was dressed nicely was given a slightly higher score. In the last study, student performances from a variety of times of day were tape recorded. Independent judges rated them (1) at the end of two days of listening, (2) a week later, and (3) two months later. In all cases, the rating closely matched the scoring given on the day of the competition.

From this I have to conclude that the judging is extremely reliable. Just like a sports referee who will occasionally make a miscall, I am sure there are some inaccurate individual scores, but overall these judges are extremely consistent, fair, and accurate. In most states, they have to go through some sort of training to become a judge, and most are experienced teachers used to working with this age group.

As a parent, I encourage you to avoid being swept up in all the myths that surround these events. A relaxed and supportive attitude toward your child, your child's teacher, and the judges will help ensure a positive experience for all involved.

A Final Word on Competitions

Competitions themselves are fairly neutral (with the possible exceptions of marching band competitions that can truly take on a high-stakes winner-take-all mentality). The benefit or harm to the student comes not from the competition, but from the adults surrounding the child—specifically the parents and teachers of the child.

The advantages can outweigh the disadvantages. Expert judges who will offer helpful and honest suggestions for improvement critique your child. Your child will have the opportunity to hear many other musicians of a similar ability level—something not often available—and your child will have a musical goal to aim for while practicing.

Unfortunately, these advantages are all diminished if the parent or teacher assumes the attitude that the final score is all that matters. In these cases, the pressure to succeed leaves the student in a position where she won't be open to constructive criticism and suggestions for making her a better musician.

I suggest you encourage your child to do his or her best and relax about the score. There will be enough pressure on your child without your adding to it. On the day of the event, stop by the bake sale sponsored by the band parents' organization, buy a couple of brownies and something to drink, and try to keep everything in perspective.

Chapter 14

Music, Teenagers, and the Home

When I first outlined this book, I did not include a chapter on the topic of teenagers and home life. After teaching teenagers for years, I thought I was an expert on their musical development. Not until I lived surrounded by three teens did I see how little of the picture I was seeing as a teacher. Therefore, I started reading all I could on this topic and realized it warranted an entire chapter.

Music may never be as important to the life of a person as it is during the teen years. Between seventh and twelfth grade, average American teenagers listen to about 10,500 hours of popular music. This is about the same amount of time they will spend in the classroom from kindergarten through high school. It also appears that girls listen to more music than boys do and that this has seemed to stay constant over the years.[1]

But it is not only interesting to see *how much* teens listen to music, but *where* they listen. Sixty-nine percent of this listening is done in private, usually alone in the teen's room. Twenty-three percent of the time is listening with others. But 82 percent of all active listening is in the home.[2]

Another important factor in this mix is that the music listened to the most during the teen years will become that person's music for life. The music listened to during a person's late adolescence and early adulthood is a musical style they will identify with for their entire life.[3] Radio stations know this. When they are trying to target a certain age population, they simply look at the hits from the years when that group was between fifteen and twenty-five and create a play list based on those hits. It seems to work. Thus, the late teen years are some of the most influential years from a musical standpoint. Since most of the music experienced happens in the home, the home environment plays a large role in this development.

What do teens listen to?

In Chapter 3, I talked about the importance of being able to put music into categories. It is important to hear a piece of music and think "this is from a musical" or "this is jazz." This type of grouping is the first step toward understanding.

Research has shown that teens put music into just a few categories, usually about five.[4] They know rock music and all its subcategories (rap, heavy metal, pop, and blues). But that is as far as it goes with most teens. After that, they will tend to lump everything together into such categories as church music or movie music or my parents' music. These have no subcategories. It makes sense that we are attracted to things we understand. Teens understand rock and roll and therefore will be attracted to it. The more they listen, the more they will understand it. So, it is a logical cycle. From this it is easy to predict what music they listen to the most and what music they will continue to listen to the most: rock.

This won't be true for every teen, but by and large it will be true for most. There is certainly nothing wrong with listening to, and enjoying, rock. However, if you followed some of the advice about working to acquaint your children with diverse styles of music when they were young, you will probably find that they have much more diverse musical interests at this age than most of their friends. This gives them more avenues for expressing themselves both through listening and performing.

Why do they listen to it?

In addition to the cycle of understanding previously listed, there are other reasons why rock (of some sort) will be the music of choice of teens. These involve three broad categories: musical characteristics, lyrics, and group identity.

A style of music often defines social groups. In high schools there are the heavy metal kids, the rap kids, the folk kids, and so on. Perhaps no other item (except clothing) works so well to identify the group to which a teen belongs. It is both a statement of what they believe in and what they don't believe in. Music defines certain boundaries in this manner.

How powerful is this? In one interesting study, teens were shown tapes of other teens (professional actors) being interviewed.[5] There were several identical interviews with only one difference. In some interviews, the teens being interviewed mentioned they liked a certain type of music such as country, classical, soft rock, or heavy metal. In other interviews, no mention of a musical preference was made.

When boys watched the tapes of girls, some interesting things happened. Girls who said they loved classical music were rated as more sophisticated than girls who loved heavy metal. When girls watched tapes of boys, it did not matter whether they liked classical or heavy metal music, but sophistication ratings dropped when they said they liked country music.

What about romantic attraction? When the boys said they liked heavy metal their appeal went up while that of girls went down. If girls said they liked classical music, their appeal went up. When either sex said they liked country music, their romantic appeal went down.

Interestingly, a preference for soft rock in either sex was viewed as a very neutral choice. It may be that teens not wishing to bring attention to themselves will state a preference for this kind of music so they can exist in a neutral area. Other researchers reported similar findings as well.[6] Not surprisingly, the music with which teens identify is a powerful force in their lives.

As a parent, you need to be conscious of this. When you see your children listening to music and you suspect they are doing it because their friends like it, a little sensitivity will go a long way. Your children are looking for identity and examining who they are. Music is an important part of this. Try to be understanding of the power music plays in their own self-perception and the perception of others. But don't think you have to like their music. Here is the catch-22 of being a parent. Another strong reason for teens liking their music is to rebel against authority. Much teen music will have lyrics that question authority or possess musical characteristics that are meant to challenge the taste of adults. Teens know this. If you respond with shock and outrage, or try to convince your teen the music is awful, then the music becomes successful in their eyes. On the other hand, if you go out and buy a copy of the CD for yourself, your teen will think you have totally lost your sanity.

Probably the best route is one of understanding. There is some worth and value in just about any music. As a parent, try to find it. A few years ago one of my kids (I really don't remember which one) played a song for me that had completely unintelligible words— except for one. There was a certain four-letter word that kept appearing over and over (and over!). It was literally the *only* word I could understand in the entire song. After listening for a while I said something like, "Well, he certainly knows that word well. I guess he is trying to shock us, but too bad he has to be so obvious. I really like what the drummer is doing." I thought this was one of my best lines ever (and it was true). It worked. The CD was never played again (as far as I know). It did not get the desired response from me as a parent. The music had failed.

I have to believe that if I had banned the song, or tried to talk my teen out of the song, I would have ended up hearing it again. When I was a middle school music teacher, I often made this mistake. But I quickly learned one important fact. Teens are smart. They know they are using the music to get a rise out of you. If they don't, they will often move on to other music.

But not always. That is because often there are musical characteristics that make the music appealing to teens and bothersome to adults. Teens have tons of emotional and mental energy. Parents of teens are exhausted. The teens choose music that has fast tempos, lots of energy, and is loud.[7] This helps them to diffuse their excess energy, anger, and emotions in a positive way through physical and emotional excitation.

Unfortunately, the last thing parents of teens need is a way to diffuse excess energy of any sort. Therefore, there will always be a conflict here. I don't have a good solution to this one, except to be eternally grateful that most listening will be done in the privacy of their own rooms.

Can certain types of music make my kid a mass murderer?

Newspapers often contain reports about how violent music can make kids violent. They will use as evidence a certain incident in which a student who committed a violent crime listened to a certain style of music. This is a classic case of finding a relationship between two things and saying one causes the other. It is certainly clear that certain personalities will be attracted to certain types of music. A violent person will be attracted to music with violent sounds and lyrics. But I really doubt that music can make a person who is not violent into someone who is. Everyone who has listened to a Marilyn Manson record has not committed a crime. Everyone who listens to Mozart is not a genius.

Convincing research has shown that students' academic success will mold their musical taste, not the other way around. Students who are academically successful tend to develop musical tastes along non-controversial lines. Conversely, students who are failing academically are attracted to more confrontational music.[8] There clearly is a relationship, but it does not seem that the music is causing the child's behavior.

This will be an ongoing debate and one that is almost impossible to resolve. I think the important issue for a parent is to use musical choices as a possible indicator of how teens are feeling about themselves. If your teen is consistently listening to music that is violent in nature or has violent lyrics, it should be of concern in the same way as if they are attracted to violent movies or video games. By themselves, these are probably doing no harm. But if your child has an inclination toward that type of behavior, violent movies, video games, and music might certainly aggravate it or, worse yet, convince your child that it is an accepted way of behaving.

Look for music as one sign of a larger problem. Don't think for a moment that removing the music will eliminate the problem. In fact, it may make it worse by eliminating that outlet for letting off steam. Instead, try to talk with your child or get professional help if needed. There are no easy answers; to simply blame the music is much too simplistic a solution.

Teens and Hearing Loss

Much of my personal research has been in the area of hearing loss in musicians due to constant exposure to loud sounds.[9] We immediately envision rock and roll musicians when we think of hearing loss, but that is not necessarily the case. For example, many violinists have hearing loss in their left ear because they hold the violin so close to their ear while practicing. So, it is truly something all musicians (and listeners of music) need to know about.

There are two types of noise-induced hearing loss. The first is sudden and the second is gradual. The first type is created from sudden

Loud music and teenagers go hand-in-hand. Knowing the potential hearing dangers is important.

loud sounds. Being close to an explosion or other loud sound may do damage to the ear that is sudden and permanent. There is little we can do about this since we rarely know when something is going to happen that will create this kind of noise. Seldom is anything going to be this loud in a music setting unless you are close to a speaker and something goes wrong, resulting in excessive feedback or other loud sound.

The second type of hearing loss is gradual and this is of great concern. The small hairs in the inner ear that receive the sound and send it to the brain are actually destroyed by loud sounds. Once they are destroyed, they are gone forever. Luckily we have millions of these hairs and can stand to lose a few before we realize it. But we still want to avoid this as much as possible.

Much music today has the potential of doing harm over the long term. Recent concerts I have gone to have volume levels that are almost unbelievably high. The good news is that the concert only lasts for a couple of hours. In this amount of time, there is not a great deal of exposure.

Of much more concern are the situations with repeated exposure. If your child plays in a rock band, it will be important to protect hearing through the use of earplugs available at any drugstore. Probably the biggest concern is from Walkman-type headsets. These units have the potential to put the equivalent of very high volume levels directly into the ear. Most manufacturers of these units are conscientious and offer settings that will protect hearing. Encourage your child to use these settings.

I have often sat next to people who had earphones on, and I could hear perfectly everything they were hearing. This is a dangerous volume level for them. The only solution is to turn it down.

Hearing loss is permanent. Without trying to use scare tactics, it is important you make your teen aware of this if he is exposing himself to loud volumes for extended periods of time.

What is my role as a parent during the teen years?

What should be clear from this chapter is that music becomes very important in the life of a teen. It becomes teens' identity and influences their musical tastes, very often for life. Most of this music will be consumed in the home.

As a parent, you will be somewhat excluded from this musical environment by design. Your child is using the music to establish *his or her* identity, not yours. For that reason, it is important to observe from a distance and let your children explore. This will not be hard because probably most of their listening will be done in the privacy of their room or with headsets.

Still, musical behavior during this time can act as an important indicator of the mental state of your child. Listen to the music with an open mind, always mindful that it is a window to what your child is feeling and thinking.

Being critical of or demeaning their music will not accomplish much. Instead, be accepting (within limits) and try to talk about the music as much as possible. Continue to share your music with them, but not in the manner of trying to convince them of its superiority.

Try also to keep them involved with making music both in school and out. Since the amount of time spent listening to music will increase greatly during these years, it is helpful to balance that with music making. Unfortunately, some factors are working against you during this time.

In school it has been found that children are the most likely to drop out of school musical performing groups when they change from one school to another.[10] During the preteen years, your children most likely did not switch schools. During the teen years, they will probably switch twice: between elementary and middle school, and again between middle and high school (and maybe even again between high school and college). At each of these junctures, the possibility of dropping out of school music programs increases and many students stop participating in them. This is in part because new responsibilities start competing for your child's time. College preparatory courses, drivers ed, working, love life, and sports can all limit the amount of available time to devote to music. Despite these reasons, the number one factor these students report for not continuing in music when they switch schools is that "they were not sure how to continue in the new school."[11] You can play a very positive role at this point by acquainting them with the musical activities available in their new school and encouraging them to seek them out.

If your daughter is taking private lessons, the same factors will compete for her attention and time. You can help her balance these many diverse distractions and responsibilities by talking with her and helping her organize her time to include practice and music making.

During the teen years you may feel that you can't win for losing. But you can have a great impact. Keep in mind that these are formative years for musical development and most of this development happens in the home. These are years of exploration, rebelliousness, and independence. You and music are two important influences, even though sometimes it may not seem like it.

Chapter 15

Computers and Music Learning

Computers have had a major impact on every aspect of our lives, and music is no exception. Computers affect not only how and when we listen to music, but they also influence performance and learning as well. Today, recordings are digital, we listen to music on digital compact disks, we can download music from the Internet, and we create music through electronic keyboards and synthesizers. Some aspect of performing and listening to music changes almost daily because of computers.

For every action of electronics on music there seems to be a reaction as well. Walk into a music store and you will see as many acoustic (nonelectric) instruments as electronic. Electronic guitars and keyboards have not replaced their acoustic counterparts despite great advantages in price and maintenance. Research shows a recent increase in school-age children's interest in learning to play traditional orchestra instrument.[1] There is a dichotomy existing right before our eyes. Technology is here to stay, but so is traditional music making. Often the technology supports not only novel musical sounds, but also established traditions in large part by the increasing availability of all kinds of music to everyone.

Computers have changed how we make, record, and listen to music, but have computers changed how we *learn* music? Some uses of computers in music learning are effective while others seem to be diametrically opposed to the process of learning music. In this chapter, I will explore some of these uses.

Because technology seems to change almost by the minute, no other chapter in this book runs such a high risk of being outdated by the time you read it. No other area of music is changing as fast as the computer and Internet area. Instead of focusing on changing technology, I take a functional approach to this chapter. I will discuss computers and music learning by the functions that computers can serve and the benefits technology can offer toward learning about, hearing, and making music.

Computers can be used in music for a variety of purposes. Some of these purposes are perfectly suited to computers and others seem a far stretch. In the back of this book is an appendix that lists a sampling of software available at this time. These are listed under Learning Aids. As with anything dealing with software, new titles are appearing daily, so the list will be incomplete as soon as this book goes to press. If a certain piece of software is not listed, it is not intended to reflect on the software in any way. I suggest you browse your local software store and keep in mind the functions discussed next.

Drill

Perhaps one of the best uses of computers is for help with the drill and practice that are necessary in certain aspects of music. Both are important in the area of reading music and what is called ear training. The computer is also valuable in providing specific facts about music.

With ear-training software, your child can learn to recognize melodies, chord progressions, or rhythm patterns. As described in the first chapter, this is a basic type of learning important to understanding music. These patterns are the words of music. Ear-training soft-

Computers in music can be used for a variety of purposes.

ware plays a musical pattern and asks your child to make some decision about it. For example, sometimes two patterns are played back to back and the child has to decide if the second is the same or different. Although this may sound easy, it is not for a young child. Differences can also be simple or complex, with some of the more complex differences being so subtle that they challenge a skilled musician. These games are teaching your child to listen carefully to music and learn the musical patterns that are the building blocks of all music. When purchasing this type of software, you should definitely go for the fun factor. The goal is to have your child do these drills often. If the game is fun, the child will play it often without even realizing the important knowledge being gained. This is a great use of the computer.

On the other hand, there are programs that will drill your child on musical facts. These programs work much like electronic flashcards. Your child can learn key signatures, tempo markings, Italian terms, chord structure, and many other aspects of music theory. These programs are the easiest types to write, so there are many on the market. They range from boring to exciting. You can usually trust that the factual knowledge is accurate and go for the enjoyment factor. Unlike the ear-training software previously described, I am not sure these are all that much better than regular paper flashcards that can be purchased in most music stores for less than $5. However, the computer programs have the advantage of being able to be used by your child without your involvement.

The last area in which drill is important is the area of learning to read music. In these programs, a note is usually flashed on the screen and the child has to identify the note. Again, I am not sure these are all that much better than flashcards and they are certainly less effective than learning to read notes with an instrument in hand. These programs are also easy to write and therefore they are common (and often inexpensive). As parents, we had many of these programs available for our own kids, but none passed the test of being interesting enough to attract the kids to do the drill without outside encouragement.

Computers can be used very successfully for ear-training drill, but they are perhaps less useful for drilling facts or note reading.

Learning to Play an Instrument

One of the least effective uses of computers (at least at this time) is for learning to actually play an instrument. Popular magazines have always been filled with advertisements that boast "learn to play the guitar in one hour" or some such nonsense. Since the advent of computers, these types of claims have seemed to multiply. Like their pre-computer counterparts, none live up to their claims.

Without the personal interaction that takes place between a teacher and student, it is very hard to learn. A teacher can watch the student and actually correct mistakes and spot problems—something a computer cannot do. The teacher can also motivate and encourage the student along a path. Again, computers have not been able to do this successfully.

The majority of programs have value as an extra aid for your child. They can demonstrate concepts in a very visual format that can be quite entertaining. I suggest using them in addition to regular lessons, but I have not seen one that can come close to replacing the interaction that takes place in private (or even group) lessons.

As I am writing this, there is much interest in a new use of computers with lessons. Famous teachers are now offering interactive lessons over the Internet using distance learning programs. In these lessons the student plays via a camera and the teacher responds in the same way. These lessons are expensive, around $150-200 per hour. Although this type of distance learning is primarily restricted to famous teachers providing advanced study, a few teachers are using it for beginning or intermediate students. These teachers seem to utilize the technology in one of two ways: to completely provide lessons or to offer help for their students between more traditional lessons.

I contacted several teachers who were giving lessons exclusively via the Internet. All agreed to talk by phone after an e-mail contact and all were enthusiastic about the future of this type of lessons. The focus of their enthusiasm revolved around being able to provide lessons for students who have no other access to a teacher. The other major advantage was the convenience involved because there was no need for the teacher or student to leave home.

On the other hand, they were unsure how large the market was for these lessons. There is little need (and thus demand) for this type of learning because there are so many private teachers available in most areas who are capable of working with beginning and intermediate-level students. The most successful stories involved students who were truly in remote areas with no access to a teacher. All these teachers taught in a traditional face-to-face format with students as well, and all preferred this when possible.

Other teachers were using the Web in a very unique manner. They were employing the technology to check in with their students in the week between private lessons. Students would get a mini-lesson or checkup mid-week. The students play their pieces for the teacher who, in turn, gives them feedback and encouragement. This sounds like an exciting use of this technology.

Teachers using the technology in either manner referred to problems they had encountered. Students need a computer near their practice area. This was not a problem if the students had either a portable instrument such as the clarinet or saxophone, or a portable computer. If either the instrument or the computer was awkward to move, it seemed to be a problem. The teachers held reservations that the technology was not yet advanced enough to truly teach without the computer getting in the way. Further, student and teacher need extremely fast connections to avoid lost time between interactions because even small momentary breaks in the video or audio made it impossible to evaluate the student's musical performance. For the same reason, these teachers were never confident that their demonstrations were being properly heard or seen by their students.

These teachers felt they were pioneers in a completely unexplored area of teaching music. Interestingly, all were male and most, but not all, taught more popular instruments such as guitar and drums.

Enhancing Performance

Unlike software that is designed to actually teach your child how to play an instrument, there is software that can be used to enhance your child's playing ability and enjoyment of practicing. Many of these programs will provide musical accompaniment while your child is performing. One of the most popular is called Band in a Box. Another popular program is called Vivace. This software provides an accompaniment that actually responds to what your child is playing. A microphone is placed on your child's instrument. The computer follows the notes played by the performer and adjusts the accompaniment accordingly. If your child slows down, the accompaniment slows down; if your child speeds up, the accompaniment speeds up. This software attempts to mimic the experience of performing with an accompanist. Vivace takes a little getting used to, but after the initial getting acquainted period it can truly be an enjoyable and educational experience

Learning about Music and Music History

Quite a few programs are available that can be used to learn about music and music history (or what is often called music appreciation). As true of most software, there are good and bad programs and everything in between.

For the most part, music history and appreciation programs are not geared toward children. Most are appropriate for college (or high school) students. They can be excellent and provide instruction in many ways that teachers cannot. For example, such programs can explain how a composer uses a certain type of melody in his or her works and then actually play the exact excerpts from the work where the melody appears. These programs can also demonstrate what different instruments or whole orchestra sections sound like. You, as a parent, might enjoy some of these and perhaps you can use them to demonstrate certain things to your child. But I would not expect your child to enjoy using them on her own.

There are some programs that teach facts about music that are geared toward children. These tend to help the student understand terms and concepts such as "What is a melody?" or "What instruments are in the string family?" or "What is a time signature?" Here the quality is often uneven. Although the accuracy of the information is usually correct, the attractiveness of the presentation varies greatly. I suggest that you assume the information is correct and then review the software and trust your instincts as to whether the presentation is something that would appeal to your child.

Another use of the computer in this area is in addition to or as an auxiliary to a written textbook. This works exceedingly well in learning about music where, to truly understand what an author is trying to say, you have to actually hear the musical examples. Several books on the market have *added* computer software to accompany the text, yet a few have been written with the use of the software *integrated* into the text. A good example of this type of book is *Developing Musical Intuitions* by Jeanne Bamberger.[2] Throughout the book Bamberger describes projects that the reader completes through the accompanying software. The interplay between traditional text and software is often seamless and the result is truly a new way of learning about the elements of music. I expect to see more music books written this way in the future.

By and large, these programs can be very helpful and educational *if* your child will use them, and I suspect this will be an area that will expand in the future. At the present time, however, many of these programs are not geared to children younger than about fifteen years of age.

Composition

Computers seem well suited as an aid to composing music. Before computers, most composers worked at a piano. Their compositions were limited by the piano skills they had available. If they could not play it, they generally could not compose it.

Today all that has changed. Composition programs are available that enable a person to compose music on the computer screen and hear it simply by pushing a play button. These programs are available for just about any ability level. For example, the composer Morton Sabotnic wrote a commercially available program called Making Music. This program is ideal for children who are in the primary and middle grades of elementary school.

Children can compose by choosing the instrument they want (from a menu with pictures of the musical instruments) and then drawing lines on a blank music stand. The child can then hear what he or she has written, modify it, add instruments, speed it up, slow it down, or engage in a wide variety of activities. It is much like a word processor for sound.

Using this software, children can learn to compose at an early age.[3] They have to be given time and freedom to explore the software. In the early stages, their progress seems to resemble play, but over time they will create more and more sophisticated pieces.

As a parent, remember that these compositions are going to be

Computers seem well suited as an aid to composing music.

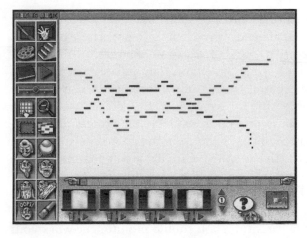

A screen from Making Music.

much like the artwork your child brings home from school (you know, the ones on your refrigerator). You do not expect a perfect landscape from your first-grade child. Likewise, do not expect a finished song. Instead, look for the signs that they are learning and encourage them to explore the sounds. If your child draws a landscape with the sun underground, you would ask about it and try to help correct it if it was not what was wanted. But if the sun were in the sky—even if it hardly looks like the sun—you would encourage it. Do the same with the music—if the basic ingredients seem to be shaping up, encourage them, even if the piece is only six seconds long. It is from these early compositions that later pieces emerge.

Elementary-age children do not generally enjoy modifying or editing a piece of music once they create it (even though the software allows them to).[4] They will be much more likely to start a completely new piece than to change something. Don't get frustrated if they do this. Like the child who gets a new piece of paper and starts a new picture instead of erasing something from an old picture, your child is exploring in an age-appropriate way.

As children get older there are more sophisticated programs. Making More Music is one intended for older students. In this program, preteens and teens can start to use actual music notation. The songs or compositions that your child makes will start to sound more like what you consider music. Also, teens are much more likely to work on revising and editing a work until it is closer to their liking. Look for programs that make composing and editing fast and easy and that allow for easy and accurate performance of the composition.

The older student can also begin to explore techniques such as sampling and sound editing with programs such as Sound Edit 16, which is an excellent user-friendly program for teens. These programs allow your child to record a sound of any kind (a note from an instrument, a spoken word, or a dog bark) and manipulate it in terms of pitch, length, and even sound. These sounds can then be combined to create a musical composition. Eventually, the older student can expand to one of the many programs available for professional composers. What is important here is that, for the first time in history, composing music is an activity available to just about anyone. No one knows how this will change music in the long run, but it seems clear that it is an activity that can certainly be used to enhance your child's musical development.

Like anything else in parenting, you should monitor the work your children do. Talk to them about their compositions and encourage, suggest, and nurture. Do not dictate or criticize their explorations. And, most important, let them explore and do it themselves. (P.S. After the kids go to bed, explore the programs yourself—they are truly fun.)

Notation

Another good use for computers is creating and printing notation. If your child has music theory or composition assignments due as part of a music class or private lessons, programs that create notation are a wonderful time-saver. Some of these programs allow you to choose each note from a menu and "drag" it on a staff. Others will convert what you play on a keyboard to standard notation. Each has its strengths and weaknesses. But any of these programs could be useful to a musician who is in middle school or older.

Software in which you choose each note from a menu is somewhat time consuming and the user must know the exact note values and pitches in order to insert them. Although these seem like disadvantages, the accuracy of this method is much greater than with other types.

For programs that use a keyboard to input sound that is converted to notation, the performer must be extremely accurate, especially in terms of rhythm, when playing. The software will print whatever is played, no matter how illogical it may be. The advantage is that this is a much faster method of inputting the information. Regardless of how the notation is put into the software, all programs can print out high-quality copies. Two of the most widely used programs of this type are Sibeleus and Finale. The music that is printed has the potential to look like music you would purchase in a music store. To get the music to this point can be quite time consuming, however, and the programs are so complex that classes are required in their use. Perhaps more appropriate for children are the many more basic programs available in most music stores. Most of these do an acceptable job without the complexity inherent in the more professional programs.

All these programs have the advantage of letting you actually hear the music that is on the page. Although the quality of sound will depend on the soundcard your computer has, even the most low-tech computers will play it well enough for the person to check the accuracy of the notation.

Multimedia

A music-related used of computers is to create musical multimedia. I won't go into great detail here, but there are programs that allow you to edit video in conjunction with music. One of the most popular programs is called Adobe Premiere. You can enter video and then edit it to a soundtrack (or anything else). Although the concept is easy, it takes a great deal of time to do the actual editing. Also, be warned that these programs are expensive and require amazing amounts of computer memory. Still, we have had a great time exploring this medium on our home computer and find it musically rewarding. I would not recommend this for students younger than high school age.

MIDI

Computers can be used to control electronic instruments such as keyboard synthesizers utilizing a format called Musical Instrument Digital Interface (MIDI). All instruments and computers use the MIDI standard, thus allowing musicians to hook up a synthesizer to a computer. Once this happens, you can compose, perform, or listen to music on your computer with all the sound resources of the synthesizer. Conversely, you can enter musical information into your computer through the synthesizer keyboard instead of the computer keyboard, which is much more user-friendly to musicians. Thus, through the use of MIDI, the computer and musical instrument can communicate with each other. Many of the software programs or instruments you will purchase will tell you that they are MIDI adaptable. This simply means you can hook the instruments to a computer if you have the appropriate software.

The Web

The Web can benefit your child's music learning in a variety of ways. It offers a wonderful means of obtaining information about music, purchasing music, investigating instruments, hearing music, and many other miscellaneous possibilities. The extent of the Web is too large to explore here, so I will only offer a few websites to get you started. These are portals to other sites that are listed in the reference section.

I have greatly enjoyed surfing the Web in relation to teaching music. I purchase about 100 percent of my music on the Web and utilize professional websites almost daily. About the only area I have found the Web lacking in is the purchasing of instruments. Buying an instrument is a very personal decision. Even within the same model and brand, each instrument will vary slightly in appearance, feel, and sound. For this reason, it is very difficult to purchase an instrument without the chance to actually play it. You may be able to save a few dollars (and truly only a few) by purchasing on the Web, but the inability to try out the instrument is a great hindrance. You will have to make your own decision, but, for most musicians, playing the instrument first is a critical part of the selection process.

Summary

Computers have changed quite a few things about music learning. Interestingly, they have left untouched some very basic aspects of music learning. For the most part, music instruction is still done with actual contact between the student and the instrument with a live teacher actively participating. It is a truly human undertaking and for this reason the computer has had limited success in actual performance instruction. The computer is also of limited use in purchasing an instrument or in learning facts about music.

On the other hand, computers have proved extremely beneficial for composition and ear training, finding information, creating notation, and learning to perform with an accompaniment. As with all technology, computers are finding their appropriate place in the field of music making and becoming a strong addition to the whole process.

Chapter 16

Finding (and Using)
Community Musical Resources

Regardless of the size of the town you live in, your community is probably rich with musical experiences. We have been able to locate ample musical resources in fairly small towns, medium-sized cities, and large urban areas. The key to finding them is knowing where to look. Unfortunately, many people don't know how to do this. Every year the U.S. government conducts a massive study called the National Assessment of Educational Progress to measure how well children and young adults can do in a specific discipline. About every eight years the focus is on music. One of the questions asked of adults is whether they are aware of concerts and musical opportunities within their communities. Surprisingly, very few (about 25 percent) know how to find out about these. Often people only know about the concerts or musical events that are sponsored by the specific radio station they listen to or those that have a major financial supporter like a beer or sporting goods company.

This is truly sad. Most communities are alive with a variety of concerts and musical groups in just about any style you can image. Newspapers do not have the room to feature every concert that takes place and most concerts are put on with a shoestring budget that eliminates the possibility of newspaper, television, or radio ads. So how do you find them?

Regardless of what you are seeking, there are four indispensable ways to get information. The first is your local music store, the second is your local newspaper, the third is the phone book, and the fourth is a local music school, either community based or as part of a college.

Music stores are much more than a place to buy music or take lessons. They often assume the role of serving as the gathering place of musicians. Interestingly, in larger cities they have become very specialized, with one store featuring school music, another the rock/pop scene, and others specializing in such areas as folk, world, classical, or traditional music. So, to find out the true extent of opportunities, you may have to visit more than one store. You may also find some of the same information at local CD stores.

Once in the store, examine the bulletin board that is probably located by the main entrance or checkout counter. These boards have become the communication hubs of local musicians and musical groups. On them you will find announcements of concerts, demonstrations, lectures, groups looking for members, music festivals, and just about anything you can imagine.

The second resource is your daily paper. Every local paper will have a section called What's Happening? or About Town or some such name. This section will contain a listing of either the events for the upcoming twenty-four-hour period or the entire week. The weekly announcements are usually printed on Fridays and will feature a wealth of concerts. Many are excellent, and since they don't have a huge advertising and promotional budget, ticket prices are often quite reasonable for a family with children.

In addition to the daily paper, larger cities will usually have a magazine devoted to events in town. This is often geared toward visitors, but is an excellent way for local residents to find concerts as well. Seek out these lists and don't assume that because there is no picture of the artist or a feature it will not be a good concert. At the university at which I teach, we are often amazed (and sometime frustrated) with what the newspapers choose to feature. We could be sponsoring six concerts in one week, and the paper will select one that is probably the least interesting to the general city audience. Why did they feature it? Often the explanation is something as simple as they liked the photo we sent for that concert. Therefore, don't take a feature story as a statement of quality. Conversely, don't assume lack of publicity as a sign of a lesser concert.

Another resource is the phone book or websites for local organizations. Call the local parks and recreation office as well as the local branch of a community college if you have one. In the Yellow Pages, you will find opportunities listed under the headings Music Instruction and Musicians. You can often find links to cultural events attached to the website of your city, chamber of commerce, or tourist bureau.

Community music schools or university music departments will often be both a resource as well as a place to find out about other resources in the community. These schools will sponsor concerts, recitals, master classes, and lectures by both their own faculty, guest artists, and their students. In addition, these institutions will often have multiple bulletin boards throughout the building announcing upcoming musical events, auditions, and resources.

When looking for community musical resources for your child, you will find that they tend to fall into three broad categories. These categories include the opportunities to (1) perform music, (2) hear music, and (3) learn about music. Naturally, much overlap occurs, and any event will provide more than one opportunity. Still, it is a helpful way to think about musical community events.

Opportunities to Perform Music

Many communities have musical ensembles for youth, most likely in the form of orchestras, bands, and choirs. Although they may seem to duplicate the experience your child is receiving in school, that is usually not the case. The community groups will be made up of the most dedicated (and usually the best) student musicians from the community. Consequently, the music they perform will be more demanding and the expectations will be higher. Such musical experiences will be most enriching for your child.

It is also beneficial for your child to work with more than one conductor. Each conductor will emphasize different aspects of the music, providing your child with a different outlook on music. Since your child will work with the same conductor every day at school (and probably for several years), it is very beneficial to experience other approaches to making music.

Besides ensembles, community theater groups often put on musicals. While most people immediately think of the opportunities for vocalists, it is important to remember that there is usually a band or orchestra in the pit. Most theater companies have more trouble finding quality instrumental musicians to perform the music than they do finding singers for the production. This type of performing is a great experience for your children. They have to be able to play at specific cues in the play, at specific tempos (for the dancers), and at specific volumes (to balance with the singers)—in short, a great training opportunity. Of course, if your child is a singer, the on-stage opportunities are beneficial as well.

Many community ethnic groups maintain musical ensembles. For example, in the Cleveland, Ohio, area the Indian community has an active musical presence and even provides lessons on authentic instruments for interested individuals. They are not unique. You can find Irish, Mexican, African, Japanese, Jewish, Polish (and more!) groups. Many will have a musical component, and some of these groups enthusiastically embrace young musicians.

When looking for performance opportunities for your child, be sure to consider local churches. Not only do churches provide numerous choral opportunities, but many also welcome instrumentalists and offer a variety of performance options from accompaniment support to solo performance. These are great opportunities. Churches are always looking for additional music and the congregations seem to really enjoy it. A call to the church office will put you in touch with the right person.

When you visit a music store to look for resources, you might come across some jam sessions when musicians bring their instruments and create an impromptu music session. These are usually only open to instruments that play jazz, folk, bluegrass, or rock, but if your child plays one of these instruments (and is old enough and good enough), these get-togethers can be educational as well as fun. Most people think jam sessions happen mainly in bars—not true. Family restaurants often feature live music, some of it in the jam-session format.

Closely related to jam sessions are coffeehouses. Many are looking for folk singers or other musicians to perform. Sometimes a musician can come and play for just a half-hour or so. To do this, you have to be an entertainer and musician, but it is lots of fun.

Sometimes even family vacations can provide an unexpected performance opportunity for a musical family. A few years ago we took a family vacation to Montana. Nathan brought his banjo and I took my madolin, hoping to have a little musical fun. We jammed every night in the motel room, but the rest of the family soon grew tired of this activity and encouraged us to play somewhere else. We started going outside the motel and playing, usually in front of the motel or in a city park. We soon learned that people really enjoyed hearing us. We really liked the smiles and words of encouragement from people passing by and some even gave us tips! I had never thought about how much fun this could be or how much people would enjoy the music. Don't be afraid to explore playing in public spaces. I suggest you do

Many communities will have ensembles specifically for adults. You can join these to be a role model for your child.

this with your child. Not everyone who passed by was polite or appreciated our efforts. But all in all, it was a great experience.

Many communities will have ensembles specifically for adults. Although this book is intended for children, I am including possible resources for you as a parent (or grandparent) because of what I have said elsewhere: A great musical influence is for your child to see *you* making music. If you are in a community band or chorus and your child comes to your concerts or sees you going to rehearsal one night a week, this will send a strong message about the importance of music.

Don't overlook the power of grandparents as role models. There are community choruses, bands, and orchestras specifically for senior adults. One group is called New Horizons Band and has chapters in over thirty cities. These groups are intended for senior citizens and usually provide lessons on the individual instruments for the adult beginner. Find out more about them at www.newhorizonsband.com.

Opportunities to Hear Music

Most communities provide a variety of opportunities to hear live music in many different styles and performance settings. Your town probably has more concerts than you ever imagined. Beyond the opportunities listed in the paper, however, are other ways to hear live music. Great resources include schools and private studios. Your children will probably relate better to musicians who are closer to their own age than to adults. Therefore, take in a choir or band concert at your local school, or the annual musical at your high school. Visit a recital of a local music teacher. As a music teacher, I found it frustrating that audiences were made up almost exclusively of parents of the performers. I always felt that the concerts would be enjoyable to others as well, but they never came.

If you have a local orchestra, they will almost certainly give at least one children's concert per year. Call the box office of the orchestra and find out what is planned. These concerts are inexpensive and are geared toward young audiences. Often they are significantly shorter than regular concerts to accommodate the attention span of the young child.

Community music schools and departments of music in colleges and universities will sponsor regular concerts that feature their students, faculty, and guest artists. These concerts are usually reasonably priced and offer a great variety of musical styles and instrumentation. Rarely can these schools afford expensive publicity, so you may have to call or check their website for upcoming events.

Do not limit your listening to concerts. Support live music in your community by going to coffeehouses or restaurants with live music. This is a great way to hear (and see) music being performed while supporting musicians in your area.

Your local library is also a gold mine of resources for hearing music. With improvements in technology, especially the CD revolution, the musical resources of most libraries have expanded dramatically. Gone are the days of scratchy LP recordings that used to define

Your local library is also a gold mine of resources for hearing music.

the library collections. Today you can sample a broad range of CD recordings with great audio fidelity. This is a wonderful way to experiment with and experience music that is new to you. You can check out something you never heard before—jazz, opera, the music of South India, rap, klezmer—and listen to it with your children at literally no expense. Try taking out one new CD every time you visit the library. Pick music you have never heard before in genres new to you or your child. This is a wonderful, inexpensive way to grow musically with your child

Opportunities to Learn about Music

All those experiences provide an opportunity to learn about music. However, some events are specifically geared toward learning. For example, before concerts there are often preconcert events at which someone will tell you about the music you will hear in a specific concert. If your child is old enough, she may enjoy these. In addition, local music stores will often offer class piano, guitar, or theory lessons.

Summary

Almost certainly there is a vibrant musical community existing around you, but you may not be aware of it. It takes just a little work to discover these outlets. Finding the musical resources in your own community will provide great experiences for your child and enjoyment for the whole family. It will also have the added benefit of supporting live music in your community. Seek and you will find.

Chapter 17

Careers in Music

Picture this: your child is a senior in high school. You have done such a great job of raising a musical child that now that child is considering a career in music. You panic. What kind of career is that?! Everyone knows musicians starve, do drugs, and play in corner bars six nights a week. Suddenly you wish you had never purchased this book.

If this is your reaction, than you have made a very common mistake. You jumped to the conclusion that a career in music is defined as one of two things: performing or teaching. At this point, you have drastically limited your child's career options.

The music industry is one of the largest industries in the country, if not the world. It employs countless individuals in a wide array of professions that together make up the music industry. It is true that performers are the ones who seem to get all the glory, yet it is often the case that they are also the least paid individuals, with the least amount of job security, in the entire pyramid of the music industry. The exceptions to this, of course, are the superstars who hit it big and become millionaires, but they constitute a very small percentage of the entire music industry. There are many secure careers in the field that will utilize your son's or daughter's musical skills and love for music. Let's look at a few of these.[1]

Performer

When we think of a career in music, performing is certainly the first option that comes to mind. Usually we envision some famous singer,

Doesn't everybody want his child to grow up to be a musician?

violinist, or group in a large performance venue with thousands of adoring fans. Actually, most career positions in performance are less visible, off-stage performance opportunities in orchestras, pit bands for both professional theater and ballet companies, and openings throughout the entire entertainment industry.

For the child interested in a career in classical music, either as a soloist, orchestra musician, opera singer, chamber music musician, or chorus member, a college degree is a must. It is during the college years that a young musician really begins to flourish. It is also in these years that the young musician can devote the time necessary to begin to perfect performance skills under the close individual supervision of a private teacher.

Being accepted into a college to major in music performance is highly selective and based largely on the quality of your child's audition (which gains entry into the music program) and the grade point average (which gains admission into the university). In many schools, an extremely good audition can earn entrance into the university even if the GPA is not of the level normally required. This points to the importance of the audition.

Preparation for this audition actually begins early in the high school years. For the teen interested in a career as a classical musician, private lessons on his instrument or voice needs to continue throughout the high school years. A private teacher will work with the teen to bring the playing ability to the level required for admission. As the audition approaches (normally in the junior year or early in the senior year), the private teacher will help prepare the actual audition. In addition to performing, many auditions include a test in both ear training and music theory. Each college will have its own requirements for auditions, available from the music department at that school. Although the audition process is rigorous, a successful audition will often be rewarded with both acceptance into a program and an offer of a scholarship.

The serious high school student also needs to have ensemble experience. This experience should be through high school ensembles and may also include community groups designed for outstanding young musicians. Both the private lessons and ensemble experiences are necessary.

The College Music Society lists over 1,100 colleges that offer degrees in music. Choosing the right college is a combination of finding the right fit for your child as well as the right match in music.

One of the first considerations is the size of the music program. If your child was majoring in English literature or political science, it might not matter how many other students are also majoring in that subject. However, in music, size does matter. So much of music learning happens in groups that the learning experience is impacted directly by the quality and quantity of the other students. A music program needs a certain critical mass of music majors to properly create an orchestra, wind ensemble, opera, chorus, and chamber music program. Small programs depend on the same students to play or sing in all the groups, rely extensively on nonmusic majors (who usually do not have the same performance ability or commitment), or do not offer a healthy balance of diverse musical experiences such as large and small ensembles or ensembles from different time periods and different cultures.

The second consideration is the quality and reputation of the program, the private teacher, and the ensemble director. Your child will spend many hours during the college years with the private teacher and the ensemble director. It is important that there is a match both in personality and playing style. Once your child is accepted to the college or university program, the teacher will take over the primary responsibility for preparing your child for a career beyond college.

While choosing the right college is important, choosing the proper major is equally important. Within the broad category of music major, there are many specific types, from music education to music business to music performance. For the student interested in a career as a performer, the rigor of the performance degree is necessary.

Entering the field of music as a performer involves an audition. Symphonies, ballet orchestras, opera companies, and the like hold regular auditions and competition is fierce for these positions. To win an audition requires proof of excellent performance skills and proper training.

If your child is more interested in a career as a performer outside the classical arena, many opportunities are available. For example, positions such as playing in the orchestra for a Broadway musical or being a full-time musician at Disney World are lucrative jobs for a musician. The positions with institutions like Disney are attractive because of the job security and benefits inherent in working for a large corporation. These musicians are usually protected by a union contract under the guidelines of the American Federation of Musicians.

In large entertainment and recording centers such as Los Angeles, New York, and Nashville there are many freelance musicians who make a living by performing on movie or television soundtracks, as background musicians on recordings, or as pick-up ensembles for traveling performers. This last option is one that is not often realized by the general public. Many performers who require a medium to large instrumental accompaniment while on tour do not travel with all those musicians because of the tremendous cost involved. The same is true of many touring musicals and ballet companies. Instead of bringing an entire orchestra, these performers travel with either a small core group of musicians or just a conductor. When these performers come to a city, they depend on hiring local musicians to make up the balance of the group. Many musicians earn a comfortable living performing regularly in these groups.

Another area for employment for a musician is in church music. Some churches employ full-time musicians and just about every church hires part-time musicians. In these positions, the person may play the organ or keyboards for services, conduct an adult or children's choir, direct a praise band, lead a handbell choir, and organize all musical activities for the church. This is an excellent position for a diverse musician with good people skills and a strong religious belief.

Yet another area of employment for performing is playing at weddings, bar mitzvahs, and dinner clubs and bars. The night club and party scene has no guarantees whatsoever and a person tends to live from gig to gig. Still, many people make a comfortable living doing just this type of work.

To perform in a band or be a freelance musician requires one to have business skills as well as musical ones. In essence, these musicians are running a small business with themselves as the product to sell; this involves marketing, budgeting, and people and administrative skills.

Teacher

There are basically two types of careers as a music teacher. The first is as a teacher in the public or private schools whose primary responsibility is teaching classes or ensembles. The second is as a teacher who gives private lessons either as a part of an organization or as a self-employed teacher.

The schoolteacher will specialize in choir, band, orchestra, or general music. The general music teacher tends to teach in the elementary grades and the more specialized music teachers will teach middle school and high school.

Public and private school teaching is an extremely stable and exciting profession. A music teacher enjoys all the benefits and pay of any other teacher and sometimes receives an additional stipend because of outside duties such as evening concerts or marching band shows.

To become a school music teacher, you will need a bachelor's degree in music education. In most colleges and universities, this degree will meet the requirements of both the state department of education and the National Association of Schools of Music. Because of this, curricula at different schools, and even in different states, tend to be fairly consistent. Students will take courses in music theory, music history, private lessons, conducting, methods of teaching, and will play or sing in ensembles. In addition, students seeking these degrees are usually required to attain some level of proficiency on *all* band and orchestra instruments. This may seem extreme, but for a conductor to be able to help students on all instruments in a band or orchestra, that person must have some knowledge of each and every one. The final semester or quarter of their college career will be spent student teaching in a special area (band, orchestra, chorus, or general music) of the student's choosing.

Once this degree is received, an individual is usually certified to teach any aspect of music from kindergarten through grade 12.

Although each state issues its own certification, most states have reciprocity with each other. This means that if you have your certification from Maryland, you can obtain certification in another state, such as Wyoming, simply by doing some paperwork. Some states may require an additional college class, but usually it is an easy procedure to switch states.

The second type of music teacher, the private teacher, will give lessons on a specific instrument such as saxophone or piano. Sometimes the teacher will work through a music store or in a community music school, or teach from home. Some people make private teaching a full-time occupation. Many, however, teach part-time to augment the salary of a performance career or a career in another field.

There are no requirements or degrees necessary for this position. Literally anyone who plays an instrument well can give lessons. However, in reality, many private teachers have college degrees in music. These degrees can be in music education, performance, or music pedagogy. If your son or daughter is interested in a career in private teaching, a degree in pedagogy would be extremely valuable because it emphasizes techniques and materials for teaching privately. In addition, courses in business would be beneficial because many private teachers are actually running their own small businesses.

Music Therapist and Medicine

Music therapy combines music and therapy to train an individual to use music in therapeutic ways. For example, a person who is recovering from a stroke may be given piano lessons to help regain some motor skills. Music can also be used to assist people with emotional problems or even help with the rehabilitation of criminals.

Hospitals, universities, correctional institutions, or nursing homes often hire music therapists. To become a music therapist, a bachelor's degree in music therapy is required. This leads to certification as a registered music therapist in much the same manner as someone becomes a registered nurse.

It is difficult to describe the availability of positions as a music therapist—they seem to fluctuate with time and also with the community in which the person lives. Larger cities tend to have more opportunities for music therapists than small or medium-sized ones.

Somewhat related to music therapy is the area of music medicine. This is a fascinating career in which a medical doctor specializes in disorders or physical characteristics unique to musicians. These include ailments such as repeated stress disorders and hearing loss. However, there is also great interest in preventative practices for musicians and even using some medical technologies, such as biofeedback, to improve a musician's performance. If your son or daughter is interested in medical school and is also a musician, this profession might allow a rewarding combination of skills.

Recording Engineer

When you listen to a recording, you probably concentrate on the performers. Yet the person who is in charge of the recording process often has as much, if not more, to do with how the end product sounds than the actual musicians. There are many examples of excellent musicians who have sounded terrible in recordings and terrible musicians who came across quite well. This is a tribute the power of the recording engineer.

The engineer will run the recording studio. Recording engineers often have to be excellent musicians themselves to bring out the best in the performer or group being recorded. Where they place the microphones, how they balance the different parts during recording, how accurately they listen to the actual mix of the sound will all be reflected in the final product. Here is one of the few areas in which a musician can have great creative freedom without actually making music.

There are several different avenues to becoming a recording engineer. The best way is to get a degree (bachelor or associate) in recording engineering. Many universities and community colleges offer these programs. Another avenue for entering the field involves working as an apprentice or intern in a recording studio. However, most internships are administered through colleges or universities, and are often open to students who are not getting degrees in engineering. Some music schools, for example, offer internships in recording studios for their students in the belief that this increases their musical skills.

A fairly recent way to work as a recording engineer is to build your own studio. Although this would have been a totally implausible suggestion just a few years ago, with the advent of digital electronics, recording studio equipment has become more affordable and there are now many recording studios located in people's basements or bedrooms. With this equipment at your child's fingertips, along with the many current excellent magazines and books published on home recording studios, your child could develop engineering skills even while in high school.

The Military

The military uses many musicians in its bands. These bands perform at official military functions as well as military social events. The musician is an enlisted soldier and must complete boot camp just like anyone else. After that, the soldier's full-time job is to perform. Without exception, these musicians are fabulous. The daily playing under strict discipline produces fine performers.

Many military musicians decide to continue and make it a career. This is a viable career option for a musician who also has the temperament for the military. These positions are available by audition and can be discussed with a military recruiter.

Composer/Arranger

The stereotype of a composer is one of a person sitting at a piano for hours at a time, shunning the world, uncompromising as an artist, and living in poverty. We rarely think of a businessperson who is comfortable with executives and is part of a decision-making team. Yet very often these skills characterize the composer of today. Every time you watch a movie or television show you hear the creative work of a composer. Even video and computer games use music, all of which is created by someone. In addition to being talented musicians, the composers of this type of music need to be good at working with others, communicating their ideas, and serving as part of a creative team.

Some composers only write for concert performances. These individuals are often employed by universities or support themselves from commissions or grants from arts organizations. Although many composers probably aspire to be working at this pure art level, few will have the luxury of doing so.

Another area of employment for composers is as a songwriter. One hit song can make a songwriter rich. Aspiring songwriters seem to be everywhere, however, and hit songs are limited. If your children have a talent for writing songs, I suggest they write them, record them, and enter them in songwriting competitions. The other avenue for getting into the field is to hire an agent who will work to sell your songs.

A word of caution is necessary here. Because so many people feel they can write songs, and so few can actually write good ones, a large market exists for exploiting these naive people. Avoid many of the places that advertise in the backs of magazines because these are frequently scams or vanity operations. These ads will often promote services whereby, for a fee, a company will record your song and present it to major record labels. In reality, what will happen is that you send your money to someone who will record your song in a home studio with hired musicians. These musicians will record song after song in a mass-produced way. You will receive a copy and a copy will be mailed to the major recording studios with a cover letter. The company has thus fulfilled its obligation. During this process, it will charge you for all the expenses involved and also try to sell you many copies of the CD.

What happens to the CD that was sent to the recording studios? It is either thrown away or returned unopened. For legal reasons, most major recording labels will not listen to unsolicited songs that are not represented by an agent. If a representative of a major label listened to a song you wrote, and then one of their own artists released a song that was in any way similar (title, chords, melody, theme, whatever), the company could be sued. Because recording labels have many people under contract who are writing songs, the risk of their producing something similar is just too great.

If your child has a gift for writing songs, I would recommend finding a good local recording studio, even one that may be located in someone's basement, and contract to have the song recorded. You will usually pay a per-hour fee and it will take about two to three hours to record and mix one song. Once you have a good recording, find a song agent who will promote the song. Reputable agents usually require no up-front fee, but will take a commission if and when the song is sold. Agents listen to many songs and are known for being extremely blunt. If an agent does not feel your son or daughter has much promise as a songwriter, he will usually let you know this pretty clearly. However, even that advice can be very valuable.

Many issues are involved in songwriting, including finding a good agent, copyrights, commissions, and learning how to do it. If your child enjoys writing songs, I suggest you explore the offerings of Writers Digest Books (www.writersdigest.com), which publishes several highly respected books on everything from learning to write songs to publishing them. Two other interesting websites are those of the Songwriters Guild of America at www.songwriters.org and Renascent Music Publishers (www.renascent.org). Both have links to other sites as well as pages of frequently asked questions that can be helpful to parents.

Another career in the composing area is writing or arranging music specifically for school music groups. School music groups have very specific needs. This music has to be at appropriate levels, interesting to students, and educational. For these reasons, writing music that serves an educational purpose is a huge business. Also important is arranging music for such groups. For example, when the movie *Titanic* opened, there was an immediate demand for arrangements of the music from the soundtrack for many different levels of performance ability. Arrangers spent late nights getting them produced and published while the movie was still popular. Although this is a viable career option, it involves working with copyrighted material and therefore is usually done in conjunction with an established publisher. Music should never be arranged for performance without copyright permission.

Instrument Sales

Musicians will often tell you about the karma or personality of their specific instrument. Musicians create a strong bond with their instruments; many even give them a name. The feel of the wood, the craftsmanship, and the sound become a source of pride. For this reason, it seems natural that most people who sell instruments are first and foremost musicians themselves. They are drawn to selling so that they can be surrounded by instruments they love and help others to find just the right one for them.

For a salesperson to be of help to a buyer, the representative must know something of the product. Who knows a bassoon better than a bassoonist does? Therefore, music stores will seek out individuals who are familiar with the instruments they sell. Larger stores will often have a salesperson who is an expert in percussion, another who is a guitar expert, still another with reed expertise, and will try to have as many diverse experts as they can afford. Therefore, a viable career for a musician is to work in, or own, a music store. Musical skill on an instrument, good interpersonal skills, and a good business sense are requirements for this career.

Instrument Building, Repairs, and Technician

Just like a car, most instruments need regular maintenance from a professional technician. Pianos need tuning, guitar actions must be adjusted, pads on wind instruments have to be replaced, and countless other alignments unique to each instrument are necessary. This regular maintenance keeps the instrument sounding good and easy to play.

Again, as with a car, accidents happen. When instruments are carried back and forth to rehearsals or performances, all sorts of things can and do happen. If something breaks, it needs to be repaired by a professional. (*An aside*: Parents, please refrain from attempting to fix anything but the most basic problems on your child's instrument. As a teacher, I have enough horror stories to fill another book of a well-meaning father or grandfather who attempted to fix an instrument with catastrophic results.)

To adjust the tone or playing action of an instrument, the repairperson must know how the instrument is supposed to sound. For this reason, most instrument technicians are musicians themselves. Like salespersons, they often choose this line of work because they love the instruments.

A related career is instrument building. It requires not only an understanding of the instrument, but also of the physics of sound and, depending on the instrument, an understanding of electronics. Independent instrument builders who can support themselves from making instruments are rare, but large commercial companies are constantly working to design new products and improve old ones and they do maintain design and production divisions.

Conductor

Almost any time a musical group becomes larger than seven or eight members, a conductor is required to lead the musicians in the interpretation and performance of the music. Although we are used to seeing conductors in the center of the stage during a performance, in reality their most important work is done with the ensemble during rehearsals that lead up to the public performance.

Because leadership is such an important aspect of being a conductor, often interpersonal skills such as the ability to motivate others, demand respect, and take charge are as important as the necessary musical skills. This is not to diminish the level of musical skill required for becoming a successful conductor. Understanding the characteristics of all the instruments, knowing how to read multiple musical parts (the score) at once, and acute listening skills are all necessary. Thus, the successful conductor is not only a highly trained manager with exceptional people skills, but also a superior musician.

To develop these skills, conductors of a large professional ensembles such as orchestras, bands, or choruses undergo a rigorous training program, with advanced degrees in music and frequently a long period of apprenticeship. All conductor positions of this nature require a stringent audition.

Conductors of smaller ensembles such as pit orchestras or stage bands often need less formal training, but must still have an extremely high level of musicianship and leadership ability. Likewise, conductors of amateur or community groups are often public school directors or other experienced musicians with leadership and organizational skills.

Musical Theater

The last decade has seen a resurgence of musical theater on the Broadway stage, in touring companies, and in animated movies. This has reopened the field of vocalist for many people. This is a position in which an individual is judged solely on vocal and acting abilities. All positions are through audition.

To find out about these auditions, consult in the classified or arts listing section of your daily paper, which will often list future auditions. When a touring company of a musical is in your town for performances, it will often hold auditions. Likewise, local and community theaters are a great resource.

Here is one of the few professional musical opportunities for young children. Musicals such as *Les Misérables, Oliver, The King and I,* and *Annie* include children as cast members. This is a wonderful opportunity for the child with a strong voice and good stage presence.

Like many other areas of the performing arts, acting positions in musical theater are extremely competitive. If your child has interest and ability in musical theater, you should strive to provide as much experience and training as possible at a young age. Community theater groups as well as pubic and private schools offer valuable learning experiences. As young adults, a college degree in musical theater can further refine and polish their skills.

Management, Publicist, or Lawyer

Music is big business. Billions of dollars pass through the music industry annually. For this reason, there are armies of people behind the scenes. The list of possible careers in these auxiliary professions would take up this entire book, but as a sampling, we could look at such professions as managers, publicists, and entertainment law.

Negotiating contracts for records, performances, instrument endorsements, copyrights, and just about anything related to the professional musician is the domain of entertainment law. Being a musician is not a necessity, yet it is certainly helpful in understanding the unique needs and sensitivities of musicians. The people who manage musicians are also often musicians. A manager is the person who oversees all aspects of the musician's business. This person arranges the concerts, handles the finances, and performs a million other duties that guide the musician's career and direction. In many ways, the manager is the person who takes care of all the nonmusical aspects of a musician's career so that the musician can concentrate on making the music.

The publicist's job is to make sure the public knows about the musician. This person writes press releases, arranges interviews, promotes concerts, and does just about anything involving publicity about the musician. Although musical skills are not necessary, it certainly helps if this person has knowledge of music that can be used to help communicate with the general public.

Multimedia

The visual and musical arts are becoming interwoven in ways only dreamed of just a few years ago. Today, with the accessibility of computer graphics and editing as well as inexpensive digital and traditional video, the linkage between sight and sound is all around us, from rock videos to films and commercials to pure art forms that blur the lines between these previously separate disciplines. Because of this, an entirely new area called media arts has developed. In media arts, the artist combines visuals and sounds to create a totally new experience. To be able to do this successfully, a knowledge of and sensitivity to music and visuals are critical. The field of media arts is exciting and one that is attractive to many young people. With the prevalence of home computers and easy-to-use multimedia software, many young people begin to experiment with the form during their high school years. For those who wish to continue this exploration, college degrees in media arts will usually allow them to develop their musical and artistic skills in equal partnership.

Summary

The music industry is huge. I have presented just a few of the major types of career opportunities and each of these categories could be further divided and refined. I have attempted to show you that a realistic, lucrative professional career can be pursued within the music industry as long as you maintain an open mind. Although the parallel images of both the starving artist and the world-famous superstar remain in many of our heads, the reality is that most musicians are somewhere in the middle, leading financially comfortable and rewarding careers. This mix creates a profession that looks a lot like most careers. For someone passionate about music, a career in one of the many venues of the music business can offer lifelong rewards and a lot of fun as well.

Chapter 18

Da Capo al Fine

Da capo is an Italian musical term that means go back to the beginning; *al fine* means until the end. I want to take you back to the beginning of this book and then jump to some concluding thoughts.

This book started:

Let's stop and review before we go any further. The title of this book is *Raising Musical Kids*. This title is not to be taken lightly. It is intended to imply something that I have come to believe in very strongly over the last twenty-five years of teaching music, researching musical learning, and raising three children. What I believe is simply this: musical children are not born—they are raised.

While writing this book, I have been forced to research and question many aspects of musical development. At the start of my work I believed that musical kids are raised that way by their parents. Now, my beliefs are even stronger.

In the first chapter, I introduced my three kids—Nathan, age fifteen, Madeline, age thirteen, and Melanie, age eleven. It is now three years later and they are eighteen, sixteen, and fourteen, respectively. They have changed, but not as much as the field of music education has in that short time. As my own children progressed through their teen years, I entered this period with confidence, having taught teenagers in the public schools for many years, and later college students. But seeing teens in home life is completely different from see-

Success in musical parenting is not measured by whether your children get a "1" rating at a competition or if they perform recitals every year or pursue a career in music.

ing them in school. This difference was so pronounced that it prompted me to add an entire chapter on teens and the home.

As a parent intent on raising musical kids, let me share a few personal details about my own kids. My son, Nathan, graduated from high school last year, and as a graduation present he received a new set of drums. Although he was excited to get them, he has no plans to make music a career. Instead, he plays in a band for the fun of it. He also has learned to play the banjo during the three years I spent writing this book. He enjoys jamming with his friends at home and gets the occasional gig. I think he will probably always do this to some degree because music making is a part of his life.

I point this out for a very important reason. I never intended this book as a way to create professional musicians. Success in musical parenting is not measured by whether your children get a "1" rating at a competition or if they perform recitals every year or pursue a career in music. Instead, success is measured by whether or not music becomes an important part of your child's life. Imagine a future generation of stockbrokers who play music on the weekends, CEOs who sing in choirs, and moms or dads who have friends over to play a few songs, much like they would come to watch a movie today.

On the other hand, it seems as if my daughter Melanie is headed for a career in music. She lives for music and practices for the sheer joy and challenge of it. This is great, but it does not show any more success in musical parenting than the other. Success is measured by the degree to which parents can help children fit music into their lives in ways appropriate for them. (Just for the record, Madeline is somewhere in between the two and is totally involved in musical theater.) I believe all three have chosen musical experiences appropriate to their abilities and interests. As a parent, it was my responsibility to provide those opportunities.

Now I want to change hats and talk from the music teacher perspective. Over the last twenty-five years I have worked with many students. I used to be disappointed when an enthusiastic and accomplished student musician chose to follow a career path that was not music. I was wrong. As a music teacher I should not judge my success by how many students go on to major in music in college (still a very common measure of a music program), but rather whether music has become a part of their lives. The real disappointments are the students who put their horns away after four years of band in high school and never play again. It is these students we have somehow failed, in both our teaching and our parenting.

As a teacher, I see far too many of these kids. Some of my first students are now in their mid-thirties. (Maybe you were one of my former students!) I run into them from time to time as our paths cross. One former student said something I hear all too often: "I really should play my trumpet; I really used to like it." That hurts.

On the other hand, when a student writes to share ongoing musical involvement, I am thrilled and I know my efforts have met with success. But I have come to understand also that the teacher is only one part of the equation. You as the parent are the other, bigger piece of the puzzle.

The field of music teaching has changed radically in recent years. It is easier now to be a musical nurturing parent than at any other time. Advances in technology have brought about the biggest change, especially the flourishing of the Internet. We now have more resources for hearing music than ever. As a parent, you can find all kinds of information and resources, but the Internet, or computer software, or even your local newspaper will not do it all for you. The tools are suddenly at your fingertips, yet they are only tools. You and your child will need to use them. It is your responsibility as a parent to provide the encouragement.

When I started writing this book, there was no talk of the Mozart Effect or that music would make us smarter in math or any of these things. Now I worry that parents who are not musical themselves will push their kids toward music to help them in school. Many will be disappointed. Far worse, such children will get the wrong message about music. Instead of looking for the joy in music, they will be focused on its effects. This book emphasizes the joy of participating in music for its own sake and establishes music as a lifelong activity that begins almost from birth.

Despite changes in society, music, and technology, one thing will remain the same: we are still human beings. Music is unique to being human. When we make music, listen to music, or experience music we are reinforcing what it means to be human. Music is so powerful and so instinctive to our mental, physical, and emotional well-being that it will always be a part of our lives. This book is intended to make music a more central part of more lives.

This book was written to make a difference to the musical lives of you and your children. Once music becomes a central part of your daily lives, it will be hard to remove it. Enjoy making music with your children and your actions will someday make a difference in the life of your children's children and maybe even their children. What more could we possibly hope for?

Appendix A

Resources for Parents

Educational Programs

Bands of America, Inc.
526 Pratt Avenue North
Schaumburg, IL 60193-4555
(847) 891-2263
(800) 848-BAND (2263)
Fax: (847) 891-1812
E-mail: boainfo@bands.org
Website: www.bands.org

> Nonprofit educational organization presenting performance opportunities and workshops, including the national concert band festival, summer band symposium for students and directors, grand national and regional marching band championships, regional concert band festivals, and Band of America express summer camps.

Campsearch.Com
Website: www.campsearch.com

> A website that is a search engine for finding youth camps of all types. Search under the heading "music" for music camps.

Directory of Summer Music Programs
6716 Eastside Drive, N.E.
Tacoma, WA 98422
(206) 972-3269

Written by Sandy Cavaziel, et al., this book can help you locate a summer music program for your child.

Disney Magic Music Days
Walt Disney World
P.O. Box 10,000
Lake Buena Vista, FL 23830
(800) 833-9806
Fax: (407) 828-4664
Website: www.disney-go.com

Various youth programs offering performance opportunities in many different types of performing groups.

Idyllwild Arts
P.O. Box 38
Idyllwild, CA 92549-0038
(909) 659-2171
Fax: (909) 659-5463
E-mail: iasumpro@aol.com
Website: www.idyllwildarts.og

A summer arts program and boarding arts high school. The summer program provides intensive arts experiences in dance, music, theater, visual arts, and writing to students of all ages and abilities. The academy offers college preparatory academics and preprofessional training in the arts to talented students from around the world. Financial aid is available to talented and deserving students.

Interlochen Center for the Arts
P.O. Box 199
Interlochen, MI 49643
(231) 276-7200
Website: www.interlochen.org

A year-round school of the arts for children K-12. Offers extensive summer camps in the arts.

International Music Camp
1725 11th Street SW
Minot, ND 58701
(701) 838-8472
Fax: (701) 838-8472
E-mail: imc@minot.com
Website: www.musiccamp.minot.com

A nonprofit summer arts camp located at the International Peace Garden on the border of the United States and Canada that features thirty one-week summer programs for students in the fine and performing arts. Now in its forty-third season, the camp attracts students from sixty-three countries, including every state and province in North America.

Kids Camp.com
5455 N. Federal Hwy, Suite O
Boca Raton, FL 33487
E-mail: info@kidscamp.com
Website: www.kidscamps.com

Music Works Northwest
2003 Maple Valley Highway #213
Renton, WA 98055
(425) 228-4506
Fax: (425) 235-6084
E-mail: gmurray@musicworksnw.org
Website: www.musicworksnw.org

> A nonprofit organization that offers winter and summer music programs to Puget Sound youth. Programs include jazz ensembles (3 levels), jazz combo, percussion ensemble, and youth choir. We also sponsor the Pacific Northwest Music Festival, the Imperials Percussion Invitational, and numerous other clinics and workshops throughout the year.

Summer Music Festival and Institute
Hartwick College
Oneonta, NY 13820
(607) 431-4801
(800) 388-0337
Fax: (607) 431-4813
E-mail: zvengrowski@hartwick.edu
Website: www.hartwick.edu/hcsmfi/FrameR.html

> Students experience a full range of music study. Fifteen large ensembles, chamber music, classes in music theory, history, computer technology, and so on; high school and college credit available. Private lessons.

World of Music Festivals
(858) 268-8825

(800) 748-5579
Fax: (858) 282-9951
Website: www.worldofmusic.com

> Lists national festivals around the country at various theme parks for a broad range of ensembles.

Gifts

Four Seasons Orchestra
4982 East Paradise Lane
Scottsdale, AZ 85254
(602) 493-3118
E-mail: carolyn@www.fourseasonsorchestra.org

> Gifts for orchestra lovers.

Friendship House
29313 Clemens Road, Suite 2-G
Westlake, OH 44145-0623
(216) 871-8040
(800) 791-9876
Fax: (216) 871-0858
Website: www.friendshiphouse.com

> Musical gifts, awards, and teaching aids for teachers, students, and music lovers.

The Music Stand
c/o Genesis Direct, Inc.
P.O. Box 1663
Secaucus, NJ 07094-1663
(800) 717-7010

> A large mail-order store of musical gifts, fashions, and fun. Extensive free catalog available.

Music in Motion
P.O. Box 833814
Richardson, TX 75083-3814
(800) 445-0649
Website:www.Music-in-motion.com

A music education and gift catalog store for all ages. Large, free catalog available.

Music Treasures Company
P.O. Box 9138
Richmond, VA 23227
(804) 730-8800
(800) 666-7565
Fax: (888) MUSICTC (687-4282)
E-mail: musict@musictreasures.com
Website: musictreasures.com

Music and dance gifts, awards, learning resources, music software, Gill recorders, T-shirts, and totes. Over 6,000 gifts offered in a 125-page catalog.

Learning Aids

Carousel Publications
1304 Route 42
Sparrowbush, NY 12780
(212) 758-9399
Fax: (212) 758-6453
E-mail: worldntune@aol.com
Website: www.Carousel-Music.com

Teaching materials; world instruments; World in Tune™ (a global music curriculum for the classroom that covers math, history, and humanities, with music as the core). Authentic instruments included.

The Children's Group, Inc.
1400 Bayly Street, Suite 7
Pickering, Ontario L1W 3R2, Canada
(905) 831-1995
Fax: (905) 831-1142
E-mail: childgroup@gta.igs.net
Website: www.childrensgroup.com

Produces the Classical Kids series of audio and video recordings introducing children to classical music. Includes a complete range of teacher resources, interactive CD-ROMs, and books for music education professionals.

Coda Music Technology
6210 Bury Drive
Eden Prairie, MN 55346-1718
(612) 937-9611
(800) 843-2066
Fax: (612) 937-9760
E-mail: dhawley@codamusic.com
Website: www.codamusic.com

Creators of interactive music software for notation and accompaniment.

Dancing Dots
130 Hampeden Road, 3rd Floor
Upper Darby, PA 19082-3110
(610) 352-7607
Fax: (610) 352-4582
E-mail: ddots@netaxs.com
Website: www.netaxs.com/~ddots

Specialists in developing and adapting software for the blind musician.

Electronic Courseware Systems, Inc.
1210 Lancaster Drive
Champaign, IL 61821
(217) 359-7099
(800) 832-4965
Fax: (217) 359-6578
E-mail: sales@ecsmedia.com
Website: www.ecsmedia.com

Publisher of music education software and multimedia products for kindergarten to college-level instruction.

eMedia Corp.
2403 East Aloha Street
Seattle, WA 98112
(206) 329-5657
Fax: (206) 329-0235
E-mail: bartgtr@aol.com
Website: www.emedia.org

Produces the eMedia Guitar Method on CD ROMs.

GuitarEncycloMedia
P.O. Box 20564
Dayton, OH 45420-0564
Fax: (937) 253-3142
E-mail: mike@guitarencyclomedia.com
Website: www.guitarencyclomedia.com

> Publishers of the GuitarEncycloMedia, a reference source for guitar knowledge.

Harmonic Vision, Inc
68 East Walker Place, 7th floor
Chicago, IL 60601
(313) 332-9200
(800) 474-0903
Fax: (312) 726-1946
E-mail: sales@harmonicvision.com
Website: www.harmonicvision.com

> Developer and publisher of music education software for beginning and intermediate music students. Titles include the award-winning Music Ace and the new Music Ace 2.

Homespun Tapes, Ltd.
P.O. Box 694
Woodstock, NY 12498
(914) 246-2550
(800) 338-2737
Fax: (914) 246-2582
E-mail: hmspn@aol.com
Website: www.homespuntapes.com

> Carries hundreds of instructional videos, CDs, and audiocassettes in a wide variety of musical instruments, styles, and levels.

Huiksi Music Creative Resources for Musicians
2350 Broadway, Suite 816
New York, NY 10024
(212) 724-3256
(800) 484-1333
Fax: (212) 724-3515
E-mail: juliehmus@aol.com
Website: members.aol.com/julielyonn

Books, videos, and audio series that emphasize new avenues to music making such as whole-brain, whole-body approaches, improvisation, and world music.

MiBAC Music Software
P.O. Box 468
Northfield, MN 55057-0468
(507) 645-5851
(800) 645-3945
Fax: (507) 645-2377
E-mail: info@mibac.com
Website: www.mibac.com

Manufacturer of music education software for Macintosh and IBM computers.

Minnesota Orchestra Visual Entertainment
1111 Nicollet Mall
Minneapolis, MN 55403
(612) 371-7119
(888) 666-6837
Fax: (612) 371-7191
Website: mnorch@mnorch.org

Producer of NotesAlive!™ StoryConcert children's videos that combine children's books, 3D animation, live action, and classical orchestral music performed in concert by the Minnesota Orchestra.

Music for Little People
1144 Redway Drive
Redway, CA 95560
(707) 923-3991
(800) 346-4445
Fax: (707) 923-3241
E-mail: musicforlittlepeople@mlfp.com
Website: mflp.com

An independent producer and distributor of audio and audio-related products, including instruments, video, and gifts.

Music Minus One Music Group, Inc.
50 Executive Boulevard
Elmsford, NY 10523-1325
(914) 592-1188

(800) 669-7464
Fax: (914) 592-31

Play-along and sing-along accompaniment cassette tapes and CDs.

Musicware, Inc.
8654 54th Avenue NE
Redmond, WA 98052
(425) 881-9797
(800) 99 PIANO (74266)
Fax: (425) 881-9664
E-mail: musicware@musicwareinc.com
Website: www.musicwareinc.com

Publisher and distributor of music education software for IBM and MAC platforms. Major titles include Music Lab, Piano, SING! Nightingale, Rhythmaticity, and Inner Hearing.

Music Together LLC
66 Witherspoon Street
Princeton, NJ 08542
(609) 430-0341
(800) 728-2692
Fax: (609) 924-8457
E-mail: adriana@musictogether.com
Website: www.musictogether.com

Program for infants through age four and their parents or caregivers. Teacher training in developmentally appropriate practices for parent/child, preschool, and daycare programs. Tapes and CDs, song collections, instruments, and music development guides for parents. Founded in 1987 and developed by the Center for Music and Young Children.

Peg Hoenack's MusicWorks
8409 Old Seven Locks Road
Bethesda, MD 20817-2006
(301) 635-1818
(800) 466-TOOT (8668)
Fax: (301) 469-9252
E-mail: phoenack@ix.netcom.com
Website: www.netcom.com/phoenack

Integrated music literacy programs for recorder, keyboard, autoharp, and Orff and classroom instruments, including the Sing & Play, Write & Read method. Stand-up student books, workbooks, fingering charts, teachers' books, CDs, tapes, and transparencies. Free program and products guide on request.

Note Family, Inc.
P.O. Box 789
Manchester, MO 63011-1089
(314) 227-5846
Fax: (314) 391-2714
E-mail: NFI@landofmusic.com
Website: www.landofmusic.com

The Land of Music Series, a music theory course for K-5 featuring characters, songs, movement, drama, stories, activities, and colorful visuals.

Notes & Strings Flashcards
P.O. Box 476
Hotchkiss, CO 81419
(970) 872-3142
(800) 587-3056
Fax: (970) 527-6792
E-mail: notesnstings@mail.tds.net
Website: www.earthbound.com/notesnstrings

Note reading and fingering flashcards with note on one side and note name and finger positions illustrated on the other. Specific instruments include violin, viola, cello, bass, guitar, flute, clarinet, saxophone, trumpet, and French horn. Also, general music note cards with theory questions.

PG Music, Inc.
29 Cadillac Avenue
Victoria, BC V82 1T3, Canada
(250) 475-2874
(800) 268-6272
Fax: (877) 475-1444
E-mail: sales@pgmusic.com
Website: www.pgmusic.com

Makers of music software programs, including Band-in-a-Box™, PowerTracks Pro Audio™, and eighteen live MIDI performance collections. These include The Pianist™, a library of more than 800 classical selections, The Modern Jazz Pianist, and The Jazz Soloist™, a resource for students of improvisation.

Piano Partners, Inc.
531 East 72nd Street
New York, NY 10021-4001
(212) 628-3918
Fax: (212) 628-3912
E-mail: ppmls@aol.com

> Offers schools (K-12) an integrated music learning system using IBM computers and MIDI keyboards. Includes an open-ended, comprehensive curriculum based on multimedia instructional software, customized music stations for cooperative learning, coordinated supporting resource materials, assessment system, and teacher training.

PureGold Teaching Tools, Inc.
P.O. Box 16622
Tucson, AZ 85732
(520) 747-5600
Fax: (520) 571-9077

> Publisher of child-friendly teaching tools including oversized grand staff kit; big colorful music symbols and Italian term flashcards; coloring books; card games, puzzles; rhythm cards; and memo boards. Call for a free brochure.

SoundTree
316 South Service Road
Melville, NY 11747-3201
(516) 393-8535
(800) 963-8733 (outside New York City metro area)
Fax: (516) 393-8548
E-mail: soundtre@korgusa.com
Website: www.soundtree.com

> Providers of music technology for education, including Korg keyboards, Apple and Compaq computers, and a variety of software and print materials.

TeAch-nology
11220 West Florissant, Suite 303
St. Louis, MO 63033
(800) 474-6447

Fax: (618) 466-1798
Website: www.teach-nology.com

Success-oriented computer music series for learners of all ages and stages.

Themes & Variations
30 Dixon Crescent
Red Deer, Alberta T4R 2H4, Canada
(403) 346-2741
E-mail: tvmusic@agi.net

Classroom music teaching materials such flashcards, charts, Christmas concerts, recorder music, song collections, and musical revues. All teaching materials are reproducible.

Thinking Cap/Education Software Development
59 Acres Drive
Hamilton Square, NJ 08690
(690) 587-5945
E-mail: cbakalian@earthlin.net
Website: www.home.earthlink.net/~cbakalian

Software development with music games for children ages four to twelve.

Professional Organizations

American Bandmasters Association
Website: www.tntech.edu/www/aba

The objectives of this organization are the recognition of outstanding achievement in the field of the concert band and its music; helpfulness and fellowship among members; an increasingly higher standard of artistic excellence for the concert band, its performers, its conductors and its literature; and a constantly greater contribution through the concert band to the musical life and culture of all peoples.

American Choral Directors Association
502 SW 38th Street
Lawton, OK 73505
(580) 355-8161

Fax: (580) 248-1465
E-mail: acda@acdaonline.org
Website: www.acdaonline.org

The American Choral Directors Association (ACDA) is a nonprofit music education organization whose central purpose is to promote excellence in choral music through performance, composition, publication, research, and teaching.

American Music Conference
5790 Armada Drive
Carlsbad, CA 92008
(760) 431-9124
(800) 767-6266
Fax: (760) 438-7327
E-mail: sharonm@namm.com
Website: www.amc-music.com

Promotes music making and music education.

American Music Therapy Association
8455 Colesville Road, Suite 1000
Silver Spring, MD 20910-3315
(301) 589-3300
Fax: (301) 589-5175
E-mail: info@musictherapy.org
Website: www.musictherapy.org

An association dedicated to advancing the public awareness of music therapy benefits and increasing accessibility to quality music therapy services. Brochures, books, videos.

American Orff-Schulwerk Association
P.O. Box 391089
Cleveland, OH 44139-8089
(440) 543-5366
Fax: (440) 543-2687
E-mail: hdqtrsaosa@aol.com
Website: www.aosa.org

Professional music and movement education association whose purpose is to promote the teachings and philosophy of Carl Orff and Gunild Keetman. Most states have chapters.

American String Teachers Association
1806 Robert Fulton Drive
Reston, VA 20191
(703) 476-1316
Fax: (703) 476-1317
E-mail: asta@erols.com
Website: www.astaweb.com

An organization specializing in the needs of string teachers.

Dalcroze Society of America
2812 Fairmont Blvd.
Cleveland Hts. OH 44118
Website: www.dalcrozeusa.org

Music training featuring eurhythmics, solfege, and improvisation.

Gordon Institute
P.O. Box 874
Narberth, PA 19072
(610) 660-6146
Website: www.unm.edu/~audiate/giml.htm

The broad purpose of this Institute is to ensure that Dr. Gordon's work
realizes its potential to serve as the foundation for future research and
to revitalize music education for generations to come.

International Society for Music Education
P.O. Box 805
3500 AV Utrecht
The Netherlands
Tel: 31 30 236 1258
Fax: 31 30 236 1217
E-mail: b.2.isme@lokv.nl
Website: www.isme.org

Organization formed by UNESCO for worldwide promotion of music
as a part of general education.

Music Educators National Conference
1806 Robert Fulton Drive
Reston, VA 20191
(703) 860-4000
(800) 336-3768

Fax: (703) 860-1531
Website: www.menc.org

The largest professional organization of music educators in the country. It is an umbrella organization that serves all specializations within the music education profession.

Music Teacher National Association
The Carew Tower
441 Vine St. #505
Cincinnati, OH 45202
(888) 512-5278
Fax: (513) 421) 2503
E-mail: MTNA@MTNA.org
Website: www.mtna.Org

A nonprofit organization of 24,000 independent and collegiate music teachers committed to furthering the art of music through programs that encourage and support teaching, performance, composition, and scholarly research.

National Band Association
P.O. Box 121292
Nashville, TN 37212
(615) 385-2650
Website: www.Nationalbandassoc.org

A professional organization dedicated to promoting the musical and educational significance of concert bands.

Organization of American Kodály Educators
1612 29th Avenue South
Moorhead, MN 56560
(701) 235-0366
FAX: 701) 241-7051
E-mail: oake@oake.org
Website: http://oake.org

OAKE was founded in 1973. Its purpose is to promote Kodály's concept of music for everyone through the improvement of music education in schools.

Richards Institute
25702-C Holiday Circle

Stevenson Ranch, CA 91380
(661) 255-1863
Fax: (661) 253-3885
E-mail: ETM@quicknet.com
Website: www.educationthroughmusic.com

> Association organized on the teaching method "education through music" aimed at general education via music.

SPEBSQSA (Society for the Preservation and Encouragement of Barber Shop Quartet Singing in America)
6315 Third Avenue
Kenosha, WI 53143-5199
(414) 653-8440
(800) 876-7464
Fax: (414) 654-4048
E-mail: bashleigh@spebsqsa.org
Website: www.spebsqsa.org

> Music education materials for four-part male a cappella singing in the barbershop style.

Sweet Adelines International
5334 East 46th Street
Tulsa, OK 73135
(918) 622-1444
Fax: (918) 665-0894
E-mail: education@sweetadelineintl.org
Website: www.sweetadelineintl.org

> Publisher of barbershop-style music arranged for young women's voices. Producer of newsletters and festivals through its Young Women in Harmony program.

Appendix B

Songs That "Americans, of All Ages, Should Know and Can Sing"

Compiled by the Music Educators National Conference.

All Through the Night (traditional)
Amazing Grace (Newton/traditional)
America (My Country, 'Tis of Thee) (Smith/traditional)
America the Beautiful (Bates/Ward)
Auld Lang Syne (traditional)
Battle Hymn of the Republic (Home/traditional)
Blue Skies (Irving Berlin)
Both Sides Now (Joni Mitchell)
Camptown Races (Stephen Foster)
Clementine (traditional)
Danny Boy (Londonderry Air) (traditional)
De colores (traditional)
Dona Nobis Pacem (traditional)
Do-Re-Mi (Rodgers and Hammerstein)
Down by the Riverside (traditional)
Down in the Valley (traditional)
Edelweiss (Rodgers and Hammerstein)
Erie Canal (traditional)
Ev'ry Time I Feel the Spirit (traditional)
Five Hundred Miles (Hedy West)
Follow the Drinkin' Gourd (traditional)
Frère Jacques (traditional)
Getting to Know You (Rodgers and Hammerstein)
Give My Regards to Broadway (George M. Cohan)
God Bless America (Irving Berlin)
God Bless the U.S.A. (MAAG)

Green, Green Grass of Home (traditional)
Guantanamera (Pete Seeger and Jose Martí)
Havah Nagilah (traditional)
He's Got the Whole World in His Hands (traditional)
Home on the Range (traditional)
I Love the Mountains (traditional)
I've Been Working on the Railroad (traditional)
I've Got Rhythm (George Gershwin)
If I Had a Hammer (The Hammer Song) (Hays/Seeger)
Irene Goodnight (Huddie Ledbetter)
It's a Small World (Richard and Robert Sherman)
Jamaica Farewell (Irving Burgie)
Kum Ba Yah (traditional)
Let It Be (Lennon and McCartney)
Let Me Call You Sweetheart (traditional)
Let There Be Peace on Earth (Miller/Jackson)
Lift Ev'ry Voice and Sing (Johnson)
Make New Friends (traditional)
Michael (Row the Boat Ashore) (traditional)
Midnight Special (Huddie Ledbetter)
Music Alone Shall Live (traditional)
My Bonnie Lies Over the Ocean (traditional)
My Favorite Things (Rodgers and Hammerstein)
Oh! Susanna (traditional)
Oh, What a Beautiful Mornin' (Rodgers and Hammerstein)
Old MacDonald Had a Farm (traditional)
Over My Head (traditional)
Over the Rainbow (Harold Arlen)
Peace Like a River (traditional)
Precious Lord (Thomas Dorsey)
Puff the Magic Dragon (Yarrow/Tipton)
Red River Valley (traditional)
Rock Around the Clock (Max Freedman and Jimmy DeKnight)
Rock-A-My Soul (traditional)
Sakura (traditional)
Shalom Chaverim (traditional)
She'll Be Comin' 'Round the Mountain (traditional)
Shenandoah (traditional)
Side by Side (Harry Woods)
Simple Gifts (Shaker Hymn)
Sometimes I Feel Like a Motherless Child (traditional)
The Star Spangled Banner (Key/Traditional)
Swing Low, Sweet Chariot (traditional)
Take Me Home, Country Roads (John Denver/Bill Danoff/Taffy Danoff)

Take Me Out to the Ball Game (Norworth/von Tilzer
This Land Is Your Land (Woody Guthrie)
This Little Light of Mine (traditional)
To Every Season (Turn! Turn! Turn!) (Pete Seeger)
Try to Remember (Harvey Schmidt and Tom Jones)
The Water Is Wide (traditional)
We Shall Overcome (Horton, Seeger, Carawan)
What a Wonderful World (Theile/Weiss)
When Johnny Comes Marching Home (Patrick Gilmore)
When the Saints Go Marching In (traditional)
Where Have All the Flowers Gone (Pete Seeger)
Yankee Doodle (traditional)
Yesterday (Lennon and McCartney)
You Are My Sunshine (Davis/Mitchell)
You Are the Sunshine of My Life (Stevie Wonder)
You're a Grand Old Flag (George M. Cohan)
You've Got a Friend (Carole King)
Zip-A-Dee-Doo-Dah (Gilbert/Wrubel)

Appendix C

The National Standards for Music Education

Each of these nine umbrella standards is broken down into specific skills that should be addressed at each age level. The complete book of standards can be purchased through the Music Educators National Conference.

1. Singing, alone and with others, a varied repertoire of music.
2. Performing on instruments, alone and with others, a varied repertoire of music.
3. Improvising melodies, variations, and accompaniments.
4. Composing and arranging music within specific guidelines.
5. Reading and notating music.
6. Listening to, analyzing, and describing music.
7. Evaluating music and music performances.
8. Understanding relationship between music, the other arts, and disciplines outside the arts.
9. Understanding music in relation to history and culture.

Appendix D

Suggestions for Listening

This list was compiled from a variety of suggestions. Many come from the music faculty at the University of Arizona, but others are from such sources as "The 100 most important musical works of the twentieth century" (www.npr.org/programs/specials/vote/list100.htm).

Although this list provides good variety, it is not meant to be comprehensive. When you look for music, the important feature is whether it engages your child.

MUSIC/ALBUM	COMPOSER/PERFORMER
Adagio for Strings	Barber
Annie	Broadway show (Charnin/Strouse)
Appalachian Spring	Copland
Mother Goose	Prokofiev
Baby Beluga	Raffi
Blue Moon of Kentucky	Monroe
Bolero	Ravel
Born to Run	Springsteen (for older children)
Brandenberg Concertos (1-6)	Bach
Canon in D	Pachelbel
Carmina Burana	Orff
Carnival of the Animals	Saint-Saëns
City of New Orleans	Guthrie
Come Swing with Me	Sinatra
Edward Scissorhands	Soundtrack (Elfman)
Eine Kleine Nachtmusik	Mozart

Fantasia	Disney film (multiple composers)
Fantasia 2000	Disney film (multiple composers)
Foggy Mountain Breakdown	Scruggs
Grand Canyon Suite	Grofé
Hard Day's Night	Beatles
Hound Dog	Presley
I'm So Lonesome I Could Cry	Williams
In the Mood	Glenn Miller Orchestra
La Mer	Debussy
Music of Eastern Europe	Various Composers (American Folklife Center)
Music of Southeast Asia	Various Composers (American Folklife Center)
Music of the Middle East	Various Composers (American Folklife Center)
Night on Bald Mountain	Mussorgsky
Nutcracker Suite	Tchaikovsky
Piano Rags	Joplin
Original Version	Guthrie/Leadbelly (Folkways Records)
Peter and the Wolf	Prokofiev
Rhapsody in Blue	Gershwin
Rite of Spring	Stravinsky
Rhythm Saved the World	Armstong
Rocky Mountain Christmas	John Denver
Rodeo	Copland
The Seasons	Vivaldi
Singable Songs	Raffi
Singin' in the Rain	Soundtrack
Symphony No. 5	Beethoven
Symphony No. 6	Beethoven
Symphony No. 40	Mozart
Three Places in New England	Ives
Toccata and Fugue in D minor	Bach
Young Person's Guide to the Orchestra	Britten
Water Music	Handel
West Side Story	Soundtrack (Bernstein/Sondheim)
Vision Shared	Springsteen/Nelson and others (Folkway Records)

Notes

CHAPTER 1

1. R. A. Cutietta, D. L. Hamann, and L. M. Walker, *Spinoffs: The Extramusical Advantages of a Musical Education* (Chicago: UMI Publications, 1994).
2. R. Radocy and J. D. Boyle, *The Psychological Foundations of Musical Behavior*, 3rd ed. (Springfield, IL: Charles C. Thomas, 1997).
3. "Profile of SAT and Achievement Test Takers" (College Entrance Examination Board, 1987, 1988, 1989, 1990, 1991, 1992, 1993).
4. W. Jennings and J. Nathan, "Startling/Disturbing Research on School Program Effectiveness," *Phi Delta Kappan* (March 1977): 589.
5. C. Fowler, *Strong Arts, Strong Schools* (New York: Oxford University Press, 1996).
6. E. E. Gordon, *The Nature, Description, Measurement, and Evaluation of Music Aptitudes* (Chicago: G.I.A. Publications, Inc., 1987).

CHAPTER 2

1. F. A. Raucher, G. L. Shaw, and K. N. Ky, "Music and Spatial Task Performance," *Nature*, 365 (1993): 611.
2. E. Winner and L. Hetland, "The Arts and Academic Improvement: What the Evidence Shows," *Journal of Aesthetic Education* (Fall 2000): 3.
3. G. Schlaug, L. Jancke, Y. Huang, and H. Steinmetz, "In Vivo Evidence of Structural Brain Asymmetry in Musicians," *Science*, 267 (January-March 1995): 699-701.
4. Ibid.
5. R. A. Cutietta, D. L. Hamann, and L. M. Walker, *Spinoffs: The Extramusical Advantages of a Musical Education* (Elkhart, IN: UMI Press, 1995).

6. C. Fowler, *Strong Arts, Strong School* (New York: Oxford University Press, 1996), 42.
7. H. Gardner, *Frames of Mind: The Theory of Multiple Intelligences* (New York: Basic Books, 1983).

CHAPTER 3

1. D. L. Walters, "Edwin Gordon's Music Aptitude Work," *The Quarterly*, 2, 1 (1991): 68.
2. E. E. Gordon, *The Nature, Description, Measurement, and Evaluation of Music Aptitudes* (Chicago: G.I.A. Publications, Inc., 1987).
3. Walters, 67.
4. For more information on this topic, see F. H. Raucher, "Music Exposure and the Development of Spatial Intelligence in Children," *Bulletin of the Council for Research in Music Education*, 142 (1999): 35–47, and P. R. Huttenlocher, "Synapse Elimination and Plasticity in Developing Human Cerebral Cortex," *American Journal of Mental Deficiency*, 88 (1984): 488–96.
5. R. A. Cutietta, "Edwin Gordon's Impact on the Field of Music Aptitude," *The Quarterly*, 2, 1 (1991): 73.
6. J. A. Sloboda, *The Musical Mind: The Cognitive Psychology of Music* (New York: Oxford University Press, 1997).
7. J. E. Ormrod, *Human Learning* (Englewood Cliffs, NJ: Prentice-Hall, 1990).
8. C. S. Zwink, "Verbal Categorization of Holistic Musical Stimuli by Preschool Children: Implications for Cognitive Categorization" (master's thesis, Kent State University, 1988).
9. R. A. Cutietta, "An Analysis of Musical Hypotheses Created by the 11-16 Year Old Learner," *Bulletin of the Council for Research in Music Education*, 84 (1985): 1–13.
10. M. K. Berke, "The Ability of Preschool Children to Recognize Chord Changes and Audiate Implied Harmony" (Ph.D. diss., University of Arizona, 2000); Lineburgh, "The Effects of Incidental Exposure to Musical Prototypes on the Stylistic Discrimination Ability of Kindergarten and Second Grade Children" (Ph.D. diss., Kent State University, 1994).
11. H. Chang and S. E. Trehub, "Auditory Processing of Relational Information by Young Infants," *Journal of Child Psychology*, 24 (1977): 323–31; H. Chang and S. E. Trehub, "Infant's Perception of Temporal Grouping in Auditory Patterns," *Child Development*, 48 (1977): 1666–70; H. Moog, *The Musical Experience of the Pre-school Child*, trans. C. Clarke (London: Schott, 1976).
12. P. S. Campbell, *Songs in Their Heads* (New York: Oxford University Press, 1998).

13. Sloboda, 206.
14. R. Radocy and J. D. Boyle, *Psychological Foundations of Musical Behavior* (Springfield, IL: Charles C. Thomas, 1979); D. Sergeant, "Experimental Investigation of Absolute Pitch," *Journal of Research in Music Education*, 17 (1969): 135–43; P. T. Brady, "Fixed-scale Mechanism of Absolute Pitch," *Journal of the Acoustical Society of America*, 48 (1970): 883–887; L. L. Cuddy, "Training the Absolute Identification of Pitch," *Perceptual Psycophysiology* 8 (1970): 265–69.
15. Sloboda, 196.
16. P. E. Wilkin, "The Foetal Auditory Environment—Possible Effects of Music on the Human Infant," *Human Biology: An Integrative Science*, 4:371–80.
17. P. E. Wilkin, "Prenatal and Postnatal Responses to Music and Sound Stimuli—A Clinical Report," *Canadian Music Educator* (research edition), 33 (1991): 223–32.
18. P. E. Wilken, "A Comparison of Fetal and Newborn Responses to Music and Sound Stimuli with and without Daily Exposure to a Specific Piece of Music," *Bulletin of the Council for Research in Music Education*, 127 (1996): 163–69.
19. Sloboda, 199.
20. Sloboda, 200.
21. Sloboda, 202.
22. H. Gardner, "Do Babies Sing a Universal Song?" *Psychology Today*, 15, 12 (1981): 70–76.
23. Moog, 1976.
24. Recorders are also sometimes used, especially in schools. They are often regarded as pre-band instruments to allow students to begin learning how to read notation and play in a group before they begin instruction on an instrument in the school band. This is an unfortunate stereotype because the recorder can be a beautiful instrument in its own right. Still, it is excluded from this discussion because it is not too common to find a child learning the recorder outside the classroom.
25. C. Kepner, "The Effect of Performance Familiarity, Listening Condition and Type of Performance Effort on Correctness of Performance Error Detection by 50 High-School Instrumentalists as Explained Through a Sensory Blocking Theory" (Ph.D. diss., Kent State University, 1986).
26. W. F. Cramer, "The Relation of Maturation and Other Factors to Achievement in Beginning Instrumental Music Performance at the Fourth Through Eighth Grade Levels" (Ph.D. diss., Florida State University, 1958); L. A. Hartley, "A Comparison of Factors Related to Participation and Achievement in Instrumental Music Students Who Began in Fifth Grade and Those Who Began in Sixth Grade," *Journal of Band Research*, 26, 2 (1991); L. A. Hartley, "The Relationship of Student Attitude, Enrollment, and Retention in Instrumental Music to

Beginning Instructional Grade and Grade Level Organization" (Ph.D. diss., Kent State University, 1991); G. H. Shull, "An Instrumental Alternative That Works," *Music Educators Journal*, 70, 5 (1984): 51-52; T. E. Silliman, "The Effect of Entrance Age on Achievement and Retention in the Beginning Band Instrument Program" (Ph.D. diss., University of Maryland, 1971); E. E. Strachen, "The Designation of the Appropriate Grade Level for Beginning Instrumental Study" (Ph.D. diss., Colorado State College, 1964).

CHAPTER 4

1. An excellent review of this literature can be found in R. E. Klinedinst, "Predicting Performance Achievement and Retention of Fifth-Grade Instrumental Students," *Journal of Research in Music Education*, 39, 3 (1991): 225–38.
2. J. D. Boyle and R. E. Radocy, *Measurement and Evaluation of Musical Experiences* (New York: Schirmer Books, 1987).

CHAPTER 5

1. M. B. Holbrook and R. M. Schindler, "Some Exploratory Finding on the Development of Musical Tastes," *Journal of Consumer Research*, 16 (1989):119–24; H. Stipp, "Musical Demographics: The Strong Impact of Age on Music Preferences Affects All Kinds of Businesses," *American Demographics* (August 1990): 48–49.
2. There are close to twenty research reports with similar findings to support this. For an excellent review of this literature, see Leif Finnas "How Can Musical Preferences Be Modified: A Research Review," *Bulletin of the Council for Research in Music Education*, 102 (Fall 1989): 1–59.
3. J. A. Sloboda, *The Musical Mind: The Cognitive Psychology of Music* (New York: Oxford University Press, 1997), 211.
4. S. L. Schleuter and L. J. Schleuter, "The Relationship of Grade Level and Sex Differences to Certain Rhythmic Responses of Primary Grade Children," *Journal of Research in Music Education*, 32 (1985): 23–29.

CHAPTER 6

1. B. S. Bloom, *Developing Talent in Young People* (New York: Ballantine Books, 1985).

CHAPTER 7

1. J. E. Ormrod, *Human Learning* (Englewood Cliffs, NJ: Prentice-Hall, 1990).
2. W. F. Cramer, "The Relation of Maturation and Other Factors to Achievement in Beginning Instrumental Music Performance at the Fourth Through Eighth Grade Levels" (Ph.D. diss., Florida State University, 1958); L. A. Hartley, "The Relationship of Student Attitude, Enrollment, and Retention in Instrumental Music to Beginning Instructional Grade and Grade Level Organization" (Ph.D. diss., Kent State University, 1991); L. S. Hartley, "A Comparison of Factors Related to Participation and Achievement in Instrumental Music Students Who Began in Fifth Grade and Those Who Began in Sixth Grade," *Journal of Band Research*, 26, 2 (1991); G. H. Shull, "An Instrumental Alternative That Works," *Music Educators Journal*, 70, 5 (1984). 51–52; T. E. Silliman, "The Effect of Entrance Age on Achievement and Retention in the Beginning Band Instrument Program (Ph.D. diss., University of Maryland, 1977); F. D. Strachen, "The Designation of the Appropriate Grade Level for Beginning Instrumental Study" (Ph.D. diss., Colorado State College, 1964).
3. J. K. Delzell and D. A. Leppla, "Gender Association of Musical Instruments and Preferences of Fourth-Grade Students for Selected Instruments," *Journal of Research in Music Education*, 40 (1992): 93–103; S. O'Neill and M. Boulton, "Boys' and Girls' Preferences for Musical Instruments: A Function of Gender?" *Psychology of Music*, 24, 2 (1996): 171–83; J. Zervoudakes and J. Tanur, "Gender and Musical Instruments: Winds of Change?" *Journal of Research in Music Education*, 42 (1994): 58–67.
4. R. A. Cutietta and P. A. McAllister, "Student Personality and Instrumental Participation, Continuation, and Choice," *Journal of Research in Music Education*, 45 (1997): 282–94; A. E. Kemp, "Personality Differences between the Players of String, Woodwind, Brass, and Keyboard Instruments, and Singers," *Bulletin of the Council for Research in Music Education*, 66 and 67 (1981): 33–38; A. E. Kemp, "Personality Structure of the Musician, I: Identifying a Profile of Traits for the Performer." *Psychology of Music*, 9, 1 (1981): 3–14; A. E. Kemp, "Personality Structure of the Musician, III: The Significance of Sex Differences," *Psychology of Music*, 10, 1 (1982): 48–58; R. Bruce, and A. Kemp, "Sex-Stereotyping in Children's Preferences for Musical Instruments," *British Journal of Music Education*, 10, 3 (1993): 213–18.
5. E. E. Gordon, "Final Results of a Two-Year Longitudinal Predictive Validity Study of the Instrument Timbre Preference Test and the Musical Aptitude Profile," *Bulletin of the Council for Research in Music Education*, 89 (1986): 8–17.
6. Ibid.

CHAPTER 8

1. This next section regarding learning and reinforcement is based on a large body of psychological research. Instead of citing extensive numbers of studies, I refer you to two excellent and authoritative sources; each cites literally hundreds of research studies to support these points. The sources are E. Hilgard and G. Bower, *Theories of Learning*, 4th ed. (Englewood Cliffs, NJ.: Prentice-Hall, 1975); and J. E. Ormrod, *Human Learning* (Englewood Cliffs, NJ.: Prentice-Hall, 1990).

CHAPTER 9

1. G. R. Doan, "An Investigation of the Relationships Between Parental Involvement and the Performance Ability of Violin Students" (Ph.D. diss., Ohio State University, Columbus, 1973); J. P. Brokaw, "The Extent to Which Parental Supervision and Other Selected Factors Are Related to Achievement of Musical and Technical-Physical Characteristics by Beginning Instrumental Music Students" (Ph.D diss., University of Michigan, 1983); and J. A. Sloboda, J. W. Davidson, M.J.A. Howe, and D. G. Moore, "The Role of Practice in the Development of Performing Musicians," *British Journal of Psychology*, 87 (1996): 287–309.
2. H. Jorgensen, "Teaching/Learning Strategies in Instrumental Practice" (paper presented at the Third RAIME [Research Alliance of Institutes for Music Education] Symposium, Florida State University, Tallahassee, Florida, April 6–10). Published in Jack A. Taylor (ed.), *Transatlantic Roads of Music Education: World Views* (Tallahassee, FL: Center for Music Research, 1997); N. H. Barry and V. McArthur, "Teaching Practice Strategies in the Music Studio: A Survey of Applied Music Teachers," *Psychology of Music*, 22 (1994).
3. N. H. Barry, "The Effects of Practice Strategies, Individual Differences in Cognitive Style, and Gender upon Technical Accuracy and Musicality of Student Instrumental Performance," *Psychology of Music*, 20 (1992): 112–23.
4. K. Miklaszewski, "Individual Differences in Preparing a Musical Composition for Public Performance," in M. Manturzewska, K. Miklaszewski, and A. Biatkowski (eds.), *Psychology of Music Today* (Warsaw: Fryderyk Chopin Academy of Music, 1995); P. Ghent, "Expert Learning in Music" (master's thesis, University of Toronto, Ontario, 1989); D. B. McLaughlin, "An Investigation of Performance Problems Confronted by Multiple Woodwind Specialists" (Ed.D. diss., Columbia University Teachers College, 1985); S. Hallam, "Approaches to Learning and Performance of Expert and Novice Musicians" (Ph.D. diss.,

University of London, 1992); S. Hallam, "Professional Musicians' Orientations to Practice: Implications for Teaching," *British Journal of Music Education*, 12, 1 (1995): 3–19; S. Hallam, "Professional Musicians' Approaches to the Learning and Interpretation of Music," *Psychology of Music*, 23, 2 (1985): 111–28.

5. E. R. Guthrie and F. F. Powers, *Educational Psychology* (New York: Ronald Press Co., 1950).

6. S. Hallam, "Approaches to Learning and Performance of Expert and Novice Musicians" (Ph.D. diss., University of London, 1992).

7. S. L. Ross, "The Effectiveness of Mental Practice in Improving the Performance of College Trombonists," *Journal of Research in Music Education*, 33 (1985): 221–30; J. Wapnik, M. Gilsig, and T. Hummel, "Relative Effects of Psychomotor Practice, Mental Rehearsal and Guided Mental Rehearsal on Performance of Undergraduate Brass and Piano Music Majors" (paper presented at the meeting of the Music Educators National Conference, San Antonio, TX, 1982).

8. M. Folts, "The Relative Aspects of Two Procedures as Followed by Flute, Clarinet, and Trumpet Students While Practicing on the Development of Tone Quality and on Selected Performance Skills" (Ph.D. diss., New York University, 1973, abstract in *Dissertation Abstracts International*, 34, 1312-A); R. K. Rosenthal, "The Relative Effects of Guided Model, Model Only, Guide Only and Practice Only Treatments on the Accuracy of Advanced Instrumentalists' Musical Performance," *Journal of Research in Music Education*, 32 (1984): 265–73; R. K. Rosenthal, M. Wilson, M. Evans, and L. Greenwalt, "Effects of Different Practice Conditions on Advanced Instrumentalists' Performance Accuracy," *Journal of Research in Music Education*, 36, 4 (1988): 250–57; E. Hodges, "The Effects of Recorded Aural Models on the Performance Achievement of Students in Beginning Band Classes," *Journal of Band Research*, 12 (1975): 30–34; W. Z. Zurcher, "The Effects of Model-Supportive Practice on Beginning Brass Instrumentalists" (Ed.D. diss., Teachers College, Columbia University, 1992); V. Puopolo, "The Development and Experimental Application of Self-Instructional Practice Materials for Beginning Instrumentalists," *Journal of Research in Music Education*, 19 (1971): 342.

9. C. Kepner, "The Effect of Performance Familiarity, Listening Condition and Type of Performance Effort on Correctness of Performance Error Detection by 50 High-School Instrumentalists as Explained Through a Sensory Blocking Theory" (Ph.D. diss., Kent State University, 1986).

10. M. Folts, "The Relative Aspects of Two Procedures as Followed by Flute, Clarinet, and Trumpet Students While Practicing on the Development of Tone Quality and on Selected Performance Skills" (Ph.D. diss., New York University, 1973); R. K. Rosenthal, M. Wilson, M. Evans, and L. Greenwalt, "Effects of Different Practice Conditions on

Advanced Instrumentalists' Performance Accuracy," *Journal of Research in Music Education*, 36, 4 (1988): 250–57.

11. H. G. Bastian, *Leben fur Musik. Eine Biographie-Studie uber usikalische (Hoch)-Begabungen* (Nainz, Germany: Schott, 1989); B. S. Bloom, *Developing Talent in Young People* (New York: Ballantine, 1985); J. P. Brokaw, "The Extent to Which Parental Supervision and Other Selected Factors Are Related to Achievement of Musical and Technical-Physical Characteristics by Beginning Instrumental Music Students" (Ph.D. diss., University of Michigan, 1983); J. Davidson, M. Howe, and J. Sloboda, "What Motivated Instrumental Learning?" (paper presented at the VIIth European Conference on Developmental Psychology, Krakow, August 23–27, 1995); J. W. Davidson, J. A. Sloboda, and M. J. A. Howe, "The Role of Parents and Teachers in the Success and Failure of Instrumental Teachers," *Bulletin of the Council for Research in Music Education*, Special Issue, 127 (Winter 1995–96): 40–44, The International Society for Music Education, July 9–15, University of Miami, Florida; M. F. Heaney, "The Components of a String Education: A Qualitative Study of Selected Members of the Philadelphia Orchestra String Section" (Ph.D. diss., Florida State University, Tallahassee, 1994); M. Howe and J. Sloboda, "Young Musicians' Accounts of Significant Influences in Their Early Lives. 2. Teachers, Practising and Performing," *British Journal of Music Education*, 8, 1(1991): 53–63; L. A. Sosniak, "Learning To Be a Concert Pianist," in B. S. Bloom (ed.), *Developing Talent in Young People* (New York: Ballantine Books, 1985); J. Sperti, "Adaptation of Certain Aspects of the Suzuki Method to the Teaching of the Clarinet: An Experimental Investigation Testing the Comparative Effectiveness of Two Different Pedagogical Methodologies," *Bulletin of the Council for Research in Music Education*, 37 (1970): 46–48; P. Vacher, "An Investigation into Piano Practising Techniques" (master's thesis, University of Reading, 1992).

12. J. B. Shea and R. L. Morgan, "Contextual Interferance Effects on the Acquisition, Retention and Transfer of a Motor Skill," *Journal of Experimental Psychology: Human Learning and Memory*, 5 (1979): 179-87.

CHAPTER 10

1. This brief history is based on information gleaned primarily from the following three sources: Harold F. Abeles, Charles R. Hoffer, and Robert H. Klotman, *Foundations of Music Education*, 2nd ed. (New York: Schirmer Books, 1994); Michael L. Mark, *Contemporary Music Education*, 2nd ed. (New York: Schirmer Books, 1986); and Lloyd Fred-

erick Sunderman, *Historical Foundations of Music Education in the United States* (Metuchen, NJ: Scarecrow Press, 1971).

CHAPTER 11

1. *The School Music Program: Descriptions and Standards* (Reston, VA: Music Educators National Conference, 1986).
2. L. A. Hartley, "The Relationship of Student Attitude, Enrollment, and Retention in Instrumental Music to Beginning Instructional Grade and Grade Level Organization" (Ph.D. diss., Kent State University, 1991).
3. E. J. Kvet, "Excusing Elementary School Students from Regular Class-room Activities for the Study of Instrumental Music: The Effect on Sixth-Grade Reading, Language and Mathematics Achievement," *Journal of Research in Music Education*, 33 (1985): 45–54.
4. B. Friedman, "An Evaluation of the Achievement in Reading and Arithmetic of Pupils in Elementary School Instrumental Music Classes" (Ph.D. diss., New York University, 1959).
5. F. H. Groff, "The Effect on Academic Achievement of Excusing Elementary School Pupils from Classes to Study Instrumental Music" (Ph.D. diss., University of Connecticut, 1963).

CHAPTER 13

1. Dan Bell ,"The Relationship Between Judges' Scores and Time of Day in a National Jazz Band Competition" (unpublished paper, the University of Arizona); Ron Blackely, "The Relationship Between Select Variables and Judges' Scores" (unpublished paper, The University of Arizona).
2. Thomas Zampella, "Factors Affecting Musical Judging Accuracy at the High School Level" (Ph.D. diss., Kent State University, 1995).

CHAPTER 14

1. Davis, 1985, reports this total number of 10,500. However, Lyle and Hoffman, 1972; Brown et al., 1986; and Sun and Lull, 1986, all report that American teens listen to music from three to four hours per day, which is slightly less than Davis's total number if listening is constant for all seven of the teen years; J. D. Brown, K. Campbell, and L. Fischer, "American Adolescents and Music Videos: Why Do They Watch?" *Gazette*, 37 (1986): 19–32; S. Davis, "Pop Lyrics: A Mirror and Molder of Society," *Etcetera* (Summer 1985): 167–169; J. Lyle and H. R. Hoff-

man, "Children's Use of Television and Other Media," in U.S. National Institute of Mental Health, *Television in Day-to-Day Life: Patterns of Use Television and Social Behavior, Reports and Papers*, Vol. IV, E. A. Rubinstein, G. A. Comstock, and J. P. Murray (eds.), 129–256 (Washington, DC: U.S. Government Printing Office, 1972); S. W. Sun and J. Lull, "The Adolescent Audience for Music Videos and Why They Watch," *Journal of Communication*, 36, 1 (1986): 115–54.

2. M. S. Andreasen, "Patterns of Family Life and Television Consumption from 1945 to the 1990s," in D. Zillmann, J. Bryant, and A. C. Huston (eds.), *Media, Children, and the Family: Social Scientific, Psychodynamic, and Clinical Perspectives* (Hillsdale, NJ: Erlbaum, 1994), 19–36.

3. M. B. Holbrook and R. M. Schindler, "Some Exploratory Findings on the Development of Musical Tastes," *Journal of Consumer Research*, 16 (1989): 119–24.

4. R. A. Cutietta, "An Analysis of Musical Hypotheses Created by the 11–16 Year Old Learner," *Bulletin of the Council for Research in Music Education*, 84 (1985): 1–13; W. S. Fox and M. H. Wince, "Musical Taste Cultures and Taste Publics," *Youth and Society*, 7, 2 (1975): 198–224; J. K. Skipper, Jr., "How Popular Is Popular Music?: Youth and Diversification of Musical Preferences," *Popular Music and Society*, 2, 2 (1973): 145–54.

5. D. Zillmann and A. Bhatia, "Effects of Associating with Musical Genres on Heterosexual Attraction," *Communication Research*, 16, 2 (1989): 263–88.

6. S. L. Sargent and J. B. Weaver, "Exploring the Impact of Expressed Media Preferences on Perceptions of Opposite Gender Peers" (paper presented at the annual conference of the International Communication Association, Chicago, May 1996); J. C. Turner, "Social Categorization and the Self-Concept: A Social-Cognitive Theory of Group Behavior," in E. J. Lawler (ed.), *Advances in Group Processes: A Research Annual*, Vol. 2 (Greenwich, CT: JAI Press, 1985), 77–121; D. Zillmann, et al., "Radical Rap: Does It Further Ethnic Division?" *Basic and Applied Social Psychology*, 16, 1 and 2 (1995): 1–25.

7. In case you need research to convince you of this, see J. J. Wakshlag, R. J. Reitz, and D. Zillmann, "Selective Exposure to and Acquisition of Information from Educational Television Programs as a Function of Appeal and Tempo of Background Music," *Journal of Educational Psychology*, 74 (1982): 666–77.

8. K. Roe, *Mass Media and Adolescent Schooling: Conflict or Co-existence?* (Stockholm: Almqvist and Wiksell, International, 1983); K. Roe, "The School and Music in Adolescent Socialization," in J. Lull (ed.), *Popular Music and Communication* (Newbury Park, CA: Sage Publications, 1987), 121–230.

9. R. A. Cutietta, J. Millin, and D. Royse, "Noise Induced Hearing Loss among School Band Directors," *Bulletin of the Council for Research in Music Education,* 101 (1989): 41–49; R. A. Cutietta, R. J. Klich, D. Royse, and H. Rainbolt, "The Incidence of Noise-Induced Hearing Loss among Music Teachers," *Journal of Research in Music Education,* 42 (1994): 318–30; R. A. Cutietta and R. J. Klich, "Audio Imaging of High School Band Compositions to Imitate Common Patterns of Noise-Induced Hearing Loss as Found among Instrumental Music Teachers," in D. Laufer, K. Chesky, and P. Ellis (eds.), *Music as a Human Resource: Drafts and Developments* (Cologne: Dohr, 2000).

10. L. A. Hartley, "The Relationship of Student Attitude, Enrollment, and Retention in Instrumental Music to Beginning Instructional Grade and Grade Level Organization" (Ph.D. diss., Kent State University, 1991).

11. A. Delano and D. Royse, "Factors Influencing the Decision of College Freshmen to Participate or Not to Participate in Music Ensembles," *Contributions to Music Education,* 14 (1987): 9–18.

CHAPTER 15

1. D. L. Hamann. "The Status of Orchestra Programs in the Public Schools," *Journal of Research in Music Education,* 46, 1 (1998): 75–86.

2. Jeanne Bamberger, *Developing Musical Intuitions* (New York: Oxford University Press, 2000).

3. There are several extremely good research projects in this area. Among them are J. Kratus, "Use of Melodic and Rhythmic Motives in the Original Songs of Children Aged Five to Thirteen," *Contributions to Music Education,* 12 (1985): 1–8; J. Kratus, "Time Analysis of the Compositional Process Used by Children Ages Seven to Eleven," *Journal of Research in Music Education,* 37, 1 (1989): 5–20; J. Kratus, "Characterization of the Compositional Strategies Used by Children to Compose a Melody," *Canadian Music Educator,* 33 (1991): 95–103; J. Kratus, "Relationships among Children's Music Audiation and Their Compositional Processes and Products," *Journal of Research in Music Education,* 42, 2 (1994): 115–30; J. Kratus, *The Ways Children Compose* (Tampa, FL: ISME Yearbook, XXI, 1994), 128; S. L. Stauffer, "Composing with Computers: Meg Makes Music," *Bulletin of the Council for Research in Music Education* (in press); S. L. Stauffer, "Sociological and Cultural Cues in the Composition of Children and Adolescents," in M. S. Barrett, G. E. McPherson, and R. Smith (eds.), *Children and Music: Developmental Perspectives.* Proceedings of the Second Asia-Pacific Symposium on Music Education Research, Launceston, University of Tasmania; S. L. Stauffer, "Beginnings of the Composition Process Among Children and Adolescents" (paper presented at the

national biennial Desert Skies Symposium on Research in Music Education, University of Arizona, Tucson, Feb. 20–22, 1999; S. L. Stauffer, "Learning Through Composing" (paper presented at the conference on Cognitive Processes of Children Engaged in Musical Activity, School of Music, University of Illinois at Urbana-Champaign, Urbana, IL June 3–5, 1999); P. R. Webster, *Thinking in Sound: Studying Children's Improvisations* (Tampa, FL: International Society of Music Education Yearbook, XXI, 1994), 146; R. S. Quant, "Effects of Computer Software Format on the Musical Composition Process of Adolescents" (Ph.D. diss., University of Arizona, 1999).

4. "Beginnings of the Composition Process Among Children and Adolescents" (paper presented at the national biennial Desert Skies Symposium on Research in Music Education, the University of Arizona, Tucson, 1999).

CHAPTER 17

1. For more information on careers in music, I recommend the following books devoted specially to this topic: M. William Krasilovsky, Sidney Shemel, and John Gross, *This Business of Music: The Definitive Guide to the Music Industry* (New York: Watson-Guptill Publishers, 2000) and David Baskenville, *Music Business Handbook and Career Guide* (Newbury Park, CA: Sage Publications, 2000).

References

Following is a list of recommended titles, some for parents alone, and some for reading with children. All have been personally selected as titles of lasting value for parents trying to raise musical kids. While some of these titles are no longer available in bookstores, or even in print, most will be available in good public libraries, and parents can and should seek them out.

Adams, Noah. 1997. *Piano Lesson: Music, Love and True Adventures*. New York: Delta Trade Paperbacks.

Anderson, David. 1982. *The Piano Makers*. New York: Pantheon Books.

Andress, Barbara, ed. 1989. *Prekindergarten Music Education*. Reston, VA: Music Educators National Conference.

Arnold, Caroline. 1985. *Music Lessons for Alex*. New York: Clarion Books.

Aronoff, Frances Webber. 1982. *Move with the Music*. Pittsburgh: Music Innovations.

Barlowe, Amy. 1992. *Happy Listening Guide*. New York: Warner Brothers.

Beranek, Vratislav. 1994. *The Illustrated History of Music*. London: Sunburst Books.

Bloom, Benjamin S., ed. 1985. *Developing Talent in Young People*. New York: Ballantine.

Campbell, Don G. 2000. *The Mozart Effect for Children: Awakening Your Child's Mind, Health, and Creativity*. New York: William Morrow.

Campbell, Patricia S. 1998. *Songs in Their Heads: Music and Its Meaning in Children's Lives*. New York: Oxford University Press.

Campbell, Virginia. 1985. *Puzzling, Patterning, Practicing: A Guide to More Effective Piano Study*. Chapel Hill, NC: Hinshaw.

Chang, Nai Y. 1994. *An Illustrated Treasury of Songs: National Gallery of Art, Washington*. New York: Rizzoli.

Chroninger, Ruby. 1994. *Teach Your Kids about Music*. New York: Walker.

Danes, Emma. 1993. *The Usbourne First Book of Music*. London: Usbourne.

Fierabend, John. 1989 *Music for Little People*. New York: Boosey & Hawkes.

———. 1986. *Music for Very Little People*. New York: Boosey & Hawkes.

Gardner, Howard. 1985. *Frames of Mind*. New York: Basic Books.

———. 1991. *The Unschooled Mind: How Children Think and How Schools Should Teach*. New York: Basic Books.

Goffstein, M. B. 1984. *A Little Schubert*. Boston: David R. Godine.

Greves, Margaret. 1989. *The Magic Flute: The Story of Mozart's Opera*. New York: Henry Holt.

Habermeyer, Sharlene. 2000. *Good Music, Brighter Children: Simple and Practical Ideas to Help Transform Your Child's Life Through the Power of Music*. Roseville, CA: Prima Publishing.

Hausherr, Rosemarie. 1992. *What Instrument Is This?* New York: Scholastic.

Hayes, Phyllis. 1981. *Musical Instruments You Can Make*. New York: Franklin Watts.

Healy, Jane M. 1990. *Endangered Minds: Why Our Children Don't Think*. New York: Simon & Schuster.

Krull, Kathleen. 1992. *Gonna Sing My Head Off*. New York: Knopf.

Levinson, Harold N., M.D. 1984. *Smart but Feeling Dumb*. New York: Warner Books.

McDonald, Dorothy, and Gene M. Simons. 1989. *Musical Growth and Development: Birth Through Six*. New York: Schirmer Books.

Machover, Wilma, and Marienne Uszler. 1996. *Sound Choices: Guiding Your Child's Musical Experiences*. New York: Oxford University Press.

Martin, Bill, Jr. 1994. *The Maestro Plays*. New York: Henry Holt.

Ortiz, John M. 1999. *Nurturing Your Child with Music: How Sound Awareness Creates Happy, Smart, and Confident Children*. Hillsboro, OR: Beyond Words Editing & Publishing

Phillips, Kenneth H. 1996. Teaching Kids to Sing. Belmont, CA: Wadsworth Publishing Co.

Schwartz, Elliott, and Daniel Godfrey. 1993. *Music Since 1945*. New York: Schirmer Books.

Shaw, Gordon L. 2000. *Keeping Mozart in Mind*. New York: Academic Press.

Streeter, Elaine. 1993. *Making Music with the Young Child with Special Needs: A Guide for Parents*. London: Kingsley.

Tompson, Wendy. 1991. *Composer's World Series: Biographies of Beethoven, Haydn, Mozart, and Schubert*. New York: Viking.

Wilson, Frank R. 1986. *Tone Deaf and All Thumbs: An Invitation to Music Making for the Late Bloomer and Non-prodigies*. New York: Viking Penguin.